SYSTEMATIC SOFTWARE DEVELOPMENT
USING VDM

Prentice-Hall International
Series in Computer Science

C. A. R. Hoare, Series Editor

BACKHOUSE, R.C., *Program Construction and Verification*
BACKHOUSE, R. C., *Syntax of Programming Languages, Theory and Practice*
de BAKKER, J. W., *Mathematical Theory of Program Correctness*
BJORNOR, D., and JONES, C.B., *Formal Specification and Software Development*
CLARK, K. L., and McCABE, F. G., *micro-PROLOG: Programming in Logic*
DROMEY, R. G., *How to Solve it by Computer*
DUNCAN, F., *Microprocessor Programming and Software Development*
ELDER, J., *Construction of Data Processing Software*
GOLDSCHLAGER, L., and LISTER, A., *Computer Science: A Modern Introduction*
HEHNER, E. C. R., *The Logic of Programming*
HENDERSON, P., *Functional Programming: Application and Implementation*
HOARE, C. A. R., *Communicating Sequential Processes*
HOARE, C. A. R. and SHEPHERDSON, J. C., (Eds.) *Mathematical Logic and Programming Languages*
INMOS LTD., *Occam Programming Manual*
JACKSON, M. A., *System Development*
JOHNSTON, H., *Learning to Program*
JONES, C. B., *Systematic Software Development Using VDM*
JOSEPH, M., PRASAD, V. R., and NATARAJAN, N., *A Multiprocessor Operating System*
LEW, A., *Computer Science: A Mathematical Introduction*
MacCALLUM, I., *Pascal for the Apple*
MacCALLUM, I., *UCSD Pascal for the IBM PC*
MARTIN, J. J., *Data Types and Data Structures*
POMBERGER, G., *Software Engineering and Modula-2*
REYNOLDS, J. C., *The Craft of Programming*
TENNENT, R. D., *Principles of Programming Languages*
WELSH, J., and ELDER, J., *Introduction of Pascal, 2nd Edition*
WELSH, J., ELDER, J., and BUSTARD, D., *Sequential Program Structures*
WELSH, J., and HAY, A., *A Model Implementation of Standard Pascal*
WELSH, J., and McKEAG, M., *Structured System Programming*

SYSTEMATIC SOFTWARE

DEVELOPMENT

USING VDM

CLIFF B JONES

The University, Manchester, England

Prentice / Hall PHI International

ENGLEWOOD CLIFFS, NEW JERSEY   LONDON   MEXICO   NEW DELHI
RIO DE JANEIRO   SINGAPORE   SYDNEY   TOKYO   TORONTO   WELLINGTON

Library of Congress Cataloging-in-Publication Data

Jones, C. B. (Cliff B.), 1944–
  Systematic software development using VDM.

  Bibliography: p.
  Includes index.
  1. Computer software—Development.   I. Title.
  II. Title: VDM.
  QA76.76.D47J66   1986   005.1′1   85-31178
  ISBN 0–13–880725–6

British Library Cataloguing in Publication Data

Jones, Cliff B.
  Systematic software development using VDM. —
  (Prentice-Hall International series in computer
  science)
  1. Computer software——Development
  I. Title
  005.1   QA76.76.D47

  ISBN 0-13-880725-6

PRENTICE-HALL, INC., *Englewood Cliffs, New Jersey*
PRENTICE-HALL INTERNATIONAL, UK, LTD., *London*
PRENTICE-HALL OF AUSTRALIA PTY., LTD., *Sydney*
PRENTICE-HALL CANADA, INC., *Toronto*
PRENTICE-HALL HISPANOAMERICANA, S.A., *Mexico*
PRENTICE-HALL OF INDIA PRIVATE LIMITED, *New Delhi*
PRENTICE-HALL OF JAPAN, INC., *Tokyo*
PRENTICE-HALL OF SOUTHEAST ASIA PTE., LTD., *Singapore*
PRENTICE-HALL DO BRASIL LTDA., *Rio de Janeiro*
WHITEHALL BOOKS LIMITED, *Wellington, New Zealand*

Printed and bound in Great Britain for
Prentice-Hall International (UK) Ltd,
66 Wood Lane End, Hemel Hempstead, Hertfordshire, HP2 4RG
at the University Press, Cambridge.

3 4 5   90 89 88 87

ISBN 0-13-880725-6

ISBN 0-13-880717-5 PBK

In memory of
George Henry Jones
1907–1985

Contents

List of Figures

Foreword

It is well known that ninety-nine percent of the world's problems are not susceptible to solution by scientific research. It is widely believed that ninety-nine percent of scientific research is not relevant to the problems of the real world. Yet the whole achievement and promise of modern technological society rests on the minute fraction of those scientific discoveries which are both useful and true.

The problems involved in the development and use of computer programs are well described and well appreciated, particularly by those who have suffered from them. Efforts of many researchers have been devoted to elucidate the theoretical basis of computer programming. This book shows how the results of the research are immediately and directly relevant in practical solution of the real problems of programming. By the clarity of its exposition, it makes the solution accessible to every student of computing science and to every professional programmer. A rigorous approach to software development will enable our society to reap the full benefit promised by the invention of the electronic digital computer.

Read it, study it, learn from it, enjoy it; but above all, put its lessons into practice.

C.A.R.Hoare
Oxford

Preface

In Ephesus ... when an architect accepts the charge
of a public work, he has to promise what the cost of
it will be. ... when more than one fourth has to be
spent in addition on the work, the money required
to finish it is taken from his property.
Vitruvius

The development of any large system must be preceded by the construction
of a specification of what is required. Without such a specification, the
people charged with development will have no firm idea of the needs of the
would-be users of the system; these users will be the ones who, in more ways
than one, are likely to pay for the inevitable misunderstandings.

The need for precision in a specification is accepted in most engineering
disciplines. An aircraft designer, for example, has to be fully trained in
the use of appropriate mathematical techniques such as partial differential
calculus. Computer systems need precise specifications. Unfortunately, the
current practice in the software industry is to employ an informal mixture
of text and pictures. In order to achieve precision, a specification must be
written in a language which has a formal basis. Clear use of natural language
obviously has a place in describing systems—but English cannot be relied
upon as the sole specification language.

The history of the specification of the concrete syntax of programming
languages is revealing. Before the publication of the ALGOL report, the
syntax of programming languages was given in *ad hoc* ways. Since the *BNF*
(*Backus-Naur Form*) notation has been fully understood, no sensible language designer has described syntax in English sentences—however carefully
written. The use of such notation has also made it possible to construct tools
like parser generators.

This book explains *formal methods*—the term embraces formal specification and verified design. Many aspects of a computer system must be specified including performance and cost. In this book attention is focused on *functional specification* (i.e. what the system does); the term *specification* is, however, used below without qualification to avoid heaviness. Formal specification employs mathematical notation in order to achieve precision and conciseness. The description of the intended behaviour of a computer system requires that the meaning of its operations be specified. This is done by recording properties (pre- and post-conditions) which the operations should enjoy. This is one way in which a specification can avoid, or rather postpone, issues which arise in implementations.

Another key technique for making specifications more concise than their implementations is to use data objects which match the system being specified. This can be contrasted to the use of data objects which belong to the machine or language on which the system is to be implemented.

Some notation and conventions beyond standard mathematics are required in writing formal specifications. *VDM* (see Bibliography) is used in this book because it has achieved a level of maturity and acceptance: it has been widely taught for many years and has been used in a variety of environments. But, since it is the concepts which are important, elaborate syntactic frameworks, as in most programming languages, are avoided here. Indeed, the reader should be able to understand the essential concepts and rewrite the examples in some other specification language.

The VDM notation has itself been carefully defined. This has made it possible to establish the soundness of proof rules for program design steps. An understanding of the underlying concepts makes it possible to introduce new notation (e.g. relations) if required for some class of applications. (The more fluid research areas of formal methods tackle subjects like parallelism and are not addressed in this book.)

The other major aspect of formal methods is verified design. The idea that programs are mathematical texts opens up the possibility of reasoning about their correctness. Arguments can be constructed which, because they address all cases, present an exciting alternative to running test cases as a way of checking programs.

Verified design uses the concept of proof as a way of checking design steps. Steps in a systematic development can be based on, and verified against, a formal specification. This makes it possible to use proofs in the development process and to detect errors before further work in undertaken.

The elimination of errors at the earliest moment is a key to improving the productivity of the development process.

Organization

This book is intended to be used in courses on formal methods. It is used at university undergraduate level and the material has evolved from courses for industry. The only prerequisites are a knowledge of programming and some familiarity with discrete mathematics. The notation of both logic and set theory are described but a reader who is totally unfamiliar with this material should first study a textbook such as *Set Theory and Related Topics* by S. Lipschutz.

The book contains ten chapters. The chapters are divided into sections and the main ideas of most sections can be presented in one-hour lectures. The text contains some mathematical comments which printed as footnotes. Terms are italicized at the point of introduction and are described in the Glossary of Terms. A Glossary of Symbols is also provided. Rather than disrupt the flow of the text with references, an Annotated Bibliography is provided. The index contains, in addition to technical terms, references to examples which run through the text (e.g. "QREL" for the equivalence-relation problem).

The approach taken is formal with an emphasis on proof. It is possible to understand the material on specifications without following all of the proofs. A first reading might omit Sections 2.2, 2.3, 3.2, 3.3, 4.3, 5.2, 6.2, 7.3, and Chapters 8 to 10. The study of proofs is, however, rewarding and experience shows that notation is understood more deeply if practice is gained with its manipulation. The study of a proof also deepens the appreciation of a theorem and reinforces one's memory of it.

The exercises are an integral part of the material and should be attempted by the reader who hopes to be able to use the methods described. Those exercises marked with an asterisk are more difficult and open-ended: they are best tackled in a group effort with some guidance available.

A set of *Teacher's Notes* are being printed as a technical report. These contain supporting material including answers to the unstarred exercises and sample exam questions. These notes can be obtained from the author by academic faculty members.

Acknowledgements

My sincere thanks go to the many people who have helped with the creation of this book. The original notes were typed onto the Vuwriter system by Julie Hibbs. Comments on the first draft were received from Lynn Marshall, Brian Monahan, Maurice Naftalin, Jim Toher and Colin Walter. Major reviews were undertaken by Derek Andrews and Roger Shaw. Input on the second draft was received from Howard Barringer, Ian Cottam, Tobias Nipkow and Harald Søndergaard. A Major review was made by Ian Hayes to whom I am also grateful for help in removing some unnecessary differences between "Z" and the notation used here. The long fight to transfer the word processor files to LaTeX was led by Mario Wolczko and undertaken by Lon Barfield and Rachel Lunnon. Peter Aczel reformulated the operation decomposition proof obligations. Tony Hoare has provided inspiration and encouragement. Further inspiration has come from the meetings of IFIP Working Group 2.3. Support from the UK Science and Engineering Research Council has also been received. My thanks also go to the staff of Prentice-Hall International.

SYSTEMATIC SOFTWARE DEVELOPMENT
USING VDM

Chapter 1

Logic Notation

If you are faced by a difficulty or a controversy in science, an ounce of algebra is worth a ton of verbal argument.

J.B.S.Haldane

In writing specifications, it is useful to adopt notation from established branches of mathematics. One of the most useful bodies of notation is that of mathematical logic. In this chapter, the basic ideas of both propositional and predicate calculus are explained.

One reason for the importance of logic notation is the central role it plays in the notion of proof. The use of specifications in the justification of design is described in Chapters 8 and 10. But, even when considering specifications on their own, there are a number of important proof obligations. The concept of formal proof is explored in Section 2.1.

1.1 Propositional Operators

A *proposition* is an expression which has the value true or false. Thus, under the usual interpretation of arithmetic symbols:

$$2 + 3 = 5$$

is true, but:

$$2 + 2 = 5$$

is false. Propositions can be formed by writing relational operators (e.g. $=,<,\leq$) between arithmetic *terms* built up from constants and operators.

Another way of forming propositions is by using truth-valued functions. These functions are discussed in more detail in the next section. For now, an intuitive reading should suffice—thus:

   is-prime(7)

is true providing that the truth-valued function *is-prime* has the value true for exactly those natural numbers which are normally considered to be primes; whereas:

   is-prime(8)

is false.

The language which can be built by such propositions is rather limited since truths can only be stated about constants. One way to extend the language is to permit identifiers to occur in expressions. The truth of expressions like:

   $$2 + i = 5$$

depends on the value of i. Such expressions are called *predicates* in this book. The identifier i, in the example above, is said to be a *free variable*, and the interpretation for such free variables must come from their context. The truth of a predicate depends on the interpretation of its free variables; the example above is true in a context in which i is bound to the value 3. Several different ways of providing contexts, or bindings, for free variables are given in subsequent sections.

Propositions and predicates can be thought of as truth-valued expressions. Predicates simplify to propositions when their free variables are replaced by values. This section introduces operators which are used to form composite truth-valued expressions; the operators are known as "propositional" operators. For example:

   $$(2 + 3 = 5) \lor (2 + 2 = 5)$$

is a true proposition built by combining two simpler (constituent) propositions with a symbol which can be read as "or". Such propositional operators can be compared with the familiar arithmetic operators ($+,*$ etc). Just like their arithmetic counterparts, propositional operators can be used in combinations to form long (or deeply nested) expressions; furthermore, they share the property that there are general laws about the equivalence of expressions. Thus:

$$x + y = y + x$$

is the commutative law for addition and:

$$E_1 \lor E_2 \iff E_2 \lor E_1$$

expresses the fact that "or" is commutative.

Such laws apply even when predicates, or more complex logical expressions, are written in place of E_1 etc. In this section the E_i can be replaced by arbitrary truth-valued expressions; later, arbitrary logical expressions are substituted for such names.

Whereas arithmetic expressions are concerned with an infinite set of numeric values, propositions—when evaluated—yield one of the two truth values. In recognition of the key role that George Boole played in the development of logic, these are often called "Boolean values". This set is named:

$$\mathbf{B} = \{\text{true}, \text{false}\}$$

The term "logical value" is also used below. The typography of the Boolean value true distinguishes it from the word "true" used in a normal sentence. Strictly one should write "E_i evaluates to true"; but, unless a special point has to be made, the less heavy "E_i is true" is used.

The fact that the set of Boolean values is finite provides a very simple way of expressing the meaning of logical operators. *Truth tables* display the value of a compound proposition for all combinations of the possible values of constituent propositions.

An expression whose principal operator is "or" is called a *disjunction*. Since this operator is binary (i.e. two-place), there are four cases to be considered in the truth table:

E_1	E_2	$E_1 \lor E_2$
true	true	true
true	false	true
false	true	true
false	false	false

This shows that the operator is used in a way which corresponds to the use of the word "or" in English. Notice that the first row of this truth table shows that the "or" is inclusive. The reader may be familiar with truth tables which are presented in the more compact style:

∨	true	false
true	true	true
false	true	false

The longer form is used here because of the intention to illustrate the evaluation of expressions.

A *negation* is a logical expression whose principal operator is the symbol (¬) for "not". Since it is a unary (one-place) operator, its truth table is simpler:

E	$\neg E$
true	false
false	true

Logical expressions whose principal operator is "and" are called *conjunctions*. Again, the truth table corresponds to natural language usage:

E_1	E_2	$E_1 \wedge E_2$
true	true	true
true	false	false
false	true	false
false	false	false

It is possible to investigate properties of propositional operators via truth tables. One useful law (named after de Morgan) is that:

$$\neg(E_1 \wedge E_2)$$

has, for any propositions E_i, the same value as:

$$\neg E_1 \vee \neg E_2$$

This equivalence can be verified as follows:

E_1	E_2	$\neg E_1$	$\neg E_2$	$E_1 \wedge E_2$	$\neg(E_1 \wedge E_2)$	$\neg E_1 \vee \neg E_2$
true	true	false	false	true	false	false
true	false	false	true	false	true	true
false	true	true	false	false	true	true
false	false	true	true	false	true	true

Two logical expressions which have the same logical values are said to be *equivalent*. Notice that, in forming the column for $\neg(E_1 \wedge E_2)$ the "not" operator is applied to a composite proposition: its value is still derived from the truth table. A similar observation applies to $\neg E_1 \vee \neg E_2$ where

the *disjuncts* (operands of the disjunction) are negations. The basic truth
tables are used in a step-by-step evaluation of larger expressions in the same
way that complex arithmetic expressions are evaluated one step at a time.

The operators given above match the intuitive meaning suggested by
their name. If used carefully, the same can be said of *implications*—that
is, logical expressions whose principal operator is "implies". Consider the
expression:

$$i = 2 \Rightarrow i^2 = 4$$

This implication (under the usual arithmetic interpretation) is intuitively
true. The following table considers the truth of the *antecedent* (left-hand
side) and *consequent* (right-hand side) of the expression for various values
of i:

i	$i = 2$	$i^2 = 4$
2	true	true
-2	false	true
1	false	false

This example should give some credence to all but the second row of the
truth table for implication:

E_1	E_2	$E_1 \Rightarrow E_2$
true	true	true
true	false	false
false	true	true
false	false	true

The second row should yield the value false for situations like:

$$i = 1 \Rightarrow i^2 = 4$$

in a context where i takes the value 1. These examples are not intended to
do more than motivate the truth table. The truth table is itself a definition
and no justification need be given. Problems of interpreting implications
arise only when the antecedent and consequent of an implication have no
causal connection; such expressions are avoided in this book.

A useful equivalence is that the implication:

$$E_1 \Rightarrow E_2$$

can be shown to be equivalent to:

$\neg E_1 \lor E_2$

by:

E_1	E_2	$\neg E_1$	$\neg E_1 \lor E_2$	$E_1 \Rightarrow E_2$
true	true	false	true	true
true	false	false	false	false
false	true	true	true	true
false	false	true	true	true

The fact that implications can be defined in terms of other operators does not, however, argue that they should be avoided. The implication used above is made more opaque when written:

$$\neg(i = 2) \lor i^2 = 4$$

The logical expression corresponding to the assertion of equality between arithmetic expressions is the *equivalence*. Its truth table is:

E_1	E_2	$E_1 \Leftrightarrow E_2$
true	true	true
true	false	false
false	true	false
false	false	true

Notice that, although the operator does yield the value true exactly when the operands have the same value, a special symbol ($\Leftrightarrow$) is used to show that the equality is between Boolean values.

The list of propositional operators is given in Figure 1.1. Just as in the construction of arithmetic expressions, the need for parentheses can be reduced by ranking the precedence of the operators. This order is also shown. In fact, some use of the high precedence of the "not" operator is made above. More useful examples, such as writing:

$$\neg E_1 \lor E_2 \Rightarrow E_3 \land E_4 \lor E_5$$

for:

$$((\neg E_1) \lor E_2) \Rightarrow ((E_3 \land E_4) \lor E_5)$$

are encountered below.

Having established the language of propositional logic, it is possible to discuss general properties of expressions in the language. Some logical expressions evaluate to true for all possible values of their constituent propositions. Such expressions are called *tautologies*. A simple example is:

operator	read as	priority
¬	not	highest
∧	and	
∨	or	
⇒	implies	
⇔	is equivalent to	lowest

Figure 1.1: Propositional Operators

$$E_1 \Rightarrow (\text{false} \Rightarrow E_2)$$

The obvious way of checking whether an expression is a tautology is by the construction of a truth table. One can, however, reason about such expressions. For example:

> the consequent of the principal implication would be true for any value of E_2, thus the overall expression must also be true for any value of E_1

With practice, such *rigorous* arguments can be conducted safely on quite complex expressions. However, the final security for such arguments is that a completely formal check is possible. In this Section, the truth tables provide such a formal method; other, more efficient, methods are considered in the exercises of Section 7.4; Chapter 2 provides an alternative method which relies on the construction of proofs.

Some expressions which are not tautologies are false for all values of their constituent expressions: these are called *contradictions*. For example:

$$E \vee \text{true} \Rightarrow E \wedge \text{false}$$

is a trivial contradiction. Expressions which may be false or true, depending on their constituent propositions, are called *contingent*. For contingent expressions, the sets of values—of their constituent propositions—for which they are true can be found. For example:

$$E_1 \Rightarrow E_2 \wedge E_1$$

is true in any "world" where E_1 has the value false or E_2 has the value true (or both). Each row of a truth table corresponds to a world. The column, in which the value of the overall expression is found, gives the result of the expression. A tautology is an expression in which the result is true in every row; a contradiction has the result false in every row; and a contingent expression has some results true and others false.

A tautology is, in fact, a special case of a *sequent*:

$$\Gamma \models E$$

(where Γ is a list of logical expressions). Such a sequent records a fact about the constituent logical expressions: it asserts that E is true in those worlds where every expression in Γ is true. If truth tables were constructed for the expressions in Γ, all rows in which any expression evaluates to false would be ignored; in the rows which remain, E must evaluate to true. For example:

$$E_1 \wedge (E_2 \vee E_3) \models E_1 \wedge E_2 \vee E_1 \wedge E_3$$
$$E_1 \Leftrightarrow E_2 \models E_1 \Rightarrow E_2$$
$$E_1 \wedge E_2 \models E_1 \Leftrightarrow E_2$$
$$\neg(E_1 \vee E_2) \models E_1 \Leftrightarrow E_2$$

E_1	E_2	E_3	$E_1 \wedge (E_2 \vee E_3)$	$E_1 \wedge E_2 \vee E_1 \wedge E_3$
true	true	true	true	true
true	true	false	true	true
true	false	true	true	true
true	false	false	false	—
false	true	true	false	—
false	true	false	false	—
false	false	true	false	—
false	false	false	false	—

Figure 1.2: Example of Sequent Evaluation

The $\models$ symbol is often called a (double) *turnstile*. The validity of sequents can be checked using truth tables: once the *hypotheses* (elements of the list on the left of the turnstile) of the sequent have been evaluated, the *conclusion* (right-hand-side) need only be evaluated in those rows where the hypotheses are all true. The truth table for the first of these examples is given in Figure 1.2. Notice that this example needs a truth table with eight rows, but that the conclusion of the sequent need not be evaluated for the last five rows. Here again, a rigorous argument can be constructed. For example:

> for a sequent to be false there must be some world where its hypothesis is true and its conclusion false; if $E_1 \wedge (E_2 \vee E_3)$ is true, both E_1 and at least one of E_2 or E_3 must be true; thus, either $E_1 \wedge E_2$ or $E_1 \wedge E_3$ (or both) must be true; therefore no world can be found in which the conclusion is false while the hypothesis is true

A tautology is a sequent with no hypotheses—for example:

$$\models E_1 \Rightarrow (\text{false} \Rightarrow E_2)$$

Sequents can be formed with more than one hypothesis—in such cases they are separated by commas—thus:

$$E_1, \; E_2 \vee E_3 \models E_1 \wedge E_2 \vee E_1 \wedge E_3$$
$$E_1, \; E_2 \models E_1 \Rightarrow E_2$$
$$\neg E_1, \; \neg E_2 \models E_1 \Leftrightarrow E_2$$

There are obviously similarities between $\models$ and $\Rightarrow$. In fact, in classical logic they turn out to be interchangeable. However, this is a result (the deduction theorem) which logic textbooks come to only after a sound understanding of the different concepts has been built. In the logic used here, implications and sequents are anyway not interchangeable[1]. Here, then, it is even more important to understand the distinction. The implies symbol is a logical operator whose meaning is given by its truth table. The correctness of a sequent is determined by discussing the complete truth table for all of the expressions occurring as its hypotheses or consequences. The sequent makes a claim about all models, or worlds, for the contained expressions: it is, in some senses, a meta-level statement about the contained logical expressions.

An example, which is used below, illustrates rigorous argument. Two ways of expressing that r is the absolute value of i are:

$$i < 0 \wedge r = -i \vee i \geq 0 \wedge r = i$$
$$(i < 0 \Rightarrow r = -i) \wedge (i \geq 0 \Rightarrow r = i)$$

To express that the second is a consequence of the first, write:

---

[1]The technical details of this point are explored in Section 3.3.

$$E_1 \wedge E_2 \vee \neg E_1 \wedge E_3 \models (E_1 \Rightarrow E_2) \wedge (\neg E_1 \Rightarrow E_3)$$

or, treating implication as an abbreviation:

$$E_1 \wedge E_2 \vee \neg E_1 \wedge E_3 \models (\neg E_1 \vee E_2) \wedge (E_1 \vee E_3)$$

In the case that $E_1 \wedge E_2$ is true, the first conjunct of the conclusion is true (because E_2 is the second disjunct) and so is the second conjunct (because E_1 is the first disjunct); therefore the conjunction is true; the case for $\neg E_1 \wedge E_3$ is similar.

The language which is built up from proposition variables (E_i) and the propositional operators is known as the *propositional logic*. This notation, together with rules for determining the truth of its expressions, forms the *propositional calculus*. For sequents with n distinct propositions, a truth table with 2^n rows can be used to determine its truth in all possible worlds.

A logical calculus in which the truth or falsity of any expression can be determined is said to be *decidable*. The propositional calculus is decidable. To determine whether a sequent is true or not, it is only necessary to construct the truth table and evaluate the expressions using the truth tables given above.

The truth tables provide a way in which propositional expressions can be evaluated. An alternative way of generating true statements is by selecting a small set of such statements from which all others can be generated. This proof-theoretic approach is considered in Chapter 2.

Exercises

1. Replace the question marks below by propositional operators so as to make the pairs of expressions equivalent (if in doubt, check using truth tables):

   (a) $E_1 \wedge E_2$ $E_2 \; ? \; E_1$

   (b) $E_1 \wedge (E_2 \wedge E_3)$ $(E_1 \; ? \; E_2) \; ? \; E_3$

   (c) $E_1 \wedge (E_2 \vee E_3)$ $E_1 \; ? \; E_2 \; ? \; E_1 \; ? \; E_3$

   (d) $\neg(E_1 \vee E_2)$ $? \; E_1 \; ? \; ? \; E_2$

   (e) $\neg\neg E$ $? \; E$

   (f) $E_1 \Rightarrow E_2$ $? \; E_2 \Rightarrow \; ? \; E_1$

   (g) $E_1 \Leftrightarrow E_2$ $(E_1 \; ? \; E_2) \wedge (E_2 \; ? \; E_1)$

   (h) Why are no parentheses required in the second expression in (c)?

(i) Commutative and associative laws for conjunctions are given in
(a) and (b). Write the equivalent laws for disjunctions.

(j) The law for distributing "and" over "or" is given in (c). Write
the distributive law for "or" over "and".

2. Replace the question marks with a Boolean value to make the following
pairs of expressions equivalent:

(a) $E \wedge ?$ E

(b) $E \wedge ?$ false

(c) write analogous rules to these two for "or".

(d) $? \Rightarrow E$ true

(e) $E \Rightarrow ?$ true

(f) $? \Rightarrow E$ E

(g) $E \Rightarrow ?$ $\neg E$

3. Check which of the following are correct (use truth tables or a rigorous
argument recording any other results on which the argument relies):

(a) $E_1 \vee E_2 \models E_1$

(b) $E_1, E_2 \models E_1$

(c) $E_1 \wedge E_2 \models E_1 \vee E_2$

(d) $E_1 \vee E_2 \models E_1 \wedge E_2$

(e) $E_2 \models E_1 \Rightarrow E_2$

(f) $\neg E_1 \models E_1 \Rightarrow E_2$

(g) $E_1 \Rightarrow E_2, E_1 \models E_2$

(h) $\neg E_1 \models \neg(E_1 \wedge E_2)$

(i) $\neg E_1 \models \neg(E_1 \vee E_2)$

(j) $E_1 \wedge (E_2 \Leftrightarrow E_3) \models E_1 \wedge E_2 \Leftrightarrow E_1 \wedge E_3$

(k) $E_1 \wedge E_2 \Leftrightarrow E_1 \wedge E_3 \models E_1 \wedge (E_2 \Leftrightarrow E_3)$

4. * Inferences about conditional logical expressions follow from:

E	if E then E_1 else E_2
true	E_1
false	E_2

Conditional expressions can be used to define each of the propositional operators. Write the five definitions.

5. * Write a truth table for an "exclusive or" operator (i.e. similar to "or" except that the result is false if both of the operands are true). Record some properties (as sequents) of this operator including the relation to ⇔ .

1.2   Truth-Valued Functions

A *function* is a mathematical abstraction of a familiar concept: a mapping between two sets of values. The domain of a function is a set of values to which it can be applied; *application* of a function to a value in its domain yields a result value. For example:

$$square(3) = 9$$

$$gcd(18, 42) = 6$$

The value 3 is in the domain of the function *square* and applying *square* to 3 yields the result 9; in such an application, 3 is also referred to as the "argument" of the function *square*. The function *gcd* (greatest common divisor or highest common factor) is applied to pairs of numbers.

It is useful to record, for any function, its *domain* (i.e. a specified set of values to which the function can be applied) and *range* (i.e. a specified set of values which contains the results of function application). The *signature* of a function is written with the domain and range sets separated by an arrow:

$$square: \mathbf{Z} \rightarrow \mathbf{N}$$

$$gcd: \mathbf{N}_1 \times \mathbf{N}_1 \rightarrow \mathbf{N}_1$$

Where the special symbols name the following (infinite) sets:

$$\mathbf{N}_1 = \{1, 2, \ldots\}$$

$$\mathbf{N} = \{0, 1, 2, \ldots\}$$

$$\mathbf{Z} = \{\ldots, -1, 0, 1, \ldots\}$$

The domain of a function of more than one argument is given as a list all of the argument sets separated by crosses[2]. Notice that the signature uses the

---

[2]Such functions can be viewed as taking one argument from the Cartesian product.

names of the sets of values (e.g. the integers, $\mathbf{Z}$, for the domain of *square*; the natural numbers, $\mathbf{N}$, for its range). The values to which a function is applied are elements of the set shown as the domain and the results are elements of the set shown as the range.

Some functions are used so frequently that it is convenient to avoid parentheses when they are applied to their arguments. This is particularly appropriate if, by writing them as *operators*, pleasing algebraic properties become more apparent. Thus:

$$2 + 3$$

is preferred to:

$$add(2, 3)$$

or even:

$$+(2, 3)$$

and the use of infix operators makes the distributive law:

$$i * (j + k) = i * j + i * k$$

clearer. By an obvious extension, the signatures of such operators can be recorded by showing, with '_', the position of values to which the operator can be applied:

$$_- + _-: \mathbf{Z} \times \mathbf{Z} \to \mathbf{Z}$$

Where no '_' are used, however, function application will be to a list of values enclosed in parentheses. As well as the obvious arithmetic operators, the examples in this chapter use the modulus operator which yields the remainder after integer division:

$$7 \bmod 2 = 1$$
$$27 \bmod 3 = 0$$

Its signature is:

$$_- \bmod _-: \mathbf{N} \times \mathbf{N}_1 \to \mathbf{N}$$

The decision as to whether a particular operator should be presented in this
mixfix style (as opposed to writing it as a function) is purely pragmatic;
similarly, there is no deep significance in the adoption of some special symbol
as opposed to a word in a special fount.

A *truth-valued function* is one whose range is the Boolean, or truth value,
set. The function which characterizes the prime numbers has the signature:

$$is\text{-}prime \colon \mathbf{N}_1 \to \mathbf{B}$$

thus:

$$is\text{-}prime(7), \ is\text{-}prime(23), \ \neg is\text{-}prime(8)$$

are true propositions. This truth-valued function is defined formally in Section 1.3.

An expression which contains the application of a truth-valued function
to an element of its domain forms a proposition. Thus:

$$is\text{-}prime(7) \ \vee \ is\text{-}prime(8) \ \vee \ is\text{-}prime(9)$$

Functions can be defined in terms of already understood functions (or
operators) and constants. The expressions in such direct definitions use
parameter names in an obvious way. For example:

$$square(i) \ \triangleq \ i * i$$

In order to distinguish the direct definition of a function from propositions
which might involve equality (e.g. $square(2) = 4$), a Greek delta ($\triangle$) is
superimposed on the equality sign in the definition.

In addition to known functions, certain other constructs can be used to
form direct function definitions. For example, conditional expressions can
be used in an obvious way to write:

$$abs(i) \ \triangleq \ \text{if } i < 0 \text{ then } -i \text{ else } i$$

Another simple device is to use let to define a value. Thus the absolute value
of the product of two integers could be found by:

$$absprod(i,j) \ \triangleq \ \text{let } k = i * j$$
$$\text{in if } k < 0 \text{ then } -k \text{ else } k$$

Extensions to the language for direct function definition (e.g. cases, recursion) are introduced below as they are required.

Such direct definitions can be written for truth-valued functions. Thus, if mod is understood, a truth-valued function (operator) which indicates whether its first argument divides its second without remainder, can be defined:

$$\_ \text{ divides } \_ : \mathbf{N}_1 \times \mathbf{N} \to \mathbf{B}$$
$$i \text{ divides } j \quad \triangleq \quad j \text{ mod } i = 0$$

Other examples include:

$$is\text{-}even : \mathbf{N} \to \mathbf{B}$$
$$is\text{-}even(i) \quad \triangleq \quad 2 \text{ divides } i$$

$$is\text{-}odd : \mathbf{N} \to \mathbf{B}$$
$$is\text{-}odd(i) \quad \triangleq \quad \neg is\text{-}even(i)$$

$$is\text{-}common\text{-}divisor : \mathbf{N} \times \mathbf{N} \times \mathbf{N}_1 \to \mathbf{B}$$
$$is\text{-}common\text{-}divisor(i, j, d) \quad \triangleq \quad d \text{ divides } i \wedge d \text{ divides } j$$

Notice how these definitions are built up on previously defined functions. The separation and naming of separate concepts plays an important part in the construction of large specifications.

Values (in its domain) for which a truth-valued function yields true, are said to *satisfy* the function. Thus:

> 7 *satisfies is-prime*
> 6 *satisfies is-even*
> *the triple of values* 42, 18, 6 *satisfies is-common-divisor.*

One way in which a free identifier in a proposition becomes bound to a value is by the application of a function to some value. Thus:

$$less\text{-}than\text{-}three : \mathbf{N} \to \mathbf{B}$$
$$less\text{-}than\text{-}three(i) \quad \triangleq \quad i < 3$$

is a definition of a truth-valued function whose application to 2 completes the proposition; it evaluates to true and thus 2 is said to satisfy *less-than-three*.

Exercises

1. Define a truth-valued function:

   is-hexable: $\mathbf{Z} \to \mathbf{B}$

   which determines whether a number can be represented as a single hexadecimal digit.

2. Define a truth-valued function which checks if its (integer) argument[3] corresponds to a leap year:

   is-leapyr: $\{1583, \ldots, 2599\} \to \mathbf{B}$

3. Define a truth-valued function which determines whether its third argument is a common multiple of its other two arguments (hint: remember to base the definition on separate functions in order to make it easier to understand).

4. It is often useful to employ an inverse operation to specify a function. This topic is covered in Chapter 3, but the reader should be able to see how a "post-condition" can be used to relate the inputs to the outputs of a function. Thus:

   $$post\text{-}sub(i,j,k) \quad \triangleq \quad i = j + k$$

   is a truth-valued function which can be used to check that $k = i - j$. Define (without using a square root operator) a truth-valued function:

   post-sqrt: $\mathbf{N} \times \mathbf{Z} \to \mathbf{B}$

   such that:

   $post\text{-}sqrt(9,3)$

   $\neg post\text{-}sqrt(9,4)$

5. Define a truth-valued function which determines whether a quotient q and remainder r represent a valid result for division of i by j. Thus:

---

[3]The restriction of the domain is to avoid any arguments about the pre-Gregorian calendar; the notation used defines a restricted set of integers.

$$post\text{-}idiv: \mathbf{N} \times \mathbf{N_1} \times \mathbf{N} \times \mathbf{N} \to \mathbf{B}$$

complete (without using division):

$$post\text{-}idiv(i, j, q, r) \quad \triangleq \quad \dots$$

such that:

$$post\text{-}idiv(7, 2, 3, 1)$$
$$\neg post\text{-}idiv(7, 2, 2, 3)$$

1.3 Quantifiers

The language for building logical expressions can be extended by including quantifiers. Their presentation in this section differs from the way in which the propositional operators are introduced in the preceding section: there, a rich set of equivalences and a simple evaluation mechanism (i.e. truth tables) made it interesting to study the propositional operators with arbitrary logical expressions. Here, the quantifiers are introduced with specific truth-valued functions.

Quantifiers extend the expressive power of the logical notation but can be motivated as abbreviations. The disjunction which appears in the preceding section can be written:

$$\exists i \in \{7, 8, 9\} \cdot is\text{-}prime(i)$$

This quantified expression can be read as:

> there exists a value in the set $\{7, 8, 9\}$ which satisfies the truth-valued function *is-prime*

The symbol $\exists$ is called an *existential quantifier*, the i is the *bound identifier*, the $\in \{\dots\}$ is the *constraint*, and the expression after the raised dot is the *body* of the quantified expression. Any free occurrences of the bound identifier within the body become bound in the quantified expression. All such occurrences refer to the bound identifier. The quantifiers thus provide a way of defining a context for free identifiers.

For finite sets, an existentially quantified expression can be expanded into a disjunction with one disjunct for each member of the set. This is a useful reminder to read $\exists$ as "there exists one or more". Thus:

$$\exists i \in \{11, 12, 13\} \cdot \textit{is-odd}(i)$$

is true because it is equivalent to:

$$\textit{is-odd}(11) \lor \textit{is-odd}(12) \lor \textit{is-odd}(13)$$

The reason that quantifiers extend the expressive power of the logic is that the sets in the constraint of a quantified expression can be infinite. Such an expression abbreviates a disjunction which could never be completely written. For example:

$$\exists i \in \mathbf{N}_1 \cdot \textit{is-prime}(i)$$

or:

$$\exists i \in \mathbf{N}_1 \cdot \neg\textit{is-prime}(2^i - 1)$$

express facts about prime numbers.

One way of establishing that a quantity with a certain property exists is by giving one. Thus the truth of the preceding existentially quantified expressions follows from:

$$\textit{is-prime}(7)$$
$$\neg\textit{is-prime}(2^8 - 1)$$

To be consistent with the position about the verification of existentially quantified expressions, it should be clear that any expression which is existentially quantified over the empty set must be false. Thus, for any truth-valued function p:

$$\neg\exists x \in \{\} \cdot p(x)$$

Existentially quantified expressions can be used in definitions of truth-valued functions. Thus the familiar "less than" relation on integers could be defined:

$$\_ < \_ : \mathbf{Z} \times \mathbf{Z} \to \mathbf{B}$$
$$i < j \;\; \triangleq \;\; \exists k \in \mathbf{N}_1 \cdot i + k = j$$

The preceding section uses mod as a given function. Although further notation is needed to provide a definition, a useful property can be stated:

$$i \bmod j = r \;\Rightarrow\; \exists m \in \mathbf{N} \cdot m * j + r = i$$

Many textbooks on logic do not provide the constraint part of quantified expressions. This is acceptable where the whole text concerns one type of value. Program specifications are, however, frequently concerned with different types of values and it is then wise to make the bound explicit in order to avoid confusion (e.g. claiming that no value can be doubled to yield an odd number and then being confronted with 1.5).

Just as a disjunction can be viewed as an existentially quantified expression, a conjunction such as:

$$is\text{-}even(2) \land is\text{-}even(4) \land is\text{-}even(6)$$

can be written as a *universally quantified* expression:

$$\forall i \in \{2, 4, 6\} \cdot is\text{-}even(i)$$

Here again, the increase in expressive power comes from universal quantification over infinite sets. For example:

$$\forall i \in \mathbf{N} \cdot is\text{-}even(2 * i)$$
$$\forall i \in \mathbf{N} \cdot is\text{-}even(i) \Rightarrow is\text{-}odd(i + 1)$$
$$\forall i \in \mathbf{N} \cdot \forall j \in \mathbf{N}_1 \cdot 0 \le (i \bmod j) < j$$

The truth-valued function *is-prime* which is used above can be directly defined by using quantifiers. The general concept of a prime number is one whose only divisors are 1 and the number itself. This is easy to express but care is necessary with the end cases: both 1 and 2 have the stated property. Disallowing the former, but not the latter, leads to:

$$is\text{-}prime(i) \quad \triangleq \quad i \neq 1 \land \forall d \in \mathbf{N}_1 \cdot d \text{ divides } i \Rightarrow d = 1 \lor d = i$$

The question of universal quantification over the empty set must be considered. It is necessary to adopt the position that, for any p:

$$\forall x \in \{\} \cdot p(x)$$

is true. The intuition behind this is less obvious than with the existential quantifier—although one could argue that there are no counter-examples in the empty set. One could also argue as follows—suppose:

$$\forall x \in X \cdot p(x)$$

were true for some X and p, then removing one element from X should not change the value of the quantified expression even when the last element is removed. These general arguments are less convincing than seeing how conveniently this end-case works in practice. For example, *is-prime* could be defined:

$$is\text{-}prime(i) \quad \triangleq \quad i \neq 1 \wedge \forall d \in \{2, \ldots, i-1\} \cdot \neg(d \text{ divides } i)$$

Where:

$$\{2, \ldots, i-1\}$$

is the set of integers which are greater than one and less than i; in the case that i is one or two, this set is empty and the truth of the quantified expression over the empty set gives the required result.

Where they are all the same, multiple quantifiers and bound sets can be combined. Thus:

$$\forall i \in \mathbf{N} \cdot \forall j \in \mathbf{N} \cdot p(i,j)$$
$$\forall j \in \mathbf{N} \cdot \forall i \in \mathbf{N} \cdot p(i,j)$$
$$\forall i \in \mathbf{N}, j \in \mathbf{N} \cdot p(i,j)$$
$$\forall i,j \in \mathbf{N} \cdot p(i,j)$$

all have the same meaning. In fact, where a logical expression contains variables which are not bound, they are considered to be bound by a universal quantifier at the outermost level. Thus, where the types are obvious:

$$i < i+1$$

can be considered to be shorthand for:

$$\forall i \in \mathbf{N} \cdot i < i+1$$

This closing-off converts a predicate into a proposition.

It is possible to build up expressions using both existential and universal quantifiers. For example:

$$\forall i,j \in \mathbf{N} \cdot i \leq j \;\Rightarrow\; \exists k \in \mathbf{N} \cdot i+k = j$$
$$\forall i \in \mathbf{N} \cdot \exists j \in \mathbf{N} \cdot i < j \wedge is\text{-}prime(j)$$
$$\exists i,j \in \mathbf{N} \cdot \forall d \in \mathbf{N}_1 \cdot is\text{-}common\text{-}divisor(i,j,d) \;\Rightarrow\; d = 1$$

all express true facts about natural numbers. It is important to realize that inversion of differing quantifiers can change the truth of an expression. For example:

$$(\exists i \in \mathbf{N} \cdot \forall j \in \mathbf{N} \cdot p(i,j)) \Rightarrow (\forall j \in \mathbf{N} \cdot \exists i \in \mathbf{N} \cdot p(i,j))$$

is true but the reverse implication is not (consider $p(i,j) \Leftrightarrow i = j$; the consequent is true but the antecedent is false).

As with the priority of propositional operators, it is possible to reduce the need for parenthesis by adopting some conventions. The body of a quantified expression is considered to extend as far to the right as possible—thus:

$$\forall m, n \in \mathbf{N} \cdot (m = n \vee (\exists p \in \mathbf{Z} \cdot (p \neq 0 \wedge m + p = n)))$$

can be written:

$$\forall m, n \in \mathbf{N} \cdot m = n \vee \exists p \in \mathbf{Z} \cdot p \neq 0 \wedge m + p = n$$

The bound variables in a closed quantified expression are somewhat like the variables in a program: they can be changed (systematically) without changing the meaning of the expression. Thus, the preceding expression is equivalent to:

$$\forall i, j \in \mathbf{N} \cdot i = j \vee \exists k \in \mathbf{Z} \cdot k \neq 0 \wedge i + k = j$$

When changing bound variables, it is necessary to ensure that the meaning is not changed by using an identifier which already occurs free.

Given the reading of universal and existential quantification as (respectively) conjunctions and disjunctions, the following forms de Morgan's laws should come as no surprise:

$$(\forall x \in X \cdot p(x)) \Leftrightarrow \neg(\exists x \in X \cdot \neg p(x))$$
$$\neg(\forall x \in X \cdot p(x)) \Leftrightarrow (\exists x \in X \cdot \neg p(x))$$

These laws permit some simple equivalence proofs[4] to be conducted:

---

[4]It is observed above that the truth of sentences in the propositional calculus is decidable (cf. checking by truth tables). Although it is less obvious, there are semi-decision procedures for the pure predicate calculus. The truth of sentences in the predicate calculus with interpreted functions and equality is, however, not in general decidable.

$$(\forall i \in \mathbf{N}_1 \cdot \exists j \in \mathbf{N}_1 \cdot i < j \wedge \textit{is-prime}(j))$$
$$\Leftrightarrow \ \neg(\exists i \in \mathbf{N}_1 \cdot \neg(\exists j \in \mathbf{N}_1 \cdot i < j \wedge \textit{is-prime}(j)))$$
$$\Leftrightarrow \ \neg(\exists i \in \mathbf{N}_1 \cdot \forall j \in \mathbf{N}_1 \cdot \neg(i < j \wedge \textit{is-prime}(j)))$$
$$\Leftrightarrow \ \neg(\exists i \in \mathbf{N}_1 \cdot \forall j \in \mathbf{N}_1 \cdot j \leq i \vee \neg\textit{is-prime}(j))$$
$$\Leftrightarrow \ \neg(\exists i \in \mathbf{N}_1 \cdot \forall j \in \mathbf{N}_1 \cdot \textit{is-prime}(j) \Rightarrow j \leq i)$$

Having accepted that $\exists$ corresponds to "there exists one or more", there are occasions where it is useful to be able to express "there exists exactly one". This is written as $\exists!$. For example:

$$\forall i,j \in \mathbf{N}_1 \cdot \textit{is-prime}(i) \wedge \textit{is-prime}(j) \wedge i \neq j \Rightarrow$$
$$\exists! d \in \mathbf{N}_1 \cdot \textit{is-common-divisor}(i,j,d)$$

This quantifier can be defined:

$$\exists! x \in X \cdot p(x)$$

as an abbreviation for:

$$\exists x \in X \cdot p(x) \wedge \forall y \in X \cdot p(y) \Rightarrow x = y$$

All of the laws of the propositional calculus remain true when general logical expressions (i.e. including quantified expressions) are substituted for the E_i. The language which is now available (propositional operators, truth-valued functions and quantified expressions) is known as the *predicate calculus*[5].

Exercises

1. Which of the following expressions are true:

   (a) $\exists i \in \mathbf{N} \cdot i = i$

   (b) $\forall i \in \mathbf{N} \cdot i = i$

   (c) $\exists i \in \mathbf{N} \cdot i \neq i$

   (d) $\exists i,j \in \mathbf{N}_1 \cdot i \bmod j \geq j$

   (e) $\forall i \in \mathbf{Z} \cdot \exists j \in \mathbf{Z} \cdot i + j = 0$

   (f) $\exists j \in \mathbf{Z} \cdot \forall i \in \mathbf{Z} \cdot i + j = 0$

[5]Strictly, in this book, only the first-order predicate calculus is used. This means that quantification will only range over simple values like natural numbers—names of truth-valued functions are not quantified.

(g) $\forall i, j \in \mathbf{N} \cdot i \neq j$

(h) $\forall i \in \mathbf{N} \cdot \exists j \in \mathbf{N} \cdot j = i - 1$

(i) $\forall i \in \mathbf{N} \cdot \exists j \in \mathbf{N} \cdot i < j < 2 * i \wedge \textit{is-odd}(j)$

(j) $\forall i \in \mathbf{N}_1 \cdot \neg \textit{is-prime}(4 * i)$

(k) $\forall i \in \mathbf{N} \cdot \exists j \in \mathbf{N} \cdot j \leq 3 \wedge \textit{is-leapyr}(i + j)$

2. Define a truth-valued function corresponding to:

$$\_ \geq \_ : \mathbf{Z} \times \mathbf{Z} \to \mathbf{B}$$

3. Express, using quantifiers, the fact that there is not a largest integer.

4. A function, *sign*, yields a value in the set:

$$\{-1, 0, 1\}$$

depending on whether its argument is negative, zero, or strictly positive. Write a definition and record some properties of *sign*.

5. * An extended modulus operator can be applied to negative (as well as positive) numbers. There are various forms of this operator. Mathematically, it is convenient to ensure that:

$$m \bmod n + (m \div n) * n = m$$

where $\div$ is an integer division operator. Define this operator.

Chapter 2

Proofs

Proofs are a central part of the program development method described
in this book. One property of a formal specification is that proofs can be
written which clarify its consequences; Chapters 8 to 10 use formal specifications as the basis of design: design steps give rise to proof obligations.
Once the methods are understood, most proof obligations can be discharged
by rigorous arguments. Such arguments are, however, only safe if they are
undertaken with a knowledge of how a formal proof could be constructed.
It is, therefore, necessary to gain practice in the construction of such formal
proofs.

Chapter 1 shows one way of verifying propositional expressions: truth
tables provide a model theory for propositional calculus. In this chapter, a
proof theory is given: Section 2.2 provides a proof theory for propositional
calculus; in Section 2.3, this is extended to cover the predicate calculus. The
combined proof theory is used in proofs throughout the book.

2.1 Concept of Proof

In order for proofs to be useful, they must possess a number of properties. Among these are the requirement that the proofs should be natural and that they should ensure certainty.

It is difficult to be precise about what constitutes a natural proof. When an argument is presented informally, large steps are made without detailed justification. This is not, in itself, wrong. The concept of informal proof is to indicate how a proof could be constructed: the major steps are given in the knowledge that further details can be provided if these major steps are in doubt.

Another aspect of what constitutes a natural proof concerns the crucial distinction between the discovery and presentation of a proof. A proof is often found by working back from the goal; sub-goals are created and discharged until the sub-goals correspond to known facts. In order to show how the steps relate, it is normal to present an argument working forwards from the known facts towards the goal. This forward presentation is more natural to read. But when readers become writers, they must learn to discover proofs one way and present their steps in a different order[1].

It should be clear that the claim that something has been proved must eliminate doubt. Unfortunately, informal arguments cannot create certainty. To provide a comparison, consider the truth tables for propositional calculus discussed in Section 1.1. It is easy to mechanize these in a way which determines the truth of sequents. Providing the program is correct, doubt about the truth of a sequent can always be eliminated by running the program. In order to achieve the same level of certainty with a proof, it is necessary to reduce proof construction to a "game with symbols": each proof step must depend only on known (i.e. proven) facts and be justified by one of a fixed set of inference rules. The inference rules themselves must require only the mechanical rearrangement of symbols. Such proofs are called *formal*.

The style of proof presented in this chapter is known in logic textbooks as "natural deduction". The proofs are formal in the sense above. The inference rules essentially show how to generate true sequents from others. One claim to the adjective "natural" is that the presentations enable a reader to understand the main steps in a proof; inner boxes present the detailed

---

[1]A purely technical characterization of a natural proof system is that there are introduction and elimination rules for each logical operator—although the system presented here also satisfies this requirement, this is not its major justification.

arguments for the major steps. The question of discovery (backward, goal-directed) versus presentation (forward) of proofs is not as easy to illustrate in a book as it is on the blackboard. The experience of teaching natural deduction proofs is, however, very encouraging and a style of proof discovery is investigated in some of the examples below.

Consider, for example, a rule for the introduction of a disjunction:

$$\frac{E_2}{E_1 \vee E_2}$$

This states that, under the assumption that some logical expression (E_2) has been proved, then—as a conclusion—a disjunction of that logical expression with any other is also true (proved). As above, the E_i stand for arbitrary logical expressions. The rule is, in fact, a schema for many inferences. Thus, if at some point in a proof:

$$post(x, f(x))$$

has been established, then:

$$\neg pre(x) \vee post(x, f(x))$$

and thus (treating implication as an abbreviation):

$$pre(x) \Rightarrow post(x, f(x))$$

is also true. There is a similar inference rule:

$$\frac{E_1}{E_1 \vee E_2}$$

These two inference rules can be expressed together as:

$$\vee\text{-I} \qquad \frac{E_i}{E_1 \vee E_2} \qquad (1 \leq i \leq 2)$$

The name ($\vee$-I) is a reminder that this rule justifies the introduction of disjunctions. Notice that the known expression can be either the first or the second disjunct because the assumption is shown as E_i. The validity of such a rule follows from the truth tables: the resulting disjunction must be true in all worlds where one of its disjuncts is true.

This inference rule, and the ones which follow, are mechanical in the sense that they can be readily checked: if it is claimed that a step of a proof follows by "or introduction" from an earlier step, then one or other of the disjuncts must exactly match the earlier expression. In general, an inference rule has a list of hypotheses and a conclusion separated by a horizontal line. If existing steps can be found which match each of the hypotheses, then a new step in the proof can be generated which matches the conclusion. The use of the matching concept should be obvious but note that, when steps involve complex expressions, matching must observe the structure of an expression as determined by the priority of its operators. Thus:

$$p \wedge r \vee r$$

matches:

$$E_1 \vee E_2$$

but not:

$$E_1 \wedge E_2$$

If there are several hypotheses for an inference rule, they can be matched in any order with existing lines in a proof.

How can conjunctions be generated in a proof? The "and introduction" rule is:

$$\wedge\text{-I} \qquad \frac{E_1;\ E_2}{E_1 \wedge E_2}$$

Here, there are two hypotheses separated by a semicolon. There are connections between inference rules and sequents which are discussed below. The reason that semicolons are used to separate hypotheses of inference rules (rather than commas as in sequents) is that some inference rules require sequents as hypotheses. The "and introduction" inference rule states that, in order to conclude $E_1 \wedge E_2$, the conjuncts must both be proved separately. As one would expect, there is more work to be done to justify a conjunction than a disjunction. On the other hand, precisely because a conjunction is stronger, the rule which permits elimination of a conjunction ($\wedge$-E) shows that either conjunct is true:

$$\wedge\text{-E} \qquad \frac{E_1 \wedge E_2}{E_i} \qquad (1 \leq i \leq 2)$$

A way is needed to record that some proposition (E) is a consequence of (i.e. can be proved from) others (Γ). This is written as a sequent with a new turnstile symbol:

$$\Gamma \vdash E$$

Using this new turnstile symbol, it can be shown how the proof rules[2], which are given above, can be applied to sequents. Thus, for example, if:

$$\Gamma \vdash p$$

has been proven, then ∨-I can be used to generate:

$$\Gamma \vdash p \vee q$$

A list of sequents can be used to record a whole proof. As an example of such a proof, "and" is shown to be associative. An *associative* operator is one in which:

$$x \text{ op } (y \text{ op } z) = (x \text{ op } y) \text{ op } z$$

For "and" it is necessary to show that:

$$p \wedge (q \wedge r) \vdash (p \wedge q) \wedge r$$

The hypothesis of this sequent matches that of the "and elimination" rule (note that E_2 in the rule is matched by a conjunction), thus:

$$p \wedge (q \wedge r) \vdash p$$

and, similarly:

$$p \wedge (q \wedge r) \vdash q \wedge r$$

The conclusion of this sequent again matches the hypothesis of the "and elimination" rule which can now be used to generate the next steps:

$$p \wedge (q \wedge r) \vdash q$$
$$p \wedge (q \wedge r) \vdash r$$

There are now known (proven) facts that—under some hypothesis—p and q are each true; the "and introduction" rule can be used to yield:

$$p \wedge (q \wedge r) \vdash p \wedge q$$

---

[2]The objective is to find enough inference rules so that all true statements of the model theory can be proven. That this is even achievable is not obvious. In fact, the notions of validity (⊨) and provability (⊢) are equivalent in a sense which is discussed in Section 3.3.

And, finally, the "and introduction" rule can again be used on this last sequent and the immediately preceding one, to give:

$$p \wedge (q \wedge r) \vdash (p \wedge q) \wedge r$$

Here again, the matching should be carefully checked. The way in which parentheses have been introduced to reflect the matching should also be noted.

Even in this simple example, (cf. upper part of Figure 2.1), the argument is not easy to follow; when more than one hypothesis is involved, the presentation becomes clumsy. The natural deduction style, which is explained in detail in the next section, shows the dependencies on hypotheses at the head of a box beginning with the keyword from; the overall goal closes the box with the keyword infer; all of the numbered lines within the box are true under the assumptions of the embracing boxes. Thus the proof of the associativity of "and" is presented in the natural deduction style as follows:

	from $p \wedge (q \wedge r)$	
1	p	$\wedge$-E(h)
2	$q \wedge r$	$\wedge$-E(h)
3	q	$\wedge$-E(2)
4	r	$\wedge$-E(2)
5	$p \wedge q$	$\wedge$-I(1,3)
	infer $(p \wedge q) \wedge r$	$\wedge$-I(5,4)

Each line is justified by writing, on the right, the inference rule which is used; in parentheses are listed either the line numbers or h (for the hypothesis) of the expressions to which the rule is applied. The relationship between these two styles of presenting the proof is shown in Figure 2.1.

For such elementary results, this level of detail is certainly excessive. It is, however, worth remembering that a simple arithmetic result like:

$$(i + j) + k = (k + j) + i$$

would take several steps of commutativity and associativity to justify formally.

The earlier discussion about forward versus backward proof presentation can be seen in this example—although it is clearer on the less obvious results of the next section. The preceding discussion has been in terms of working

1	$p \wedge (q \wedge r) \vdash p$	$\wedge$-E
2	$p \wedge (q \wedge r) \vdash q \wedge r$	$\wedge$-E
3	$p \wedge (q \wedge r) \vdash q$	$\wedge$-E(2)
4	$p \wedge (q \wedge r) \vdash r$	$\wedge$-E(2)
5	$p \wedge (q \wedge r) \vdash p \wedge q$	$\wedge$-I(1,3)
6	$p \wedge (q \wedge r) \vdash (p \wedge q) \wedge r$	$\wedge$-I(5,4)

from $p \wedge (q \wedge r)$

1	p	$\wedge$-E(h)
2	$q \wedge r$	$\wedge$-E(h)
3	q	$\wedge$-E(2)
4	r	$\wedge$-E(2)
5	$p \wedge q$	$\wedge$-I(1,3)
	infer $(p \wedge q) \wedge r$	$\wedge$-I(5,4)

Figure 2.1: Comparison of Proof Styles

forward from the known facts. But it would be possible to look at the form of the overall goal and generate (what became) lines 5 and 4 as sub-goals; lines 1 and 3 are then sub-goals to achieve line 5, and the "and elimination" steps then become the obvious way of achieving the set of collected sub-goals.

Such proofs could, of course, be presented in the reverse order (e.g. as infer/ from boxes). This is not done because one is writing proofs in order that they can be read. As pointed out above, it is easier to understand an argument which proceeds from known facts towards a goal.

The use of the rules as "tactics" for decomposing a goal should not be viewed as an algorithm to generate proofs. In general, many rules would be applicable; some of them would lead to blind alleys.

Thus the rules of the natural deduction game with symbols are that new lines can only be generated from earlier lines in the same, or some enclosing box. As when generating truth tables, any logical expression can be substituted for the E_i.

When proof rules are used in reasoning about programs, specific propositions are substituted for the E_i. In the proof of the associativity of "and", no specific propositions are used and thus the proof that:

$$p \wedge (q \wedge r) \vdash (p \wedge q) \wedge r$$

justifies a new inference rule which can be used in subsequent proofs:

$\wedge$-ass $$\frac{E_1 \wedge (E_2 \wedge E_3)}{(E_1 \wedge E_2) \wedge E_3}$$

2.2 Propositional Calculus

The entire proof theory of propositional calculus can be based on very few rules. In order to minimize the number, this section treats as basic only the operators "or" and "not" and defines the others in terms of these basic operators. An increasingly useful proof theory is constructed by justifying, using natural deduction, *derived rules*. Among other things, these rules facilitate manipulation of the defined operators "and", "implies" and "equivalence". For the reader who finds this development too detailed, all of the rules needed in subsequent chapters are given in Appendix A.

The basic inference rules include:

$\vee$-I $$\frac{E_i}{E_1 \vee E_2} \qquad (1 \leq i \leq 2)$$

$\vee$-E $$\frac{E_1 \vee E_2;\ E_1 \vdash E;\ E_2 \vdash E}{E}$$

$\neg\vee$-I $$\frac{\neg E_1;\ \neg E_2}{\neg(E_1 \vee E_2)}$$

$\neg\vee$-E $$\frac{\neg(E_1 \vee E_2)}{\neg E_i} \qquad (1 \leq i \leq 2)$$

$\neg\neg$-I $$\frac{E}{\neg\neg E}$$

$\neg\neg$-E $$\frac{\neg\neg E}{E}$$

contr
$$\frac{E_1; \neg E_1}{E_2}$$

The ∨-I rule is discussed in the preceding section. The ∨-E rule requires that E is provable from each of E_1 and E_2; this rule uses semicolons to separate hypotheses which require separate proofs. The need for rules which combine "not" and "or" is a technical matter which is discussed in Section 3.3. The two rules concerned with the double "not" manipulation can be combined using a notation (a double horizontal line) which shows that it is valid to make the inference in either direction:

¬¬-I/E
$$\frac{E}{\neg \neg E}$$

The contradiction (contr) rule only makes sense in an environment with other assumptions: if, under some assumptions, both E_1 and its negation can be deduced, then there must be some contradiction in the assumptions and anything can be deduced. The use of this rule is illustrated in the proof of *modus ponens* below.

The first formal proof to be undertaken in this section shows that "or" is commutative:

$$E_1 \vee E_2 \vdash E_2 \vee E_1$$

In contrast to the proof in the preceding section, this result and its proof use E_i for the propositions. The reader should check carefully the matches of these identifiers with the similar identifiers in the inference rules. The proof is given in Figure 2.2. The inner boxes represent subsidiary proofs of:

$$E_1 \vdash E_2 \vee E_1$$
$$E_2 \vdash E_2 \vee E_1$$

These are then used in the final "or elimination". Notice that a reference to the number of an inner box (e.g. 1) refers to the implied sequent; the hypotheses of a box can be referred to (cf. justification of 1) as h1.

Since the commutativity proof is general, it makes a derived inference rule available for future proofs:

∨-comm
$$\frac{E_1 \vee E_2}{E_2 \vee E_1}$$

from $E_1 \lor E_2$
1   from E_1
     infer $E_2 \lor E_1$ $\lor$-I(h1)
2   from E_2
     infer $E_2 \lor E_1$ $\lor$-I(h2)
  infer $E_2 \lor E_1$ $\lor$-E(h,1,2)

Figure 2.2: Proof of Commutativity of "or"

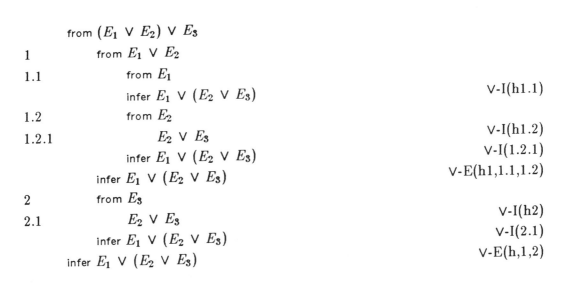

from $(E_1 \lor E_2) \lor E_3$
1   from $E_1 \lor E_2$
1.1   from E_1
     infer $E_1 \lor (E_2 \lor E_3)$ $\lor$-I(h1.1)
1.2   from E_2
1.2.1 $E_2 \lor E_3$ $\lor$-I(h1.2)
     infer $E_1 \lor (E_2 \lor E_3)$ $\lor$-I(1.2.1)
    infer $E_1 \lor (E_2 \lor E_3)$ $\lor$-E(h1,1.1,1.2)
2   from E_3
2.1 $E_2 \lor E_3$ $\lor$-I(h2)
     infer $E_1 \lor (E_2 \lor E_3)$ $\lor$-I(2.1)
  infer $E_1 \lor (E_2 \lor E_3)$ $\lor$-E(h,1,2)

Figure 2.3: Proof of Associativity of "or"

Derived rules can make proofs much clearer. Such derived rules are not, however, necessary since it would always be possible to generate appropriate additional steps in place of the use of the derived rule.

Another proof which relies heavily on ∨-E is that for the associativity of "or":

$$(E_1 \lor E_2) \lor E_3 \vdash E_1 \lor (E_2 \lor E_3)$$

This proof is shown in Figure 2.3 and presents the opportunity to say more about the structure of natural deduction proofs. Clearly, the outermost:

from Γ

$\quad \ldots$

infer E

represents:

$$\Gamma \vdash E$$

The ellipsis points elide a list of (numbered) lines which comprise a proof. The line numbering reflects the nesting of proofs. An inner from/infer box is given one line number; in addition to its hypotheses written in the from line, those of any embracing box can be used. Thus the sub-proof labeled "line 1" represents:

$$(E_1 \lor E_2) \lor E_3; \ E_1 \lor E_2 \vdash E_1 \lor (E_2 \lor E_3)$$

and the five lines contained in its from/ infer box, represent its proof: each line in the proof corresponds to a true sequent.

The proof that disjunction is associative also provides an example in terms of which it is possible to give some indication of how natural deduction proofs are discovered. The overall goal is:

from $(E_1 \lor E_2) \lor E_3$

$\quad \ldots$

infer $E_1 \lor (E_2 \lor E_3)$?

The question mark in the justification position of a line shows that it is yet to be proved. When a result has to be proved based on an assumption which is a disjunction, it is worth trying to prove the desired result from each disjunct (thus setting up a final ∨-E). Here, this heuristic gives rise to the nested boxes:

from $(E_1 \lor E_2) \lor E_3$

i   from $E_1 \lor E_2$
       infer $E_1 \lor (E_2 \lor E_3)$?

j   from E_3
       infer $E_1 \lor (E_2 \lor E_3)$?

   infer $E_1 \lor (E_2 \lor E_3)$ $\lor$-E(h,i,j)

The lines have been numbered i and j since there might be other lines to be inserted. There is no necessity when searching for a proof to tackle the sub-goals in a fixed order; here, it is quite permissible to tackle sub-goal j first. One advantage of the style of writing the applications of proof rules as though they were functions is that they can be nested; thus, the justification for the conclusion of j can be filled in as follows:

from $(E_1 \lor E_2) \lor E_3$

i   from $E_1 \lor E_2$
       infer $E_1 \lor (E_2 \lor E_3)$?

j   from E_3
       infer $E_1 \lor (E_2 \lor E_3)$ $\lor$-I($\lor$-I(hj))

   infer $E_1 \lor (E_2 \lor E_3)$ $\lor$-E(h,i,j)

This should be compared with the box labeled 2 in the complete proof in Figure 2.3. The only open step is now that labeled i; it is again subjected to decomposition by "or elimination":

from $(E_1 \lor E_2) \lor E_3$

i   from $E_1 \lor E_2$

i.m   from E_1
         infer $E_1 \lor (E_2 \lor E_3)$?

i.n   from E_2
         infer $E_1 \lor (E_2 \lor E_3)$?

     infer $E_1 \lor (E_2 \lor E_3)$ $\lor$-E(hi,i.m,i.n)

j   from E_3
       infer $E_1 \lor (E_2 \lor E_3)$ $\lor$-I($\lor$-I(j))

   infer $E_1 \lor (E_2 \lor E_3)$ $\lor$-E(h,i,j)

The relationship of this stage of the discovery process to the proof given in Figure 2.3 should be clear.

One of the advantages of the natural deduction style is that the proofs can be read, from the outer level, inwards. With practice, this also becomes a way of constructing proofs, but the hints given are no more than heuristics: insight is needed in order to discover good proofs.

Exercise 1 below proves:

$$E_1 \lor (E_2 \lor E_3) \vdash (E_1 \lor E_2) \lor E_3$$

The two parts of the associativity proof justify the following (bidirectional) derived rule:

∨-ass
$$\frac{(E_1 \lor E_2) \lor E_3}{E_1 \lor (E_2 \lor E_3)}$$

Having established associativity for "or", it is now possible to omit parentheses in expressions involving "or" (at the same level). Thus, rather than write either:

$$(E_1 \lor E_2) \lor E_3$$

or:

$$E_1 \lor (E_2 \lor E_3)$$

it is permissible to write:

$$E_1 \lor E_2 \lor E_3$$

In addition, the "or" introduction and elimination rules can be generalized as follows:

∨-I
$$\frac{E_i}{E_1 \lor E_2 \lor ... \lor E_n} \qquad (1 \le i \le n)$$

∨-E
$$\frac{E_1 \lor E_2 \lor ... \lor E_n;\ E_1 \vdash E;\ ...;\ E_n \vdash E}{E}$$

¬∨-I
$$\frac{\neg E_1;\ \neg E_2;\ ...;\ \neg E_n}{\neg(E_1 \lor E_2 \lor ... \lor E_n)}$$

¬∨-E
$$\frac{\neg(E_1 \lor E_2 \lor ... \lor E_n)}{\neg E_i} \qquad (1 \le i \le n)$$

Many of the results established in this section are familiar from Chapter 1. It must, however, be realized that the proofs here are in no way arguing from the truth tables: the formal proofs are conducted purely by playing the game with symbols. The certainty of correctness comes, here, from the fact that the game can be mechanized—a program can be written to check such proofs.

The "and" operator can be introduced by the definition:

$$\wedge\text{-defn} \qquad \frac{\neg(\neg E_1 \vee \neg E_2)}{E_1 \wedge E_2}$$

Having defined "and", rules for its manipulation can now be proved. Thus to justify:

$$\wedge\text{-I} \qquad \frac{E_1;\ E_2}{E_1 \wedge E_2}$$

the following proof is given:

from $E_1; E_2$

1	$\neg\neg E_1$	$\neg\neg\text{-I(h)}$
2	$\neg\neg E_2$	$\neg\neg\text{-I(h)}$
3	$\neg(\neg E_1 \vee \neg E_2)$	$\neg\vee\text{-I}(1, 2)$

infer $E_1 \wedge E_2$ $\qquad\qquad\qquad\qquad \wedge\text{-defn}(3)$

Here, the discovery process uses the only rule available to tackle the overall conclusion; this gives rise to the sub-goal at line 3. Line 3, in turn, matches the $\neg\vee$-I rule which gives rise to sub-goals 1 and 2; these are obvious candidates for a $\neg\neg$ rule.

Exercises 2 and 3 justify the derived rules:

$$\wedge\text{-E} \qquad \frac{E_1 \wedge E_2}{E_i} \qquad (1 \leq i \leq 2)$$

$$\neg\wedge\text{-I} \qquad \frac{\neg E_i}{\neg(E_1 \wedge E_2)} \qquad (1 \leq i \leq 2)$$

The next rule to be justified is:

$$\neg\wedge\text{-E} \qquad \frac{\neg(E_1 \wedge E_2);\ \neg E_1 \vdash E;\ \neg E_2 \vdash E}{E}$$

The proof is as follows:

from $\neg(E_1 \wedge E_2);\ \neg E_1 \vdash E;\ \neg E_2 \vdash E$

1      $\neg\neg(\neg E_1 \vee \neg E_2)$ $\wedge$-defn(h)

2      $\neg E_1 \vee \neg E_2$ $\neg\neg$-E(1)

infer E $\vee$-E(2,h,h)

Notice how the $\vee$-E uses the two sequents given in the overall premise. It is also important to notice that the inference rules must not, in general, be applied to inner expressions; the hypotheses of deduction rules are intended to match lines in the proof (not parts thereof). The reader should not find it difficult to construct examples of invalid arguments where this constraint is ignored. An exception to this restriction is that the definition rules (e.g. $\wedge$-defn) can be applied to arbitrary sub-expressions.

The commutativity of "and":

$\wedge$-comm $\qquad \dfrac{E_1 \wedge E_2}{E_2 \wedge E_1}$

can be proved by using $\wedge$-E/$\wedge$-I. The associativity of "and":

$\wedge$-ass $\qquad \dfrac{(E_1 \wedge E_2) \wedge E_3}{E_1 \wedge (E_2 \wedge E_3)}$

can be justified by repeated use of $\wedge$-E and $\wedge$-I. As with disjunctions, this justifies the use of the more general rules:

$\wedge$-I $\qquad \dfrac{E_1;\ E_2;\ \ldots;\ E_n}{E_1 \wedge E_2 \wedge \ldots \wedge E_n}$

$\wedge$-E $\qquad \dfrac{E_1 \wedge E_2 \wedge \ldots \wedge E_n}{E_i} \qquad (1 \leq i \leq n)$

$\neg\wedge$-I $\qquad \dfrac{\neg E_i}{\neg(E_1 \wedge E_2 \wedge \ldots \wedge E_n)} \qquad (1 \leq i \leq n)$

$\neg\wedge$-E $\qquad \dfrac{\neg(E_1 \wedge E_2 \wedge \ldots \wedge E_n);\ \neg E_1 \vdash E;\ \ldots;\ \neg E_n \vdash E}{E}$

There are many different ways of proving more advanced results. Although brevity is not itself the main touchstone of style, short proofs are often clearer than long ones. A very helpful rule—which provides a valid way of applying rules on inner sub-expressions—is to generalize rules like ∧-I to:

∧-subs
$$\frac{E_1 \wedge \ldots \wedge E_i \wedge \ldots \wedge E_n; \ E_i \vdash E}{E_1 \wedge \ldots \wedge E \wedge \ldots \wedge E_n}$$

The proof applies ∧-E n times, the sequent, and then n applications of ∧-I. This rule can be used as, for example, ∧-subs/∨-I to deduce:

$$E_1 \wedge E_2 \wedge E_3 \vdash E_1 \wedge (E_2 \vee E) \wedge E_3$$

Similarly, there is a derived rule:

∨-subs
$$\frac{E_1 \vee \ldots \vee E_i \vee \ldots \vee E_n; \ E_i \vdash E}{E_1 \vee \ldots \vee E \vee \ldots \vee E_n}$$

This proof uses ∨-I in n-1 sub-proofs; with the sequent in one; followed by a final ∨-E.

The distributive laws of propositional calculus are:

∨∧-dist
$$\frac{E_1 \vee E_2 \wedge E_3}{(E_1 \vee E_2) \wedge (E_1 \vee E_3)}$$

∧∨-dist
$$\frac{E_1 \wedge (E_2 \vee E_3)}{E_1 \wedge E_2 \vee E_1 \wedge E_3}$$

The general pattern of these proofs is similar; an example is shown in Figure 2.4. Distribution from the right is easy to prove—it relies on left distribution and commutativity.

Some of these elementary proofs are surprisingly lengthy but, having prepared the ground, the proofs of de Morgan's laws are very short (cf. Exercise 7).

Implication can be defined:

⇒-defn
$$\frac{\neg E_1 \vee E_2}{E_1 \Rightarrow E_2}$$

To show:

$$\neg E_1 \vee E_2, \ E_1 \vdash E_2$$

	from $E_1 \lor E_2 \land E_3$	
1	from E_1	
1.1	$E_1 \lor E_2$	$\lor$-I(h1)
1.2	$E_1 \lor E_3$	$\lor$-I(h1)
	infer $(E_1 \lor E_2) \land (E_1 \lor E_3)$	$\land$-I(1.1,1.2)
2	from $E_2 \land E_3$	
2.1	$(E_1 \lor E_2) \land E_3$	$\land$-subs/$\lor$-I(h2)
	infer $(E_1 \lor E_2) \land (E_1 \lor E_3)$	$\land$-subs/$\lor$-I(2.1)
	infer $(E_1 \lor E_2) \land (E_1 \lor E_3)$	$\lor$-E(h,1,2)

Figure 2.4: Proof of Distributivity of "or" over "and"

use:

	from $\neg E_1 \lor E_2,\ E_1$	
1	from $\neg E_1$	
	infer E_2	contr(h,h1)
2	from E_2	
	infer E_2	h2
	infer E_2	$\lor$-E(h,1,2)

Notice how the final step of the box 1 uses the contradiction rule. Using $\Rightarrow$-defn this justifies the rule:

$$\Rightarrow\text{-E} \qquad \frac{E_1 \Rightarrow E_2;\ E_1}{E_2}$$

which is known in logic textbooks as *modus ponens*.

In classical propositional calculus, it can be shown that if E_2 can be proved under the assumption E_1 (i.e. $E_1 \vdash E_2$), then $\vdash E_1 \Rightarrow E_2$ holds. This is called the "deduction theorem". Section 3.3 explains why some results of classical logic do not hold in the system used in this book. In the case of the deduction theorem, a weaker form is valid which relies on the assumption of the "excluded middle" for E_1:

$$E_1 \lor \neg E_1$$

This claim is written by stating that the expression is of type Boolean:

$E_1 \in \mathbf{B}$

The deduction theorem (here) is:

$$\frac{E_1 \vdash E_2;\ E_1 \in \mathbf{B}}{\neg E_1 \vee E_2}$$

or:

$\Rightarrow$-I $$\frac{E_1 \vdash E_2;\ E_1 \in \mathbf{B}}{E_1 \Rightarrow E_2}$$

and its justification is:

from $E_1 \vdash E_2;\ E_1 \in \mathbf{B}$

		h
1	$E_1 \vee \neg E_1$	
2	from E_1	
2.1	E_2	inf(h2,h)
	infer $\neg E_1 \vee E_2$	$\vee$-I(2.1)
3	from $\neg E_1$	
	infer $\neg E_1 \vee E_2$	$\vee$-I(h3)
	infer $\neg E_1 \vee E_2$	$\vee$-E(1,2,3)

Line 2.1 is justified by showing the use of the inference rule which is given in the hypothesis; such justifications are marked by "inf".

Finally, the equivalence operator is introduced by the definition:

$\Leftrightarrow$-defn $$\frac{(E_1 \Rightarrow E_2) \wedge (E_2 \Rightarrow E_1)}{E_1 \Leftrightarrow E_2}$$

An extensive set of derived rules in given in Appendix A; they are arranged for easy use rather than in the order of proof. It is legitimate to use any of these rules in proofs of results in subsequent sections. In fact, a relatively small set suffices for most proofs.

Exercises

1. Prove (using either $\vee$-I/$\vee$-E, or associativity in the other direction and commutativity):

$$E_1 \vee (E_2 \vee E_3) \vdash (E_1 \vee E_2) \vee E_3$$

2. Prove (hint: expand the conjunction and then use ¬∨-E and ¬¬-E):

$$E_1 \wedge E_2 \vdash E_i \qquad for 1 \leq i \leq 2$$

3. Prove (hint: begin by using ∨-I and ¬¬-I):

$$\neg E_i \vdash \neg(E_1 \wedge E_2) \qquad for 1 \leq i \leq 2$$

4. Prove (hint: remember to set up the final ∨-E):

$$(E_1 \vee E_2) \wedge (E_1 \vee E_3) \vdash E_1 \vee (E_2 \wedge E_3)$$

5. Prove (hint: use ∧-I to find a disjunction on which to base an ∨-E):

$$E_1 \wedge (E_2 \vee E_3) \vdash E_1 \wedge E_2 \vee E_1 \wedge E_3$$

6. Prove:

$$E_1 \wedge E_2 \vee E_1 \wedge E_3 \vdash E_1 \wedge (E_2 \vee E_3)$$

7. Prove the four results necessary to justify de Morgan's laws.

$$\wedge\text{-deM} \qquad \frac{\neg(E_1 \wedge E_2)}{\neg E_1 \vee \neg E_2}$$

$$\vee\text{-deM} \qquad \frac{\neg(E_1 \vee E_2)}{\neg E_1 \wedge \neg E_2}$$

8. The proofs that certain vacuous implications hold are straightforward; prove the results necessary to establish:

$$\text{vac}\Rightarrow\text{-I} \qquad \frac{\neg E_1}{E_1 \Rightarrow E_2} \qquad \frac{E_2}{E_1 \Rightarrow E_2}$$

9. Prove the result necessary to establish that the contrapositive of an implication holds:

$$\Rightarrow\text{-contrp} \qquad \frac{E_1 \Rightarrow E_2}{\neg E_2 \Rightarrow \neg E_1}$$

10. Prove:

$$E_1 \vee E_2 \Rightarrow E_3 \vdash (E_1 \Rightarrow E_3) \wedge (E_2 \Rightarrow E_3)$$

11. *

    (a) Prove the results (remember to do both for bidirectional rules) which justify:

$$\frac{(\neg E_1 \vee E_2) \wedge (E_1 \vee \neg E_2)}{E_1 \wedge E_2 \vee \neg E_1 \wedge \neg E_2}$$

$$\frac{E_1 \Leftrightarrow E_2}{E_1 \wedge E_2 \vee \neg E_1 \wedge \neg E_2}$$

$$\frac{E_1; E_2}{E_1 \Leftrightarrow E_2}$$

$$\frac{\neg E_1; \neg E_2}{E_1 \Leftrightarrow E_2}$$

$$\frac{\neg(E_1 \Leftrightarrow E_2)}{E_1 \wedge \neg E_2 \vee \neg E_1 \wedge E_2}$$

$$\frac{E_1 \Leftrightarrow E_2; E_1, E_2 \vdash E; \neg E_1, \neg E_2 \vdash E}{E}$$

$$\frac{\neg(E_1 \Leftrightarrow E_2); \neg E_1, E_2 \vdash E; E_1, \neg E_2 \vdash E}{E}$$

$$\frac{E_1 \wedge (E_2 \Leftrightarrow E_3)}{(E_1 \wedge E_2) \Leftrightarrow (E_1 \wedge E_3)}$$

    (b) Generate a counter-example (truth values) which shows that the following sequent does not hold:

$$(E_1 \wedge E_2) \Leftrightarrow (E_1 \wedge E_3) \vdash E_1 \wedge (E_2 \Leftrightarrow E_3)$$

    (c) Prove the result to justify:

$$\frac{E_1 \vee E_2 \Leftrightarrow E_1 \vee E_3}{E_1 \vee (E_2 \Leftrightarrow E_3)}$$

12. * Write inference rules for the "exclusive or" operator of Exercise 5 in Section 1.1 and develop a theory which includes some distribution properties.

2.3   Predicate Calculus

The development of the proof rules for the predicate calculus can be based on one of the quantifiers and the notion of equality. In this respect the way in which the theory is presented is very similar to that of the preceding section. There are, however, some technical problems with free variables and their substitution which make the development of the derived rules somewhat more difficult than for the propositional calculus. Relatively few rules about quantifiers are needed below. This section is restricted to presentation of those needed (in many cases, without proof); a wider-ranging set of rules is given in Appendix A.

A preliminary to the presentation of any rules is the establishment of some conventions on the use of letters. Letters at the end of the alphabet (x, etc.) are used for variables. The convention to use E_i for logical expressions is maintained, but is extended to show specific free variables; thus $E(x)$ has the variable x occurring free. It is explained above that terms are expressions (such as $2 + 3$) which denote values of some given type. The letter s—possibly subscripted—is used to denote terms.

An essential notion is that of substitution. The expression

$E(s/x)$

is formed by substituting all free occurrences of the variable x by the term s. Thus:

$$(x = 3 + 4)(7/x) \ = \ (7 = 3 + 4)$$

But the restriction to substituting free variables ensures that:

$$(\forall x \in X \cdot x = x)(7/x) \ = \ (\forall x \in X \cdot x = x)$$

There is a more ticklish problem with substitution concerning the capture of a variable. In making the substitution:

$$(y = 10 \lor \forall x \in \mathbf{N} \cdot x \neq 10 \ \Rightarrow \ x \neq y)(x/y)$$

the change from x to y should not cause a confusion between the free and bound variables. In such a case, it is sufficient to remember that bound variables can be systematically changed so that:

$$\forall x \in \mathbf{N} \cdot x \neq 10 \;\Rightarrow\; x \neq y$$

$$\forall i \in \mathbf{N} \cdot i \neq 10 \;\Rightarrow\; i \neq y$$

are equivalent. In a case where a free variable would be captured by a substitution, the danger is avoided by preceding the substitution with a suitable systematic change to the bound variable in question. Thus, the substitution above might yield:

$$x = 10 \;\vee\; \forall i \in \mathbf{N} \cdot i \neq 10 \;\Rightarrow\; i \neq x$$

Although these technicalities of substitution are important, the need to rely on them can be minimized by a careful choice of variables.

It would be possible to take either the existential or universal quantifier as basic and define the other in terms of it. Having used the disjunction as one of the basic forms for propositional calculus, it is natural to take the existential quantifier first. An obvious example of the rule for the introduction of this quantifier is:

$$7 \in \mathbf{N}_1, \text{is-prime}(7) \vdash \exists i \in \mathbf{N}_1 \cdot \text{is-prime}(i)$$

This states that knowing the type of the term (7) and knowing that it possesses a particular property (*is-prime*) establishes that there exist (one or more) values of the type which satisfy the property. In general:

$$\exists\text{-I} \qquad \frac{s \in X; \; E(s/x)}{\exists x \in X \cdot E(x)}$$

If the reader compares this rule with that for ∨-I, it can be seen as a natural generalization. The conclusion of the proof rule is essentially a disjunction over all elements of X; the second hypothesis establishes that the property does hold for some element of X. Notice that the first hypothesis establishes that the set X is not empty.

The form of the ∨-E rule shows that a conclusion which follows from a number of expressions also follows from their disjunction. The general idea of the ∃-E rule is the same. The need to show that E follows from each possible value in X is avoided by a subtle use of free variables. Thus:

$$\exists\text{-E} \qquad \frac{\exists x \in X \cdot E(x); \; y \in X, E(y/x) \vdash E_1}{E_1} \qquad (y \text{ is arbitrary})$$

The restriction that y is "arbitrary" requires that it is a variable which has not occurred in earlier proof steps. This restriction avoids certain invalid uses of the rule. It should also be the case that y does not occur as a free variable in E_1.

Once again, a comparison with the development of the propositional calculus should suggest the need for rules concerning negation. For the existential quantifier, these rules are:

$\neg\exists$-I
$$\frac{x \in X \vdash \neg E(x)}{\neg\exists x \in X \cdot E(x)}$$

$\neg\exists$-E
$$\frac{\neg\exists x \in X \cdot E(x);\ s \in X}{\neg E(s/x)}$$

The relationship between these rules and those for disjunction should be obvious when existential quantification (over finite sets) is viewed as an abbreviation for disjunction.

Other (basic) rules are required to introduce new variables and equalities. If the variable x has not been used in a proof (i.e. it is arbitrary) and the set X is not empty, the rule:

var-I
$$\frac{}{x \in X}$$ (x is arbitrary)

permits the introduction of a variable (notice that there are no hypotheses for this rule). Given two terms of a type, they are either equal or not:

=-comp
$$\frac{s_1, s_2 \in X}{(s_1 = s_2) \lor \neg(s_1 = s_2)}$$

The inequality of a term with itself yields a contradiction from which any conclusion follows:

=-contr
$$\frac{\neg(s = s)}{E}$$

The definition of the universal quantifier is given by the rule:

$\forall$-defn
$$\frac{\neg\exists x \in X \cdot \neg E(x)}{\forall x \in X \cdot E(x)}$$

This gives rise to the two generalized forms of de Morgan's rule:

$$\exists \text{deM} \qquad \frac{\neg \exists x \in X \cdot E(x)}{\forall x \in X \cdot \neg E(x)}$$

$$\forall \text{deM} \qquad \frac{\neg \forall x \in X \cdot E(x)}{\exists x \in X \cdot \neg E(x)}$$

These can be proved as derived rules.

Given the basic definition, it is possible to derive the introduction and elimination rules for the universal quantifier.

	from $x \in X \vdash E(x)$	
1	from $x \in X$	
1.1	$E(x)$	inf(h,h1)
	infer $\neg\neg E(x)$	$\neg\neg$-I(1.1)
2	$\neg \exists x \in X \cdot \neg E(x)$	$\neg\exists$-I(1)
	infer $\forall x \in X \cdot E(x)$	$\forall$-defn(2)

This justifies the rule:

$$\forall \text{-I} \qquad \frac{x \in X \vdash E(x)}{\forall x \in X \cdot E(x)}$$

Then:

	from $\forall x \in X \cdot E(x); s \in X$	
1	$\neg \exists x \in X \cdot \neg E(x)$	$\forall$-defn(h)
2	$\neg\neg E(s/x)$	$\neg\exists$-E(1,h)
	infer $E(s/x)$	$\neg\neg$-E(2)

justifies the rule:

$$\forall \text{-E} \qquad \frac{\forall x \in X \cdot E(x); \ s \in X}{E(s/x)}$$

An example of the use of this rule is to prove:

	from $\forall x \in X \cdot E_1(x) \Rightarrow E_2(x); \forall x \in X \cdot E_2(x) \Rightarrow E_3(x)$	
1	from $a \in X$	
1.1	$E_1(a) \Rightarrow E_2(a)$	$\forall$-E(h,h1)
1.2	$E_2(a) \Rightarrow E_3(a)$	$\forall$-E(h,h1)
	infer $E_1(a) \Rightarrow E_3(a)$	$\Rightarrow$-trans(1.1,1.2)
	infer $\forall x \in X \cdot E_1(x) \Rightarrow E_3(x)$	$\forall$-I(1)

From this example, it should also be clear how the change of bound variables can be formally justified.

Rules concerning negated universal quantifiers are:

$\neg\forall$-I
$$\frac{s \in X; \; \neg E(s/x)}{\neg\forall x \in X \cdot E(x)}$$

$\neg\forall$-E
$$\frac{\neg\forall x \in X \cdot E(x); \; y \in X, \neg E(y/x) \vdash E}{E} \qquad (y \text{ is arbitrary})$$

All of the rules for universal quantifiers are natural generalizations of the corresponding rules for conjunctions.

Some interesting derived rules concern the distribution of the two quantifiers over conjunctions and disjunctions.

$\exists\vee$-dist
$$\frac{\exists x \in X \cdot E_1(x) \vee E_2(x)}{(\exists x \in X \cdot E_1(x)) \vee (\exists x \in X \cdot E_2(x))}$$

$\exists\wedge$-dist
$$\frac{\exists x \in X \cdot E_1(x) \wedge E_2(x)}{(\exists x \in X \cdot E_1(x)) \wedge (\exists x \in X \cdot E_2(x))}$$

$\forall\vee$-dist
$$\frac{(\forall x \in X \cdot E_1(x)) \vee (\forall x \in X \cdot E_2(x))}{\forall x \in X \cdot E_1(x) \vee E_2(x)}$$

$\forall\wedge$-dist
$$\frac{(\forall x \in X \cdot E_1(x)) \wedge (\forall x \in X \cdot E_2(x))}{\forall x \in X \cdot E_1(x) \wedge E_2(x)}$$

The reader should understand why the converses of $\exists\wedge$-dist and $\forall\vee$-dist do not hold. Other useful derived rules are presented in Appendix A.

The equality notion ($=$) discussed above, can be used as a basis for substitution. Given two equal terms, one can be substituted for the other—but, given that they both evaluate to the same value, it is not necessary that all instances are substituted. The notation:

$$E[s_1/s_2]$$

denotes a formula obtained by substituting some occurrences of the term s_2 by the term s_1. The rule is:

$=$t-subs
$$\frac{s_1 = s_2; \; E}{E[s_2/s_1]}$$

For any given type of term:

=-term
$$\frac{s \in X}{s = s}$$

It is then possible to show that this equality is commutative and transitive:

=-comm
$$\frac{s_1 = s_2}{s_2 = s_1}$$

=-trans
$$\frac{s_1 = s_2; \ s_2 = s_3}{s_1 = s_3}$$

The proofs in Section 3.2 use definitions of functions as equalities. In some cases it would be possible to read the definitions ($\triangleq$) as equalities (=). But problems of expressions being undefined prevent this in the general case. This topic is discussed in Section 3.3. For now, some relevant rules are presented. Given a function definition:

$$f : D \to R$$
$$f(d) \ \triangleq \ e$$

it would be valid to conclude:

$$p(e) \vdash p(f(d))$$

In most cases, the required result concerns an application of the function to some arguments other than the given parameters. Writing:

$$e_0 = e(d_0/d)$$

the substitution rule becomes:

$\triangleq$-subs
$$\frac{d_0 \in D; \ E(e_0)}{E[f(d_0)/e_0]}$$

Hence, if *fact* is the normal factorial function:

$$3 \in \mathbf{N}, \ 6 = 3! \vdash fact(3) = 3!$$

To install an instance of a definition, the required rule is:

$\triangleq$-inst
$$\frac{d_0 \in D; \ E(f(d_0))}{E[e_0/f(d_0)]}$$

If f is defined by a conditional:

$$f(d) \quad \triangleq \quad \text{if } e \text{ then } et \text{ else } ef$$

the substitution which should be made depends on the value of e (after appropriate evaluation). Thus:

ifth-subs
$$\frac{d_0 \in D; \ e_0; \ E(et_0)}{E[f(d_0)/et_0]}$$

ifel-subs
$$\frac{d_0 \in D; \ \neg e_0; \ E(ef_0)}{E[f(d_0)/ef_0]}$$

Exercises

The exercises for this section are minimized, since subsequent sections provide ample examples of the use of the rules, and the development of the predicate calculus itself is not the immediate object.

1. Prove the derived rules for $\neg\forall$-I and $\neg\forall$-E.

2. * Prove the derived rules for $\exists\lor$-dist, $\exists\land$-dist, $\forall\lor$-dist and $\forall\land$-dist (remember to prove both forms of bidirectional rules).

Chapter 3

Functions

> The advantages of implicit definition over construction are roughly those of theft over honest toil.
> *B.Russell*

Several functions are directly defined in the preceding chapters. In this chapter, implicit specifications are given for functions. This mathematically familiar area provides the opportunity to illustrate the fact that implicit specifications can often be more concise than implementations (i.e. direct definitions). The next chapter develops the same idea and applies it to programs.

The second section of this chapter is concerned with proofs that direct definitions satisfy implicit specifications. In order to keep the reliance on new concepts to a minimum, most of the examples are concerned with natural numbers and their operators. Later chapters of the book extend the range of data types.

Section 3.3 reviews the reasons why the logical system which is used in this book is weaker than the classical logic presented in most textbooks: the system for dealing with partial functions is explained in detail. Some readers may choose to read only the first part of this somewhat technical section.

3.1 Implicit Specification

An *implicit specification* states *what* is to be computed whereas the direct definitions in previous chapters show *how* a result can be computed. (The term "direct definition" should not cause confusion. In these proofs of satisfaction, the direct definition is, in programming terms, being treated as an implementation, which has to be justified. It would fly in the face of mathematical convention to use a term like "implementation" and this has been avoided.) There are several reasons for preferring to record the implicit specification. Perhaps the most obvious reason is that the specification is often significantly shorter than a direct definition. For example, it is easy to state that the result of a square root function should be such that when squared it differs from the argument by at most some tolerance; a direct definition of, say, the Newton-Raphson approximation algorithm is much longer.

It must, however, be conceded that such convenient algebraic properties do not always exist. Because of the way in which UK income tax is calculated, for example, even the specification of a function which determines tax deductions is very algorithmic. However, implicit specifications are often significantly more concise than implementations, and thinking in terms of specifications can capitalize on this conciseness whenever possible. For significant problems there is a spectrum of specifications ranging from the very abstract to something which essentially describes the implementation. The full range of this spectrum becomes clear when data objects are discussed in subsequent chapters. One advantage of finding a specification far from the algorithmic end of the spectrum is that it may suggest a range of alternative implementations.

Another attribute of an implicit specification is that it can state the properties of the required result in a way which is understandable to the user. For example, the user of the square root function can be expected to be interested in the property of the final answer and to wish to leave the details of the chosen implementation to the developer.

There is, however, an attendant danger in implicit specification. Taking the same example again, the property as stated above would allow for either the negative or the positive root to be generated. This may be what is required; if not it is obvious how additional properties can be stated. An implicit specification must be such that all of the properties on which users wish to rely are consequences of the specification. Viewed from the other side, the user should rely only on the specification (and its consequences).

There are two remaining arguments for recording implicit specifications. The points are more subtle but, in practical applications, very important. Whereas any particular algorithm will yield a specific result, a specification can state a range of acceptable results. Square root (over real numbers with a tolerance) provides a good example. Moreover, an implicit specification can provide an explicit place for recording assumptions about arguments. Many computer programs are written with certain assumptions. The square root example could again be pressed into service by saying that its argument must be a positive real number (if the result is also to be a real number); but more interesting examples below illustrate how assumptions often concern the inter-relationship of values. A specification can provide a way of making explicit assumptions (pre-condition) which are otherwise hidden consequences of an algorithm.

A function which is to yield the maximum number from the set of numbers to which it is applied gives:

$$maxs(\{3,7,1\}) = 7$$

Its specification might be written:

$maxs$ (s: set of $\mathbf{N}$) r: $\mathbf{N}$

pre $s \neq \{\}$

post $r \in s \wedge \forall i \in s \cdot i \leq r$

The first line of this specification defines the signature of the function. The syntax used is slightly different from that used in Chapter 1: here, the style is intentionally closer to that of programming languages like Pascal. Names are given to both arguments and results. These names are followed by their type. Thus $maxs$ takes a finite set of natural numbers as its argument (Chapter 4 presents set notation in detail) and yields a single natural number as result. The names given are the link to the pre- and post-conditions. The identifiers used within these two truth-valued functions refer to the values of the objects which are named in the first line.

The *pre-condition* of a function records assumptions about the arguments to which it is to be applied. For this example, its type is:

$pre\text{-}maxs$: set of $\mathbf{N} \rightarrow \mathbf{B}$

Notice how the keyword pre is used in the specification but that a name is formed (in an obvious way) for the pre-condition if it is to be used out of context.

The pre-condition shows that $maxs$ is a *partial function* which is required to be defined only when it is applied to non-empty sets. The post-condition requires that the result must be a member of the argument set and that no number in that set exceeds the result. The type of the post-condition for this example is:

$$post\text{-}maxs\colon \text{set of } \mathbf{N} \times \mathbf{N} \to \mathbf{B}$$

These points are illustrated in Figure 3.1.

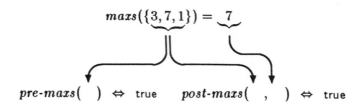

$$maxs(\{3,7,1\}) = 7$$

$$pre\text{-}maxs(\quad) \Leftrightarrow \text{true} \qquad post\text{-}maxs(\quad,\quad) \Leftrightarrow \text{true}$$

Figure 3.1: Function Specification and Application

Writing a direct definition of $maxs$ would pose a number of problems which are worth considering so as to better appreciate the implicit specification. The first problem would be one of naming. To write:

$$maxs(s) \quad \triangleq \quad \ldots$$

means that no name is available for the result. One way out is to write:

$$maxs(s) = r \quad \Rightarrow \quad r \in s \land \forall i \in s \cdot i \leq r$$

This is, in fact, an indication of the origin of post-conditions. A direct definition can be given by using recursion:

$$maxs(s) \quad \triangleq \quad \text{let } i \in s$$
$$\text{in if card } s = 1$$
$$\text{then} \quad i$$
$$\text{else} \quad max(i, maxs(s - \{i\}))$$

But this introduces a number of problems: leaving aside the max function for the moment, the arbitrary choice implied in the let is unusual; the algorithm shown does not expose the property of the result clearly; the fact that the function is partial is now a hidden property. Clearly, this is an example where the implicit specification is a useful description of the intended function.

The function which yields the larger of two integers might be specified:

$max\ (i\colon \mathbf{Z}, j\colon \mathbf{Z})\ r\colon \mathbf{Z}$

pre true

post $(r = i \lor r = j) \land i \leq r \land j \leq r$

Here there are no assumptions on the arguments (beyond their type) and the pre-condition is true. As with *maxs*, the post-condition lists several conjoined properties. In this simple example, the direct definition:

$max(i,j) \quad \overset{\Delta}{=} \quad$ if $i \leq j$ then j else i

is no longer (nor more opaque) than the specification. In general, however, decomposing a post-condition into separate (conjoined) expressions frequently results in a very clear specification. For example, it is convenient, in specifying a sort routine, to separate the properties of the order of the result and the necessity for the result to be a permutation of the starting sequence.

The VDM convention of using keywords for emphasizing the structure of a specification is followed in this book. There are obviously many alternatives. In the specification language called "Z" (see Bibliography), keywords are avoided. In work published by Manna and Waldinger, the following style is employed:

$f(a) \leftarrow$ find r such that $post\text{-}f(a, r)$
       where $pre\text{-}f(a)$

Basically, one is defining a set of pairs (the argument, result pairs of the function) and any syntax is acceptable if it clearly shows this (and, preferably, the distinction between pre- and post-conditions) without forcing the definition of an implementation.

Figure 3.2 gives the general format of an implicit function specification as used in this book. The truth-valued pre-condition can refer only to the values of the parameters; the post-condition normally refers to the values of both parameters and result. The value names are bound by the variable names within a specification. Because of the need to refer to arguments, as well as results, the name "post-condition" is not ideal, but convention has established the term and it is used throughout this book.

$$f\,(p\colon Tp)\ r\colon Tr$$

pre $\ldots p \ldots$

post $\ldots p \ldots r \ldots$

Figure 3.2: Format of Function Specification

Informally, such a specification requires that, to be correct with respect to the specification, a function must—when applied to arguments of the right type and which satisfy the pre-condition—yield a result of the right type which also satisfies the post-condition. (This statement, and the requisite proof style, are presented formally in the next section.) Notice that, for values which do not satisfy the pre-condition, nothing can be assumed about the result.

It is possible to write contradictory specifications which cannot be satisfied. Informally, it is clear that this is an error; the notion of "implementability" is used below to formalize this.

In order to specify a function which can yield any element of a set, it is necessary only to remove one of the conjuncts of the post-condition of *maxs*—thus:

$$arbs\,(s\colon \text{set of } \mathbf{N})\ r\colon \mathbf{N}$$

pre $s \neq \{\}$

post $r \in s$

Just as with the earlier discussion of square root, any algorithm would determine a particular result; the implicit specification indicates the permitted range of results.

Implicit specifications can also use quantifiers—this often avoids the recursion required in a direct definition. For example:

$$gcd\,(i\colon \mathbf{N}_1, j\colon \mathbf{N}_1)\ r\colon \mathbf{N}_1$$

pre true

post *is-common-divisor*$(i,j,r)\ \wedge$

$\qquad \neg \exists s \in \mathbf{N}_1 \cdot$ *is-common-divisor*$(i,j,s) \wedge s > r$

Thus the advantages of implicit specification over direct definition include:

- direct statement of (multiple) properties which are of interest to the user;

- characterizing a set of possible results by a post-condition;

- explicit pre-condition;

- less commitment to a specific algorithm;

- a direct naming of the result.

Where none of these points apply, a direct definition can be written. Indeed, since pre- and post-conditions are themselves truth-valued functions, it is clear that one must resort somewhere to direct definition or face an infinite regress.

Exercises

1. Write an implicit specification of a function which yields the minimum value from a set of integers.

2. Write an implicit specification of a function which performs integer subtraction. Just as one teaches children, base the post-condition on idea of "the number which would have to be added to j to get i".

3. What change would be made to the preceding specification to ensure that neither zero nor negative numbers occur as either arguments or results.

4. Write an implicit specification of a function which yields the absolute value of an integer. Do not use a conditional expression in the post-condition.

5. Specify a function which yields the smallest common multiple of two natural numbers. Build up useful sub-functions to make the specification readable.

6. Specify the mod function (over positive integers).

7. Proofs that direct definitions satisfy implicit specifications are considered below. For now check the following implementations against your specification and give a counter-example (test case value) if they are wrong.

(a) For integer subtraction:

$$sub(i,j) \quad \triangleq \quad 2 * i/j$$

(b) For natural number subtraction (cf. Exercise 3):

$$subp(i,j) \quad \triangleq \quad \text{if } i = j \text{ then } 0 \text{ else } 1 + subp(i, j + 1)$$

Would this be correct for the earlier case (Exercise 2)?

(c) For absolute value:

$$abs(i) \quad \triangleq \quad max(i, -i)$$

(d) For smallest common multiple:

$$scm(i,j) \quad \triangleq \quad i * j$$

3.2   Correctness Proofs

A direct definition of a function is said to *satisfy* an implicit specification if, for all arguments of the required type which satisfy the pre-condition, the evaluation of the direct definition yields results which are of the required type and satisfy the post-condition. This can be stated formally. Given an implicit specification[1]:

$f\,(p\colon Tp)\ r\colon Tr$

pre $\ldots p \ldots$

post $\ldots p \ldots r \ldots$

the pre- and post-conditions are truth-valued functions with the following names and signatures:

$pre\text{-}f\colon Tp \rightarrow \mathbf{B}$

$post\text{-}f\colon Tp \times Tr \rightarrow \mathbf{B}$

A direct definition:

$f\colon Tp \rightarrow Tr$

---

[1]There is a requirement that the specification itself be implementable (cf. Section 5.3).

satisfies the specification if (and only if):

$$\forall p \in Tp \cdot \textit{pre-f}(p) \Rightarrow f(p) \in Tr \wedge \textit{post-f}(p, f(p))$$

Such an expression is a *proof obligation* which, in this case, must be discharged in order to show that the direct definition satisfies the implicit specification. Thus (cf. the preceding section) the recursive function for *maxs* satisfies its specification; the same function also satisfies the specification of *arbs*. The concern in this section is with the construction of formal proofs of such statements. Notice that the oft-used phrase "... is correct" should really be interpreted as "... satisfies the ... specification". Without reference to a specification, the notion of correctness has no meaning.

The proof obligation for satisfaction, which is given above, makes the role of the pre-condition explicit: for argument values which do not satisfy the pre-condition, no constraint is placed by the specification. Thus the overall specification is satisfied by an implementation regardless of the results which it produces for those arguments which fail to satisfy the pre-condition, provided that the results are acceptable for the arguments which do satisfy the pre-condition. Similarly, a direct definition, which produces— for each argument—any answer which lies in the range of answers defined by the post-condition, satisfies the specification. Perhaps the most surprising consequence of the proof obligation is that the direct definition is allowed to produce no result (i.e. to be undefined) on arguments which do not satisfy the pre-condition.

The first examples of formal proofs are very simple in order to exhibit the general form of proof. Using **R** for the set of real numbers, the constant function *pi* can be specified:

pi $(y : \mathbf{R})$ $r : \mathbf{R}$

pre true

post $abs(\pi - r) \leq 10^{-2}$

The argument y plays no part in the post-condition: the function yields the same result for any argument. A (rather crude) direct definition might be:

$$pi(y) \quad \triangleq \quad 3.141$$

The appropriate instance of the proof obligation is:

$$\forall x \in \mathbf{R} \cdot \textit{pre-pi}(x) \Rightarrow pi(x) \in \mathbf{R} \wedge \textit{post-pi}(x, pi(x))$$

This result requires a universal quantifier; an obvious strategy is to prove the following sequent:

$$x \in \mathbf{R} \vdash \mathit{pre\text{-}pi}(x) \Rightarrow \mathit{pi}(x) \in \mathbf{R} \wedge \mathit{post\text{-}pi}(x, \mathit{pi}(x))$$

then the actual result follows from:

from $x \in \mathbf{R} \vdash \mathit{pre\text{-}pi}(x) \Rightarrow \mathit{pi}(x) \in \mathbf{R} \wedge \mathit{post\text{-}pi}(x, \mathit{pi}(x))$

1   from $x \in \mathbf{R}$

        infer $\mathit{pre\text{-}pi}(x) \Rightarrow \mathit{pi}(x) \in \mathbf{R} \wedge \mathit{post\text{-}pi}(x, \mathit{pi}(x))$ inf(h,h1)

infer $\forall x \in \mathbf{R} \cdot \mathit{pre\text{-}pi}(x) \Rightarrow \mathit{pi}(x) \in R \wedge \mathit{post\text{-}pi}(x, \mathit{pi}(x))$ $\forall$-I(1)

Here, the sequent form of the result is proved first. Clearly, the universal quantifier could be introduced in the same proof but this would result in a deeper nesting than is necessary. The use of $\forall$-I to prove the final form of the proof obligation has been made explicit. In the proofs below, only the sequent form is proved because the quantified form would always follow in the same way.

In the following proof, appeals to the definitions are shown as pi (the direct definition), $\mathit{post\text{-}pi}$ (the post clause of the implicit specification), etc. The use of different identifiers in the specification and the proof obligation is deliberate: in the first two examples it is done to clarify the substitutions being performed. The proof of the sequent form is:

from $x \in \mathbf{R}$

1      $3.141 \in \mathbf{R}$ $\mathbf{R}$

2      $pi(x) \in \mathbf{R}$ $\underline{\Delta}$-subs/pi(h,1)

3      $abs(\pi - 3.141) \leq 10^{-2}$ $\mathbf{R}$

4      $abs(\pi - pi(x)) \leq 10^{-2}$ $\underline{\Delta}$-subs/pi(h,3)

5      $\mathit{post\text{-}pi}(x, pi(x))$ $\underline{\Delta}$-subs/$\mathit{post\text{-}pi}$(h,2,4)

6      $pi(x) \in \mathbf{R} \wedge \mathit{post\text{-}pi}(x, pi(x))$ $\wedge$-I(2,5)

infer $\mathit{pre\text{-}pi}(x) \Rightarrow pi(x) \in \mathbf{R} \wedge \mathit{post\text{-}pi}(x, pi(x))$ vac$\Rightarrow$-I(6)

The general form of all of the proofs in this section is to make heavy use of the definitions and facts about the data types being manipulated with relatively little use of complex logical properties. Before seeking to understand how this proof could be discovered, the validity of the individual steps should be understood. Line 1 is a simple fact about the real numbers. Line 2 is obtained from line 1 by substitution: the value 3.141 is what is obtained when $pi(x)$ is expanded; although—in the case of a constant function—the expansion is trivial, it is necessary to ensure that the argument passed to pi is of the appropriate type; thus $\triangle$-subs/pi has to appeal to the overall hypothesis as well as line 1. Lines 3 and 4 repeat the pattern of lines 1 and 2. Line 4 is now an instance of *post-pi* with appropriate arguments; since line 4 is true so must the reference to *post-pi* be true; here again, the inference relies on assumptions about the arguments (here two); the only difference from the previous case is that the $f(d_0)$ of the inference rule constitutes the whole of line 4. Line 6 and the final conclusion use derived inference rules of propositional calculus.

But how was this proof found? There are two possibilities. It should be fairly clear how one could begin by writing what has to be proved (the overall goal) and then back-substituting into this until propositions are reached whose truth follows from a knowledge of the underlying types. It is necessary to then construct the forward proof in order to ensure that all implications are used correctly. It is, however, possible to construct the natural deduction proof more directly. Begin by writing:

from $x \in \mathbf{R}$

$\cdots$

infer $pre\text{-}pi(x) \Rightarrow pi(x) \in \mathbf{R} \wedge post\text{-}pi(x, pi(x))$?

Considering the goal, there are a collection of inference rules which could create an implication. The obvious rule would be $\Rightarrow$-I, but, noticing the special case that $pre\text{-}pi(x)$ is true, prompts to the selection of vac$\Rightarrow$-I to create:

from $x \in \mathbf{R}$

$\cdots$

k $\qquad pi(x) \in \mathbf{R} \wedge post\text{-}pi(x, pi(x))$?

infer $pre\text{-}pi(x) \Rightarrow pi(x) \in \mathbf{R} \wedge post\text{-}pi(x, pi(x))$ vac$\Rightarrow$-I(k)

(There is clearly a numbering problem when working backwards!) Line k is a conjunction and the obvious rule for its creation is $\wedge$-I, thus:

from $x \in \mathbf{R}$

    ...

i	$pi(x) \in \mathbf{R}$	?
j	$post\text{-}pi(x, pi(x))$	?
k	$pi(x) \in \mathbf{R} \wedge post\text{-}pi(x, pi(x))$	$\wedge\text{-I}(i, j)$

infer $pre\text{-}pi(x) \Rightarrow pi(x) \in \mathbf{R} \wedge post\text{-}pi(x, pi(x))$ vac$\Rightarrow$-I(k)

The reader should be able to see how such a proof would be completed. The advantage of proceeding in this way is that the ? justifications clearly mark the outstanding work. The problem with this style when tackled with "pen and ink" is knowing how much space to leave! This results in excessive use of a waste-paper basket! A simple text editor can be used to some advantage, but special-purpose systems like "Mule" (see Bibliography) can offer much more support.

Subsequent proofs are presented only in their final form (for obvious reasons) and comments on their creation are made only when some new feature is present. The reader should, however, use backwards construction when undertaking the exercises.

from $m, n \in \mathbf{N}$

1	from $m = 2$	
1.1	$m * n \in \mathbf{N}$	$\mathbf{N}$,h
1.2	$m * n = m * n$	=-term(1.1)
1.3	$m * n = 2 * n$	=t-subs(h1,1.2)
1.4	$m * n \in \mathbf{N} \wedge m * n = 2 * n$	$\wedge$-I(1.1,1.3)
1.5	$f(m, n) \in \mathbf{N} \wedge f(m, n) = 2 * n$	$\underline{\Delta}$-subs/f(h,1.4)
	infer $f(m, n) \in \mathbf{N} \wedge post\text{-}f(m, n, f(m, n))$	$\underline{\Delta}$-subs/$post\text{-}f$(h,1.5)
2	$m = 2 \in \mathbf{B}$	h
3	$m = 2 \Rightarrow f(m, n) \in \mathbf{N} \wedge post\text{-}f(m, n, f(m, n))$	$\Rightarrow$-I(1,2)

infer $pre\text{-}f(m, n) \Rightarrow$ $\underline{\Delta}$-subs/$pre\text{-}f$(h,3)

       $f(m, n) \in \mathbf{N} \wedge post\text{-}f(m, n, f(m, n))$

Figure 3.3: Proof of a Double Function

In order to illustrate the role of (non-true) pre-conditions, the following simple specification is used:

$$f\,(i:\mathbf{N},j:\mathbf{N})\ r:\mathbf{N}$$

pre $i = 2$

post $r = 2 * j$

together with the following definition:

$$f(i,j)\ \;\overset{\Delta}{=}\;\ i * j$$

The proof obligation becomes:

$$\forall m, n \in \mathbf{N} \cdot pre\text{-}f(m,n)\ \Rightarrow\ f(m,n) \in \mathbf{N} \wedge post\text{-}f(m,n,f(m,n))$$

which is discharged in Figure 3.3. This proof is similar to that for pi, but its discovery does result in an $\Rightarrow$-I because the goal is an implication which has a non-true antecedent.

It is not necessary to produce all proofs at such a fine level of detail. In particular, the substitution steps can be handled less formally (once again, given the proviso that the formal steps can be inserted should doubt arise). The proof in Figure 3.3 might be written:

from $m, n \in \mathbf{N}$

1      $m = 2\ \Rightarrow\ m * n \in \mathbf{N} \wedge m * n = 2 * n$ $\mathbf{N}, \Rightarrow$

2      $m = 2\ \Rightarrow\ f(m,n) \in \mathbf{N} \wedge f(m,n) = 2 * n$ Δ-subs$/f$(h,2)

    infer $pre\text{-}f(m,n)\ \Rightarrow$ Δ-subs$/pre\text{-}f/post\text{-}f$(h,3)

             $f(m,n) \in \mathbf{N} \wedge post\text{-}f(m,n,f(m,n))$

Direct definitions of functions can also use conditional expressions. An example is the direct definition of the max function given in Section 3.1:

$$max(i,j)\ \;\overset{\Delta}{=}\;\ \text{if } i \leq j \text{ then } j \text{ else } i$$

The implicit specification is:

$$max\ (i:\mathbf{Z},j:\mathbf{Z})\ r:\mathbf{Z}$$

pre true

post $(r = i\ \vee\ r = j) \wedge i \leq r \wedge j \leq r$

Thus the proof obligation is:

from $m, n \in \mathbf{Z}$

1	$m \leq n \vee m > n$	$\mathbf{Z}$,h
2	from $m \leq n$	
2.1	$max(m, n) = n$	max(h,h2)
2.2	$max(m, n) \in \mathbf{Z}$	2.1,h
2.3	$(n = m \vee n = n) \wedge m \leq n \wedge n \leq n$	$\mathbf{Z}$,h,h2,$\wedge$,$\vee$
2.4	$post\text{-}max(m, n, n)$	$\underline{\Delta}$-subs/$post\text{-}max$(h,2.3)
2.5	$post\text{-}max(m, n, max(m, n))$	=t-subs(2.4,2.1)
	infer $max(m, n) \in \mathbf{Z} \wedge post\text{-}max(m, n, max(m, n))$	$\wedge$-I(2.2,2.5)
3	from $m > n$	
3.1	$max(m, n) = m$	max(h,h3)
3.2	$max(m, n) \in \mathbf{Z}$	3.1,h
3.3	$(m = m \vee m = n) \wedge m \leq m \wedge n \leq m$	$\mathbf{Z}$,h,h3,$\wedge$,$\vee$
3.4	$post\text{-}max(m, n, m)$	$\underline{\Delta}$-subs/$post\text{-}max$(h,3.3)
3.5	$post\text{-}max(m, n, max(m, n))$	=t-subs(3.4,3.1)
	infer $max(m, n) \in \mathbf{Z} \wedge post\text{-}max(m, n, max(m, n))$	$\wedge$-I(3.2,3.5)
4	$max(m, n) \in \mathbf{Z} \wedge post\text{-}max(m, n, max(m, n))$	$\vee$-E(1,2,3)
	infer $pre\text{-}max(m, n) \Rightarrow$	vac$\Rightarrow$-I(4)
	$max(m, n) \in \mathbf{Z} \wedge post\text{-}max(m, n, max(m, n))$	

Figure 3.4: Proof of max Function

$$\forall i, j \in \mathbf{Z} \cdot pre\text{-}max(i, j) \Rightarrow max(i, j) \in \mathbf{Z} \wedge post\text{-}max(i, j, max(i, j))$$

The proof of the required sequent is given in Figure 3.4. As before, the reader should first check the forward steps in this proof. The generation of this proof introduces one new tactic. Line 4 is generated (as in pi) by noticing that the pre-condition is true. In the proof of pi the analysis could proceed because the definition of the function is straightforward; here, the expansion of max is a long expression which requires simplification. The best way to simplify a conditional is by case analysis. Here, the case distinction is obvious and the sub-goals generated are lines 2 and 3 (and the subsidiary proof 4). Once these are identified, the proof is straightforward.

The proofs so far are presented with a great deal of detail. The level of

detail can be chosen to suit the problem in hand and, in later proofs, several
inference steps are performed in a single line. Furthermore, as the reader
becomes confident in the construction of such proofs, only the outer boxes of
a proof need be recorded; the inner boxes can be completed if doubt arises.
The key point about such (rigorous) proof outlines is that it is clear what
needs to be done to extend them to formal proofs—for this reason, errors
are less likely.

Consider the following specification:

$abs\ (i\colon \mathbf{Z})\ r\colon \mathbf{Z}$
post $0 \leq r \wedge (r = i \vee r = -i)$

Here and below, pre-conditions which are true are omitted; thinking of the
pre-condition as permission to ignore certain argument combinations, its
omission indicates that the implementation must cater for any arguments
of the required types. Similarly, the proof obligation can be simplified to
reflect the fact that E and true $\Rightarrow E$ are equivalent expressions. Thus any
proposed implementation must be such that:

$$\forall i \in \mathbf{Z} \cdot abs(i) \in \mathbf{Z} \wedge post\text{-}abs(i, abs(i))$$

A direct definition which uses conditional expressions and arithmetic operators is considered in Exercise 4 below. Suppose, however, that the following
implementation were to be considered:

$$abs(i) \quad \triangleq \quad max(i, -i)$$

It would, of course, be possible to expand out the right-hand side of this
definition by using the direct definition of max. In the rigorous development
of programs, a high-level design step introduces components (via specifications) whose development follows the justification of the design step. The
first hint of how this works can be given by making the proof rely only on
the implicit specification, rather than the direct definition, of max. Thus,
the proof of the sequent form is as shown in Figure 3.5.

The relationship between the range of information in a function signature
and the post-condition can be understood by studying this example. If the
signature line were changed to:

$$abs(i\colon \mathbf{Z})r\colon \mathbf{N}$$

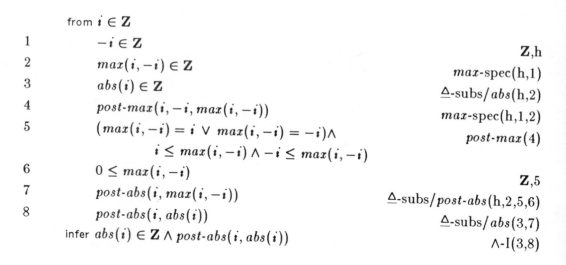

from $i \in \mathbf{Z}$

1    $-i \in \mathbf{Z}$ $\mathbf{Z}$,h

2    $max(i, -i) \in \mathbf{Z}$ max-spec(h,1)

3    $abs(i) \in \mathbf{Z}$ $\underline{\Delta}$-subs/abs(h,2)

4    $post\text{-}max(i, -i, max(i, -i))$ max-spec(h,1,2)

5    $(max(i, -i) = i \vee max(i, -i) = -i) \wedge$ $post\text{-}max(4)$
        $i \leq max(i, -i) \wedge -i \leq max(i, -i)$

6    $0 \leq max(i, -i)$ $\mathbf{Z}$,5

7    $post\text{-}abs(i, max(i, -i))$ $\underline{\Delta}$-subs/$post\text{-}abs$(h,2,5,6)

8    $post\text{-}abs(i, abs(i))$ $\underline{\Delta}$-subs/abs(3,7)

infer $abs(i) \in \mathbf{Z} \wedge post\text{-}abs(i, abs(i))$ $\wedge$-I(3,8)

Figure 3.5: Proof of abs Function

the first conjunct of $post\text{-}abs$ could be omitted. The overall proof task would
not, however, change. It would simply be necessary to rearrange the steps.
Thus the choice of whether to show constraints by type information or by
clauses in a post-condition can be made on pragmatic considerations.

Using conditional expressions, a natural way to write direct definitions
of functions is to employ recursion. A *recursive definition* of a function is
one in which, as well as using previously known functions, the right-hand
side of the definition uses the function being defined. Certain conditions
must be fulfilled for such definitions to mean anything at all—but this topic
is considered in the next section. A simple example of a recursive function
which performs multiplication of natural numbers is:

$$multp(i, j) \quad \triangleq \quad \text{if } i = 0 \text{ then } 0 \text{ else } multp(i - 1, j) + j$$

Using the proof technique considered above, the recursive use of *multp* in
this definition cannot be eliminated. In order to prove facts about recursive
functions, it is necessary to use an "inductive" proof.

The key to inductive proofs about some set of values is to recognize the
way in which all possible elements of the set can be generated. For the set of
natural numbers, the *generators* are very simple: zero is a natural number,
the function *succ* (successor or "plus one") generates natural numbers from
natural numbers—any natural number can be generated in this way. Thus:

0: **N**

$succ: \mathbf{N} \rightarrow \mathbf{N}$

For example, the number for which the normal Arabic symbol is 3 is:

$succ(succ(succ(0)))$

This unary notation may appear to be rather clumsy, but the intuition is that a unique representation is available for any natural number.

The remarkable fact is that these generators can be used to build a whole collection of operators over natural numbers. For example, the general addition function *add* is characterized by two properties:

$$\frac{j \in \mathbf{N}}{add(0, j) = j}$$

$$\frac{i \in \mathbf{N}, j \in \mathbf{N}}{add(succ(i), j) = succ(add(i, j))}$$

The more familiar way to write these properties is as a recursive definition:

$$add(i, j) \quad \overset{\Delta}{=} \quad \text{if } i = 0 \text{ then } j \text{ else } 1 + add(i-1, j)$$

In order for this definition to be understood, the subtraction operator must be explained—but, noticing that its second operand is 1, it can be treated as a predecessor (*pred*) operator whose only property is:

$$i \in \mathbf{N} \vdash pred(succ(i)) = i$$

The connection between the recursive definition and the two properties should now be obvious. General subtraction is defined as an example in the next section; multiplication is defined above in terms of addition; the development of other arithmetic operators on natural numbers is straightforward.

Here, the immediate concern is with how to prove results about recursive definitions. Just as the generators provide a way of reaching all natural numbers, they can be used to show that a property holds for all such numbers. Suppose it can be proved that some property p is true for zero and furthermore that, under the assumption that the property holds for some arbitrary natural number n, it can be proved that the property holds for the next natural number $succ(n)$—then it follows that the property holds for any natural number. This induction rule can be written:

N-ind $$\frac{p(0);\ n \in \mathbf{N}, p(n) \vdash p(n+1)}{n \in \mathbf{N} \vdash p(n)}$$

A proof using this rule is known as an *inductive proof*.

The first example to be used here establishes a property of the first *n* natural numbers. Defining:

$$sumn(n) \quad \overset{\Delta}{=} \quad \text{if } n = 0 \text{ then } 0 \text{ else } n + sumn(n-1)$$

or:

$$sumn(0) = 0$$
$$sumn(succ(n)) = succ(n) + sumn(n)$$

A proof is given that:

$$n \in \mathbf{N} \vdash sumn(n) = n * (n+1)/2$$

The proof is:

from $n \in \mathbf{N}$

1	$0 = 0 * (0+1)/2$	**N**
2	$sumn(0) = 0 * (0+1)/2$	$sumn(1)$
3	from $n \in \mathbf{N}$, $sumn(n) = n * (n+1)/2$	
3.1	$n + 1 + n * (n+1)/2 = (n+1) * ((n+1)+1)/2$	**N**,h3
3.2	$n + 1 + sumn(n) = ((n+1) * ((n+1)+1)/2$	=t-subs(h3,3.1)
	infer $sumn(n+1) = ((n+1) * ((n+1)+1)/2$	$sumn$(h3,3.2)
	infer $sumn(n) = n * (n+1)/2$	**N**-ind(2,3)

Once again, the proof here is presented in the best order for reading. In creating this proof, the rule of inference **N**-ind is used to break the overall goal into line 2 and the inner from/infer at 3.

The proof that the required property holds in the case $n = 0$ (lines 1–2) is referred to as the *basis* of the inductive proof—it arises here as the natural case distinction from the conditional expression used in the definition of *sumn*. The second part (labeled 3) is the novel feature of an inductive proof—it is known as the *induction step* and shows that the property is inherited over *succ*. In order to show this, the property is assumed to hold for *n*—this assumption (here hypothesis 3) is known as the *inductive hypothesis*.

The use, in a proof, of the inductive hypothesis has a hint of cheating! It must, however, be remembered that it is only a temporary assumption: the same expression occurring as a temporary assumption or as the final result of the proof has a very different meaning. Perhaps the best way to quieten concern about inductive proofs is to view them as recipes to create proofs for arbitrary natural numbers. Suppose someone were to doubt that a property, which had been proven by induction, were true for some particular natural number—say 7; a proof could be generated by:

- copying out the basis $(p(0))$

- copying out 7 versions of the inductive step substituting successive natural numbers in each instance.

The resulting (long and boring) text would be a proof that the property holds for 7—a proof in which no appeal was made to induction. Thus, given an inductive proof, a recipe is available for generating any required proof.

An inductive proof can be used to show that a recursively defined function, for squaring a number, satisfies the implicit specification:

$$sq\ (i\colon \mathbf{N})\ r\colon \mathbf{N}$$
$$\text{post } r = i^2$$

Given the definition:

$$sq(i) \quad \triangleq \quad \text{if } i = 0 \text{ then } 0 \text{ else } 2 * i - 1 + sq(i-1)$$

The proof is shown in Figure 3.6. Lines 1 to 6 constitute the basis of the proof and the inductive step is labeled 7. The sub-goals are generated by applying the induction rule.

The N-ind rule above is not the only possible one; another candidate— once the predecessor operator is defined—is:

N-indp $\qquad \dfrac{p(0);\ n \in \mathbf{N}_1, p(n-1) \vdash p(n)}{n \in \mathbf{N} \vdash p(n)}$

Yet another rule is introduced in Exercise 9 below.

It is possible to write equivalent specifications which differ in presentation, in the sense that the respective pre- and post-conditions could be proved to be logically equivalent. The situation with implementations (e.g. direct definitions for functions) is more interesting. Two implementations can both satisfy the same specification and yet be different in the sense

from $n \in \mathbf{N}$

1	$0 \in \mathbf{N}$	
2	$sq(0) \in \mathbf{N}$	$sq(1,1)$
3	$0^2 = 0$	$\mathbf{N}$
4	$0^2 = sq(0)$	$sq(1,3)$
5	$post\text{-}sq(0, sq(0))$	$\underline{\Delta}\text{-subs}/post\text{-}sq(\mathrm{h},4)$
6	$sq(0) \in \mathbf{N} \wedge post\text{-}sq(0, sq(0))$	$\wedge\text{-I}(2,5)$
7	from $n \in \mathbf{N},\ sq(n) \in \mathbf{N},\ post\text{-}sq(n, sq(n))$	
7.1	$sq(n) = n^2$	$post\text{-}sq(\mathrm{h}7)$
7.2	$n + 1 \in \mathbf{N}_1$	$\mathbf{N},\mathrm{h}7$
7.3	$(n + 1)^2 \in \mathbf{N}$	$\mathbf{N},7.2$
7.4	$(n + 1)^2 = n^2 + 2 * n + 1$	$\mathbf{N},\mathrm{h}7$
7.5	$= sq(n) + 2 * n + 1$	$=\text{-subs}(7.4,7.1)$
7.6	$= sq(n + 1)$	$sq(7.2,7.5)$
7.7	$sq(n + 1) \in \mathbf{N}$	$=\text{-subs}(7.6,7.3)$
7.8	$post\text{-}sq(n + 1, sq(n + 1))$	$\underline{\Delta}\text{-subs}(7.3,7.7,7.6)$
	infer $sq(n + 1) \in \mathbf{N} \wedge post\text{-}sq(n + 1, sq(n + 1))$	$\wedge\text{-I}(7.7,7.8)$
	infer $sq(n) \in \mathbf{N} \wedge post\text{-}sq(n, sq(n))$	$\mathbf{N}\text{-ind}(6,7)$

Figure 3.6: Proof of sq Function

of having dissimilar domains or even producing different answers. Specifications have to be satisfied only over those values which satisfy the precondition: two implementations can produce results outside this set and their extensions may differ. Remembering that post-conditions can be used to allow a range of results[2], it is clear that two implementations may differ by yielding different elements in this range.

The notion of an explicit function definition satisfying an implicit spec-

---

[2]It is natural to think of functions being able to produce only a unique result. In this sense, the specifications are—technically—of under-determined functions. This situation becomes more complex with programs where—because of parallelism—non-determinacy could arise. No assumptions have been made in the justification of the proof rules presented in this book which rule out the more general non-deterministic case.

ification is a special case of an ordering which can even be applied to two specifications. A specification which has a wider pre-condition and/or is more determined than another, can be said to satisfy it. Thus the specification of *maxs* can be said to satisfy the specification of *arbs*; similarly, a specification which dictated the value 7 for the function when applied to an empty set, would also satisfy the specification of *arbs*. One effect of this rule is that, if specification A satisfies specification B, then any implementations of A will also satisfy B.

Exercises

1. Prove that the specification:

   double $(x: \mathbf{Z})$ $r: \mathbf{Z}$
   post $r = 2 * x$

   is satisfied by:

   $double(x) \triangleq x + x$

2. Prove that the specification:

   conv $(f: \mathbf{R})$ $c: \mathbf{R}$
   post $c * 9/5 + 32 = f$

   is satisfied by:

   $conv(f) \triangleq (f + 40) * 5/9 - 40$

3. Prove that the specification:

   choose $(i: \mathbf{N})$ $j: \mathbf{N}$
   pre $i = 3 \lor i = 8$
   post $(i = 3 \Rightarrow j = 8) \land (i = 8 \Rightarrow j = 3)$

   is satisfied by:

   $choose(i) \triangleq 11 - i$

4. Prove that the specification:

$$abs\ (i\!:\!\mathbf{Z})\ r\!:\!\mathbf{Z}$$
$$\mathsf{post}\ 0 \leq r \wedge (r = i \ \vee \ r = -i)$$

is satisfied by:

$$abs(i) \quad \triangleq \quad \mathsf{if}\ i < 0\ \mathsf{then}\ -i\ \mathsf{else}\ i$$

5. The *sign* function can be specified:

$$sign\ (i\!:\!\mathbf{Z})\ r\!:\!\mathbf{Z}$$
$$\mathsf{post}\ i = 0 \wedge r = 0 \ \vee \ i < 0 \wedge r = -1 \ \vee \ i > 0 \wedge r = 1$$

write a direct definition and prove that it satisfies the specification.

6. Given the specification:

$$mult\ (i\!:\!\mathbf{Z}, j\!:\!\mathbf{Z})\ r\!:\!\mathbf{Z}$$
$$\mathsf{post}\ r = i * j$$

prove that:

$$mult(i,j) \quad \triangleq \quad \mathsf{if}\ i \geq 0\ \mathsf{then}\ multp(i,j)\ \mathsf{else}\ multp(-i,-j)$$

satisfies the specification. In making this proof the following properties of multp should be assumed:

$$multp\ (i\!:\!\mathbf{Z}, j\!:\!\mathbf{Z})\ r\!:\!\mathbf{Z}$$
$$\mathsf{pre}\ i \geq 0$$
$$\mathsf{post}\ r = i * j$$

7. The (general) addition of natural numbers can be implemented in terms of the simpler successor and predecessor operations using recursion. Show that:

$$add(i,j) \quad \triangleq \quad \mathsf{if}\ i = 0\ \mathsf{then}\ j\ \mathsf{else}\ add(i - 1, j) + 1$$

satisfies:

$$add\ (i:\mathbf{N}, j:\mathbf{N})\ r:\mathbf{N}$$
$$\text{post } r = i + j$$

8. Write a (recursive) definition for multp (in terms of addition) and prove that it satisfies the specification in Exercise 6.

9. * Another form of induction rule for natural numbers is:

$$\text{N-cind} \qquad \frac{m, n \in \mathbf{N}, m < n \ \Rightarrow \ p(m) \vdash p(n)}{n \in \mathbf{N} \vdash p(n)}$$

This rule (sometimes called complete induction) combines the base and inductive case; more importantly it permits an appeal to the induction hypothesis for all values less than n rather than just its predecessor. This is necessary in the proof of functions such as:

$$multp(i, j) \quad \triangleq$$
$$\quad \text{if } i = 0$$
$$\quad \text{then} \quad 0$$
$$\quad \text{else} \quad \text{if } is\text{-}even(i)$$
$$\qquad \quad \text{then} \quad 2 * multp(i/2, j)$$
$$\qquad \quad \text{else} \quad j + multp(i - 1, j)$$

Develop several useful splitting algorithms and use the complete induction rule to show that they satisfy their specifications. Include a version of Euclid's algorithm for greatest common divisor.

3.3 Logic of Partial Functions

A *total* function yields a result for any arguments in the domain—as given in the signature—of the function. Functions which do not meet this requirement are called *partial*. Much of mathematics assumes total functions. In this section, the impact of partial functions on the logic used in this book is considered.

Partial functions have been marked here by recording a non-trivial pre-condition. If the pre-condition concerns single sets, it is possible to define a new set which includes only those elements which satisfy the pre-condition; the function then becomes total over the new set. The more interesting pre-conditions are those which relate different parameters: in such cases, it is less natural to make functions total.

Consider the following simple example:

$$subp\ (i\!:\mathbf{N}, j\!:\mathbf{N})\ r\!:\mathbf{N}$$
pre $j \leq i$
post $r + j = i$

This specification is satisfied by the recursive function:

$$subp(i,j) \quad \triangleq \quad \text{if } i = j \text{ then } 0 \text{ else } subp(i, j+1) + 1$$

A term can be formed by applying a function to arguments of the appropriate type. Thus:

$$subp(5,3)$$

is a term (whose value is 2). There is, however, a problem with terms built from functions where the arguments do not satisfy the pre-condition of the function: what, for example, is to be made of the term:

$$subp(3,5)$$

In programming terms, it could be said that *subp* fails to terminate. Here, it fits the context better to say that the term does not denote a value. This leads to problems with:

$$subp(i,j)$$

since the question of whether or not this term denotes a value depends on the values (as provided by the context) of i and j.

The proof obligation for *subp* is:

$$\forall i, j \in \mathbf{N} \cdot pre\text{-}subp(i,j) \Rightarrow$$
$$subp(i,j) \in \mathbf{N} \wedge post\text{-}subp(i,j,\ subp(i,j))$$

which expands into:

$$\forall i, j \in \mathbf{N} \cdot j \leq i \Rightarrow subp(i,j) \in \mathbf{N} \wedge subp(i,j) = i - j$$

Unfortunately, when the antecedent of this implication is false, the term involving *subp* does not denote a natural number. It is tempting to say that this problem can be ignored because the implication could be considered to be true whenever its antecedent is false (regardless of the consequent). This is, in fact, one property of the logic studied here. However, the whole topic has to be put on a firm footing—for example, something must be done about the fact that the truth tables used in Section 1.1 make no mention of propositions which fail to denote a Boolean value.

Many more examples arise in this book where terms fail to denote values and the challenge is to provide a logical system which handles this problem. Far from being a contrived difficulty, this is a common feature of programs (and fragments thereof). Loop constructs may fail to terminate for some input values and the logic to be used in their proofs must have a way of discussing the set over which the loop can be safely used.

If terms fail to denote values (and hence propositions fail to denote truth values) what meaning is to be given to the logical operators? The approach adopted here is to extend the meaning of the operators in a specific way. In order to explain the extension, truth tables are again used to indicate a model theory. This model theory leads to a problem of how to mark a "non-value". Here ∗ is written; but there is no sense in which this is a new value—it is just a reminder that no value is available. Since nine rows must now be presented, the truth tables are presented in the more compact square style in preference to the series of columns used in Section 1.1. The extended truth table for disjunction is:

∨	true	∗	false
true	true	true	true
∗	true	∗	∗
false	true	∗	false

In a sense which is made formal below, this is the "most generous" extension of the truth table in that a result is given whenever possible. Notice that the truth table is symmetrical, as also is that for conjunction:

∧	true	∗	false
true	true	∗	false
∗	∗	∗	false
false	false	false	false

The table for negation is:

¬	
true	false
∗	∗
false	true

As in Section 1.1, the truth tables for implication and equivalence are derived
by viewing them as the normal abbreviations:

$\Rightarrow$	true	*	false
true	true	*	false
*	true	*	*
false	true	true	true

$\Leftrightarrow$	true	*	false
true	true	*	false
*	*	*	*
false	false	*	true

The reader should observe that the truth table for implication resolves
the problem encountered above. When the antecedent of the proof obligation
for *subp* is false, the whole implication is true even though a term in the
consequent has no value.

It is useful to think of these operators being evaluated by a program
which has access to the parallel evaluation of its operands. As soon as
a result is available for one operand, it is considered; if the single result
determines the overall result (e.g. one true for a disjunction), evaluation
ceases and the (determined) result is returned. (In order for this analogy to
hold, another condition is required. If the evaluation of an operand fails, it
must not cause the overall evaluation to fail.)

A more mathematical characterization of the chosen tables can be given.
The description in terms of a parallel program has the property that any
result, delivered on the basis of incomplete information, will not be wrong
however the information is completed (e.g. having one true operand for a
disjunction, it does not matter whether the other operand evaluates to true
or false). The concept of "v_1 could become v_2 if evaluated further" defines
an ordering relation. For the Boolean (non-value and) values this can be
written:

   * $\preceq$ true

   * $\preceq$ false

This is pictured in Figure 3.7.

A function is said to be *monotone* in an ordering if it respects the ordering in the sense that larger arguments give rise to larger results. That
is:

$$a \preceq b \Rightarrow f(a) \preceq f(b)$$

Thus, given the obvious ordering on the integers, addition is monotone in both of its operands while subtraction is monotone only in its first operand.

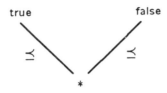

Figure 3.7: Ordering for Truth Values

The truth tables which are given above are the strongest monotonic extensions to the classical (two-valued) tables. Properties such as commutativity are natural consequences of this view.

What is to be the proof theory for this logic of partial functions (LPF)? The proof theory introduced in Chapter 2 is designed for this logic! That proof theory is consistent with the normal (two-valued) logic but cannot prove all results—it is incomplete; for LPF, whose model theory is sketched above, the axiomatization is *complete* (i.e. all true statements can be proved).

The most obvious difference between LPF and classical logic is that the so-called "law of the excluded middle" does not hold in the former. Looking at the truth table for "not" makes it clear that:

$$E \lor \neg E$$

need not be true since it relies on E denoting a value. A simple example of why this weakness is considered a virtue is that with partial functions (e.g. division) there is no reason to expect:

$$5/0 = 1 \lor 5/0 \neq 1$$

to be true. On the other hand, the useful property:

$$\forall x \in \mathbf{R} \cdot x = 0 \lor x/x = 1$$

is true in LPF and can be proved without difficulty:

from $x \in \mathbf{R}$

1       $x = 0 \lor x \neq 0$ h,$\mathbf{R}$

2   from $x = 0$

      infer $x = 0 \lor x/x = 1$ $\lor$-I(h2)

3   from $x \neq 0$

3.1 $x/x = 1$ $\mathbf{R}$,h,h3

      infer $x = 0 \lor x/x = 1$ $\lor$-I(3.1)

infer $x = 0 \lor x/x = 1$ $\lor$-E(1,2,3)

The lack of the law of the excluded middle is an intended weakness in LPF. It does, however, make certain proofs more difficult than in classical logic. For example, a shorter proof of:

$$(E_1 \lor E_2) \land (E_1 \lor E_3) \vdash E_1 \lor E_2 \land E_3$$

than that needed in LPF is possible in standard logic. The same point explains the need for a longer axiomatization for LPF: without the $\neg\lor$-E/$\neg\lor$-I rules the system would not be complete; but in classical logic these properties follow from the law of the excluded middle.

Since the law of the excluded middle does not hold, nor does:

$$E \Rightarrow E$$

Once again, it does not have a value if E does not. This has the deeper consequence that the so-called "deduction theorem" of standard logic does not hold; knowing:

$$E_1 \vdash E_2$$

does not justify:

$$\vdash E_1 \Rightarrow E_2$$

unless it is also known that E_1 is defined (i.e. $E_1 \in \mathbf{B}$).

Many of the tautologies of standard logic are not true in LPF. This is a direct consequence of the need for definedness. It is a pleasing property of LPF that it becomes classical by writing $E_i \in \mathbf{B}$, for each proposition, to the left of the turnstile.

It is an important property of a notation that it can express sufficient things. For the standard logic, "or" and "not" are *expressively complete* in that, with just these two operators, any truth table can be generated. The wholly true (respectively, false) tables can be represented by logical expressions. Because the constants cannot be generated in this way, two constants (e.g. true, *) must be explicitly brought into the axiomatization of LPF. With the basic operators listed in Appendix A, any monotone truth table can be expressed.

The proofs in the preceding section have used rules such as $\triangleq$-subs which hide a number of technical problems. It is quite possible to conduct proofs without going into the justification of these rules by simply observing their constraints. Here, the background to (and justification of) the rules is considered.

Section 2.3 contains the comment that the equality discussed there (=) is not, in general, adequate for the interpretation of definitions. The source of this difficulty is that this equality is "weak" in the sense that it is undefined if either of its operands is undefined. This is a very natural view and corresponds to that needed in most assertions. But, given the definition above, the term:

$$subp(3, 5)$$

is identical in value to:

$$subp(3, 6) + 1$$

even though both terms are undefined. The definition introduces a stronger equality. The tables which follow contrast these two notions. Here, the undefined values are shown as "bottom" elements ($\perp$).

=	0	1	2	$\ldots$	$\perp_N$
0	true	false	false		$\perp_B$
1	false	true	false		$\perp_B$
2	false	false	true		$\perp_B$
$\ldots$					
$\perp_N$	$\perp_B$	$\perp_B$	$\perp_B$		$\perp_B$

==	0	1	2	...	$\perp_{\mathbf{N}}$
0	true	false	false		false
1	false	true	false		false
2	false	false	true		false
...					
$\perp_{\mathbf{N}}$	false	false	false		true

It should be clear that strong equality (==) is not monotonic. It is characterized by a number of proof rules:

==-refl
$$\frac{}{s == s}$$

==-subs
$$\frac{s_1 == s_2;\ E}{E[s_1/s_2]}$$

==-comm
$$\frac{s_1 == s_2}{s_2 == s_1}$$

==-trans
$$\frac{s_1 == s_2;\ s_2 == s_3}{s_1 == s_3}$$

Among these, the interesting difference with weak equality comes from the rule of reflexivity, in which there is no constraint that the term s must yield a proper value. The connection with weak equality can be shown by:

==→=
$$\frac{s_1 == s_2;\ s_i \in X}{s_1 = s_2} \qquad (1 \le i \le 2)$$

=→==
$$\frac{s_1 = s_2}{s_1 == s_2}$$

Reading definitions as strong equalities, it is straightforward to prove rules such as $\triangle$-subs, with:

$$f\!:\!D \to \mathbf{R}$$
$$f(d) \stackrel{\triangle}{=} e$$
$$e_0 = e(d_0/d)$$

from $\forall d \in D \cdot f(d) == e,\ d_0 \in D,\ E(e_0)$

1        $f(d_0) == e_0$ $\forall$-E(h,h)

infer $E[f(d_0)/e_0]$ ==-subs(1,h)

Although this indicates that the derived rules (as always) could be dispensed with, it is a significant aid to the clarity of proofs to hide the notion of strong equality.

The range of bound variables is, as shown by the constraint, exactly the proper—or defined—values of the type. The importance of this point is illustrated by the proof shown in Figure 3.8, in which the result at line 9 is used (via ∀-E) to develop the required implication. This is an example where the choice of induction requires some experiment.

The rules in Appendix A use one other non-monotonic logical operator Δ. Its truth table is:

E	ΔE
true	true
false	true
$\perp_B$	false

Once again, it is possible (and desirable) to hide most of the uses of this operator.

The problem of finding a suitable logic for partial functions is currently receiving more attention and other approaches to the problem are referenced in the Bibliography.

Exercises

1. Check that the truth tables for the propositional operators are monotonic.

2. Propositional operators can be defined by conditional expressions as discussed in Exercise 4 of Section 1.1.

   (a) Draw up the truth tables for these operators.

   (b) Contrast these truth tables with the symmetrical ones defined above; why cannot the conditional expressions form the symmetrical tables?

3. Section 1.1 included an informal argument for the following sequent:

$$E_1 \wedge E_2 \vee \neg E_1 \wedge E_3 \vdash (E_1 \Rightarrow E_2) \wedge (\neg E_1 \Rightarrow E_3)$$

   (a) Produce a formal proof of this.

from $i, j \in \mathbf{N}$

1	$i - 0 = i \in \mathbf{N}$	h,N
2	$0 \in \mathbf{N}$	N
3	$subp(i, i - 0) \in \mathbf{N}$	ifth-subs/$subp$(h,1,2)
4	$0 + (i - 0) = i$	h,N
5	$subp(i, i - 0) + (i - 0) = i$	ifth-subs/$subp$(h,1,4)
6	$post\text{-}subp(i, i - 0, subp(i, i - 0))$	$\underline{\Delta}$-subs/$post\text{-}subp$(h,1,3,5)
7	$subp(i, i - 0) \in \mathbf{N} \wedge post\text{-}subp(i, i - 0, subp(i, i - 0))$	$\wedge$-I(3,6)
8	from $n \in \mathbf{N}$; $subp(i, i - n) \in \mathbf{N}$; $post\text{-}subp(i, i - n, subp(i, i - n))$	
8.1	$subp(i, i - n) + i - n = i$	$post\text{-}subp$,h8
8.2	$subp(i, i - n) = n$	N,8.1
8.3	$i \neq i - (n + 1)$	N,h,h8
8.4	$i - (n + 1) \in \mathbf{N}$	N,h,h8
8.5	$n + 1 + i - (n + 1) = i$	N,h,h8
8.6	$subp(i, i - n) + 1 + i - (n + 1) = i$	=-subs(8.2,8.5)
8.7	$subp(i, i - (n + 1)) + i - (n + 1) = i$	ifth-subs/$subp$(h,8.3,8.6)
8.8	$subp(i, i - (n + 1)) \in \mathbf{N}$	8.7,h
8.9	$post\text{-}subp(i,$	$\underline{\Delta}$-subs/$post\text{-}subp$(h,8.4,8.8,8.7)
	$\quad i - (n + 1), subp(i, i - (n + 1)))$	
	infer $subp(i, i - (n + 1)) \in \mathbf{N} \wedge$	$\wedge$-I(8.8,8.9)
	$\quad post\text{-}subp(i, i - (n + 1), subp(i, i - (n + 1)))$	
9	$\forall n \in \mathbf{N} \cdot subp(i, i - n) \in \mathbf{N} \wedge subp(i, i - n) = n$	$\forall$-I($\mathbf{N}$-ind(7,8))
10	from $pre\text{-}subp(i, j)$	
10.1	$i \geq j$	$pre\text{-}subp$(h10)
10.2	$i - j \in \mathbf{N}$	N,10.1
	infer $subp(i, j) \in \mathbf{N} \wedge subp(i, j) = i - j$	$\forall$-E(9,10.2)
11	$pre\text{-}subp(i, j) \in \mathbf{B}$	h
	infer $pre\text{-}subp(i, j) \Rightarrow subp(i, j) \in \mathbf{N} \wedge subp(i, j) = i - j$	$\Rightarrow$-I(10,11)

Figure 3.8: Proof of *subp* Function

(b) Consider the reverse sequent:

$$(E_1 \Rightarrow E_2) \wedge (\neg E_1 \Rightarrow E_3) \vdash E_1 \wedge E_2 \vee \neg E_1 \wedge E_3$$

why can this not be proved? What single additional assumption makes the proof possible?

4. Consider the following sequents and indicate additional assumptions which permit their proofs (which should then be written):

(a) $E_1 \vee (E_2 \Leftrightarrow E_3) \vdash E_1 \vee E_2 \Leftrightarrow E_1 \vee E_3$

(b) $E_1 \vee \neg(E_2 \Leftrightarrow E_3) \vdash \neg(E_1 \vee E_2 \Leftrightarrow E_1 \vee E_3)$

Chapter 4

Operations and Set Notation

> By relieving the brain of all unnecessary work, a good notation sets it free to concentrate on more advanced problems, and in effect increases the mental power of the race.
>
> *A.N.Whitehead*

The implicit specifications introduced in Section 3.1 are of mathematical functions which manipulate numbers. In two respects, these specifications need to be extended in order to cope with the tasks faced by most programmers. The major extension is to cope with the fact that most interesting programs manipulate complex data structures. It would be a mistake to write specifications in terms of the data types of some specific programming language; mathematical abstractions can be used to describe the function of a program without forcing the specification to handle the efficiency considerations which cause programs to become complicated. Section 4.2 introduces—and the remaining Sections of this chapter enlarge on—the first of these abstractions: set notation is shown to be a useful tool for writing some specifications. Further collections of notation are covered in Chapters 5 to 7.

The transition from mathematical functions to programs requires only a minor extension to the implicit specification notation of Section 3.1. This extension is described in Section 4.1. Programs, as distinct from functions, can be characterized by observing that their execution is affected by, and in turn affects, a "state". Enthusiasts for functional programming would argue that this concept brings much avoidable complexity. On the other hand, the restriction to functions necessitates making copies of those data structures which require modification. The efficiency implications of this copying are not acceptable to mainstream computing practitioners. This situation appears unlikely to change until new, special-purpose, machine architectures are developed.

It is not the intention here to take a dogmatic position on functional versus procedural programming styles. Section 4.1 shows that the notational extension from the former to cope with the latter is straightforward. More importantly, the material on data structures transcends the distinction.

4.1 Implicit Specification

Specifications can be written for whole programs, parts thereof, or even—as exercises in the notation—single statements. The most common practical use (i.e. not just for exercises) of such specifications is for something of about the size of a procedure in a programming language. A generic name is needed for these different objects—here the word *operation* is used to cover any piece of program-like text. The concern in this chapter is with the implicit specification of operations.

Functions provide a fixed mapping from input to output. For example:

$$double(i) \quad \triangleq \quad 2 * i$$

yields 4 when applied to 2 whether it has previously been applied to 99 or not. Operations have a (hidden) state which can be used to record values which affect subsequent results. For example, an accumulator operation which outputs the sum of all inputs, might respond to the first input of 2 with 2; to 99 with 101; and to a second 2 with 103.

The *state* of an operation is the collection of external variables which it can access and change. Thus, for a Pascal procedure, it would be those non-local variables of the procedure which affect, or are affected by, execution of the procedure; for a whole program, the state might be a database.

As an introductory example, consider a collection of operations for a simple calculator. The state here consists of a single external variable which is a register (*reg*) containing a natural number. This external variable is the link between the operations. An operation which stores its argument in this register is:

> $LOAD(i: \mathbf{N})$
>
> ext wr $reg: \mathbf{N}$
>
> post $reg = i$

By convention, the names of operations are written in upper-case letters. The first line of an operation specification is similar to that for a function. The second line records those entities to which an operation has external access: the variable name is preceded by an indication of whether access is read only (rd) or read and write (wr); the name of each variable is followed by its type. The post-condition is a truth-valued function of the parameters and the values of the external variables—in this case the value of reg after execution of the operation. Thus the post-condition requires that the $LOAD$ operation stores the value of its parameter into the register.

An operation which requires read only access to the register is:

> $SHOW()\ r: \mathbf{N}$
>
> ext rd $reg: \mathbf{N}$
>
> post $r = \overleftarrow{reg}$

Here, the post-condition refers to the value of reg prior to the execution of the operation. Such values are marked with a hook. In this case, since the operation only has read access, it would have made no difference had the hook been omitted. The convention below is, in fact, to omit the hook on read-only variables, thus:

> $SHOW()\ r: \mathbf{N}$
>
> ext rd $reg: \mathbf{N}$
>
> post $r = reg$

In order to clarify the difference between the access modes (rd, wr) to external variables, the reader should understand that an equivalent specification would be:

> $SHOW()\ r: \mathbf{N}$
>
> ext wr $reg: \mathbf{N}$
>
> post $reg = \overleftarrow{reg} \wedge r = reg$

The first conjunct in the post-condition is necessary since the operation is shown here as having write access and the final value would otherwise be unconstrained.

A simple incrementing operation can be specified:

$ADD(i:\mathbf{N})$

ext wr $reg:\mathbf{N}$

post $reg = \overleftarrow{reg} + i$

None of the operations $LOAD$, $SHOW$ or ADD have pre-conditions. The convention that omitted pre-conditions are assumed to be true is adopted from function specifications. A pre-condition is required for the operation which performs integer division by its parameter—yielding the result as answer and leaving the remainder in the register:

$DIVIDE(d:\mathbf{N})\ r:\mathbf{N}$

ext wr $reg:\mathbf{N}$

pre $d \neq 0$

post $d * r + reg = \overleftarrow{reg} \ \wedge \ reg < d$

The identifiers in the pre-condition are undecorated and refer to the values prior to execution of the operation. If the pre-condition is thought of as being placed before the operation and the post-condition after the operation, the undecorated values apply—in both cases—to the values of the variables at the position of the logical expression.

The states referred to in a post-condition are those prior to and after execution of an operation: any internal states which arise are of no concern to the specification.

One danger with simple examples—in particular with deterministic operations—is that the post-conditions appear to be rather like assignment statements. It is important that *post-ADD* is read as a logical expression which asserts a relationship between values. Fortunately, more interesting examples make this point clear. In *post-DIVIDE* the technique of characterizing a result by conjoined conditions is adopted from function specifications. The specification of non-deterministic operations takes over another technique and makes the role of post-conditions for operations clear.

The use of the external clause is governed by the application: it facilitates a distinction in the specification between parameters and variables which are accessed by side-effect. In the calculator example, it would be possible to replace the entities involved in the parameters/result by external variables. The decision as to where entities should appear is a pragmatic one. Thought of as procedures, the problem context governs whether an entity is to be manipulated by side-effect or be passed as an argument. All parameters are assumed here to be passed by value.

A format for specifications of operations is suggested by the following:

$OP(p\colon Tp)\ r\colon Tr$

ext rd $v_1\colon T_1$, wr $v_2\colon T_2$

pre $\dots p \dots v_1 \dots v_2 \dots$

post $\dots p \dots v_1 \dots \overleftarrow{v_2} \dots r \dots v_2 \dots$

Comparing this with Figure 4.1, the pre-condition defines the expected starting states for OP—it is, in general, a truth-valued function of the input parameters and the values of the external variables before the operation. None of these identifiers are decorated. The post-condition is a truth-valued function of the parameters, results, values of all external variables prior to execution of the operation and (for read/write variables) their values after the operation. Since there is, in post-conditions, a need to distinguish between two values for write variables, the value before execution of the operation is decorated with a hook. In both pre- and post-conditions, the undecorated identifiers refer to the values "where the condition applies". The identifiers within the pre- and post-conditions, whether hooked or not, become bound within the operation specification by the variable names.

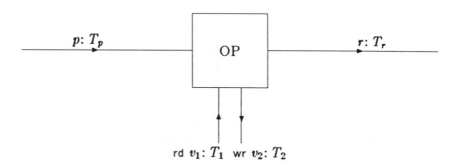

$pre\text{-}OP\colon T_p \times T_1 \times T_2 \to \mathbf{B}$

$post\text{-}OP\colon T_p \times T_1 \times T_2 \times T_r \times T_2 \to \mathbf{B}$

Figure 4.1: Operation Specification

It is conceded in Section 3.1 that the choice of the term post-condition is not entirely apposite. With operations, the post-conditions are truth-valued functions of the values of the state before and after the operation: "post" is clearly not the best term. But, here again, it is as well to follow common usage rather than coin some new term like "input/output relation".

Many different sequences of operations can result in the same state. For example, *reg* would have the value 1 after:

$LOAD(1)$
$LOAD(0); ADD(1)$
$LOAD(7); \ldots DIVIDE(3)$

Looking just at the state, there is no way of knowing which operations led to its current value. The important property is that this value determines the effect of the next operation: the history itself is not important[1]. As more complex applications are studied, the task of eliminating irrelevant detail (about the history of operations) from the state becomes important. It is precisely because the state contains the essential details of what does affect subsequent behaviour that it is an aid to perspicuous specifications.

It is the need to refer to two states, in operation specifications, which necessitates some distinguishing decoration (here hooks for old values). With functions this could be avoided, as in:

$post\text{-}f(n, f(n))$

where $f(n)$ is an expression for the result. It must be accepted that functions are more tractable mathematical objects than operations. One way to try to hide the difference is to regard operations as functions over the history of all state changes. This can be done. But this hides the fact that different histories give rise to situations which are not detectably different. The experience in the "VDM school" is that clearer specifications result from a direct acceptance of the notion of state.

Informally, it is clear that the (factorial) specification:

$FACT$
ext wr $n: \mathbf{N}$, wr $fn: \mathbf{N}$
post $fn = \overleftarrow{n}!$

is satisfied by the following fragment of program:

---

[1]Mathematically, one could say that the states induce equivalence classes on the histories.

$fn := 1;$
while $n \neq 0$ do
  begin
  $fn := fn * n;$
  $n := n - 1$
  end

Notice that the program has write access to the variable n but that its final value is not constrained by the post-condition—it is, therefore, important that the initial value of n is used in the post-condition.

This informal notion of a piece of program satisfying an operation specification can be made completely formal. Chapter 10 gives rules for such proofs. In fact, the notion of satisfaction is extended to cope with designs, or even other specifications, satisfying specifications.

As an exercise in specification, one can show how the the factorial program might be developed from its specification. The overall task ($FACT$) could be decomposed into an initialization ($INIT$) and a loop ($LOOP$). The initialization can be specified:

$INIT$

ext wr fn: $\mathbf{N}$

post $fn = 1$

Here, the variable n is not mentioned as an external. Showing what is left unchanged by an operation is sometimes known as the *frame problem*. In this style of specification, a variable which is either not mentioned or shown as read only in the operation specification cannot be changed by that operation.

There are many specifications for $LOOP$. There is a temptation to use a pre-condition of $fn = 1$ but this is not really required. It is possible to write a more general specification (i.e. one involving fewer assumptions) which specializes to the required effect in the context of the above initialization:

$LOOP$

ext wr n: $\mathbf{N}$, wr fn: $\mathbf{N}$

post $fn = \overleftarrow{fn} * \overleftarrow{n}!$

The techniques in Chapter 10 could be used to prove that the combination of the specifications for $INIT$ and $LOOP$ satisfy that for $FACT$.

The next step of development would be to decompose $LOOP$ into smaller steps. The design might be:

while $n \neq 0$ do

    begin

    $BODY$

    end

It is possible to give, to the body of the loop, a specification which does not constrain implementation to the specific two statements used above. What is really required by the loop is that the product of the variable fn and the factorial of the value of n remains constant; it is also necessary to avoid the trivial implementation which does nothing. Thus the second conjunct of the post-condition for $BODY$ requires that the value of n decreases. In order to ensure that this is possible (given the type of n) the pre-condition is required:

$BODY$

ext wr n: $\mathbf{N}$, wr fn: $\mathbf{N}$

pre $n > 0$

post $fn * n! = \overleftarrow{fn} * \overleftarrow{n}! \wedge n < \overleftarrow{n}$

One important property of implicit specifications is to avoid (or postpone) implementation commitments. Even on this small example, $BODY$ is specified so as to allow different implementations (e.g. n could be decreased by more than 1). However, the two statements in the code above can also be seen to satisfy the specification.

As might be expected, implicit specification brings certain problems— the requirement for a pre-condition for $BODY$ is one case of the general need for a check that a specification is "implementable". This point is picked up in Section 5.3, where it is treated as a formal proof obligation.

All of the arithmetic examples of the preceding chapter could be rewritten as operations rather than functions. Many would be uninstructive. The greatest common divisor problem, however, does contain some useful points:

GCD

ext wr i: $\mathbf{N}_1$, wr j: $\mathbf{N}_1$

post $is\text{-}common\text{-}divisor(\overleftarrow{i}, \overleftarrow{j}, i) \wedge$

        $\neg \exists d \in \mathbf{N}_1 \cdot is\text{-}common\text{-}divisor(\overleftarrow{i}, \overleftarrow{j}, d) \wedge d > i$

The usefulness of building up a post-condition from separate conjuncts can again be seen. It is also important to observe the interaction between the external clause and the post-condition: the final value of j is not constrained other than by its type.

Any temptation to claim that a specification is inefficient must be resisted. *Post-GCD* could be thought of as implying a massive search. The purpose of a specification is to constrain the results; its efficiency should be measured in terms of comprehension.

The case for implicitly specifying operations, rather than giving their implementations, is loaded heavily towards specification. All of the reasons which make it clearer to use implicit specifications of functions (e.g. range of results, explicit pre-condition) recur. But for operations, there is an additional argument: sequences of statements are not, as such, mathematical expressions. The equivalence of two such sequences has to be proved by mapping both of them to some common mathematical domain. For this reason, it is far easier to show that a sequence of statements satisfies a specification than it is to show that two sequences of statements compute the same result.

In Chapter 3, there are several examples where specifications can be made clearer by defining a sequence of functions each in terms of the preceding ones. It is also desirable to structure the specifications of operations. This has been done above by using functions in pre- and post-conditions. It should be obvious that it is not possible to use an operation, as such, in the pre- or post-condition of another operation: these latter are logical expressions and a state-changing operation has no meaning in such a context. This having been said, Section 5.4 introduces a way in which the specification of one operation can be used in the specification of another.

Exercises

1. Specify an operation which subtracts the initial value of j from i, where both are treated as external variables.

2. Specify an operation which has write access to two variables (say i and j); although both variables can be changed, it is required that the sum of their final values is the same as the sum of their initial values—furthermore, the operation should decrease the value in i. Assume that both variables are natural numbers.

3. Specify the operation of integer division. There are to be three external variables. The initial value (integer) in i is to be divided by the initial value (integer) in j; the quotient is to be put into register q (integer)

and the remainder left in i. Make restrictions on i and j to make the task easier. Do not use division or mod in the post-condition.

Re-specify the operation so that j is a parameter and the result is given as output from the operation.

4. Another program for factorial (using a temporary variable t and avoiding changes to n) is:

$fn : = 1;$
$t : = 0;$
while $t \neq n$ do
    begin
    $t : = t + 1;$
    $fn : = fn * t$
    end

Sketch (as above) how it might have been developed.

4.2 Set Notation

The numeric data considered so far provides a simple introduction to the key concepts of specification and proof. Many programs in the system and commercial areas do relatively little calculation; the difficulty in such programs concerns the manipulation of data structures. Attention is now turned to specification and proof techniques relating to data structures. Clearly, one would not wish to specify large systems at the bit and byte level. High-level programming languages tend to focus on particular data structures which can be implemented efficiently: APL provides a rich set of array operations, LISP provides list-processing facilities. In a specification language, it would be a mistake to favour one particular programming language. Rather, a specification language should be rich enough to model a wide range of problems prior to any commitment to a particular language.

There is, however, a more important influence on the choice of data types in specification languages. Programming languages implement those structures which can be mapped efficiently onto the target machine. In writing specifications, concern should be focussed on the task being specified and not on its eventual implementation. In general, it is possible to achieve concise specifications by using data types, like sets, which are more abstract than those, like arrays, which are governed by implementation efficiency considerations.

Abstraction is, of course, possible only at the specification level—the eventual implementation must accept the constraints of the implementation machine[2]. The process of "data reification" is considered in Chapter 8—this process can be seen as one of making commitments which achieve efficiency by capitalizing on context. In writing specifications, whenever a trade-off between efficiency and clarity has to be made, preference is always given to the latter.

Section 4.4 shows the use of set notation in specifications, but basic set notation should be familiar enough to make a simple example readable. Consider the task of checking a large text file against a dictionary of known words. Such a program is useful in the location of possible spelling errors. There are, of course, many representation details about the text file to be resolved. But the crucial design decisions undoubtedly concern the representation of the dictionary. If this is to store tens of thousands of words in a way which facilitates efficient searching, some ingenuity is required in design—this issue is returned to below as an example of data reification. Applying the dictum of abstraction, the representation issue can be postponed. For a specification the only concern is with a finite, unordered collection of distinct words—the state of this system is:

set of *Word*

Even *Word* need not be further defined at this point. Apart from the detail that the required notation is not covered until Chapter 7, there is a positive advantage in postponing this implementation-specific information: the specification is thereby made more abstract. To specify the overall system also requires the notation of Chapter 7. However, parts of the specification can already be understood. The operation which must be invoked once per word in the text can return true if, and only if, its argument is a member the state:

$CHECKWORD(w: Word)\ b: \mathbf{B}$

ext rd $dict$: set of *Word*

post $b\ \Leftrightarrow\ w \in dict$

---

[2]Strictly, one should say here, the constraints of the implementation language. It is, however, true that most languages simply transmit the constraints of the underlying machines.

The initial state for the system might be the empty set of words:

$$dict_0 = \{\}$$

An operation to add one word to a dictionary can be specified:

$ADDWORD(w: Word)$

ext wr $dict$: set of $Word$

pre $w \notin dict$

post $dict = \overleftarrow{dict} \cup \{w\}$

This specification appears simple precisely because an apposite data type is used in its state. In terms of data structures usable in, for example, Pascal, the definition would be longer and less clear. Of course, such representation details have to be faced in the design process but a concise specification is achieved by postponing unnecessary details.

It is interesting to note that the pre-condition of $ADDWORD$ is not necessary at the set level of description. It might, however, be important for the implementation and this justifies its being recorded. It can be a mistake to become so involved in the abstraction that the needs of the implementation are entirely ignored.

The specification above has used a little set notation—as have earlier chapters. It is now necessary to examine this notation in more detail. A *set* is an unordered collection of distinct objects; set values are marked by braces, thus:

$$\{a, b\} = \{b, a\}$$

The fact that the values are distinct means that there is no concept of the number of occurrences of an element in a set—elements are either present ($\in$) or absent ($\notin$). Thus:

$$a \in \{a, b\}$$
$$c \notin \{a, b\}$$

Notice that a set containing one element is distinct from that element:

$$\{a\} \neq a$$

These sets are formed by simple enumeration of their elements; sets can also be defined by *set comprehension*—this latter style defines a set which contains all elements satisfying some property—thus:

$$\{i \in \mathbf{Z} \mid 1 \le i \le 3\} = \{1, 2, 3\}$$
$$x \in \{y \in Y \mid p(y)\} \;\Leftrightarrow\; x \in Y \wedge p(x)$$

The need for a set containing an interval of the integers is common enough to justify a special notation:

$$\{i, \ldots, k\} = \{j \in \mathbf{Z} \mid i \le j \le k\}$$
$$\{1, \ldots, 3\} = \{1, 2, 3\}$$
$$\{2, \ldots, 2\} = \{2\}$$
$$j < i \;\Rightarrow\; \{i, \ldots, j\} = \{\}$$

It is possible to relax the set comprehension notation in the case that types are obvious—write:

$$\{f(i) \mid p(i)\}$$

where f is a total function on D, meaning:

$$x \in \{f(i) \mid p(i)\} \;\Leftrightarrow\; \exists i \in D \cdot p(i) \wedge x = f(i)$$

A number of sets have been named above (e.g. $\mathbf{B}, \mathbf{N}$). A way of forming new set types is to use the set of constructor applied to (the names of) known sets, for example:

$$\text{set of } \mathbf{B} = \{\{\}, \{\text{true}\}, \{\text{false}\}, \{\text{true}, \text{false}\}\}$$

Providing BS is finite:

$$\text{set of } BS = \{S \mid S \subseteq BS\}$$

The distinction between sets and their elements is crucial. Notice that set of defines a set of sets. The signature of $maxs$ is:

$$maxs\colon \text{set of } \mathbf{N} \to \mathbf{N}$$

This function can be applied to the elements of its domain, for example:

$$\{1, 7, 17\} \in \text{set of } \mathbf{N}$$

It yields an element of its range:

$$17 \in \mathbf{N}$$

The set of constructor yields only finite subsets of its base set[3]. The argument for this restriction is that it is rare, in writing specifications, that infinite sets—as such—are manipulated. Since computer stores are themselves finite it would only be possible to perform such manipulation indirectly via some finite representation.

The operators which apply to operands which are sets are first introduced by example and logical expressions. Suppose:

$$S_1 = \{a, b, c\}$$
$$S_2 = \{c, d\}$$

e_1, e_2 etc. are expressions which evaluate to sets

The *union* of two sets yields a set containing the elements of both sets (ignoring which set the elements come from and whether they are present in only one set or both):

$$S_1 \cup S_2 = \{a, b, c, d\}$$
$$e_1 \cup e_2 = \{x \mid x \in e_1 \lor x \in e_2\}$$

A natural generalization of this operator is the *distributed union* of a set of sets. This unary operator yields all of the elements present in any of the sets which are contained in its operand:

$$\bigcup\{S_1, \{e\}, S_2, \{\}\} = \{a, b, c, d, e\}$$
$$\bigcup es = \{x \mid \exists e \in es \cdot x \in e\}$$

The *intersection* of two sets is the set which contains those elements common to the two sets:

$$S_1 \cap S_2 = \{c\}$$
$$e_1 \cap e_2 = \{x \mid x \in e_1 \land x \in e_2\}$$

The *difference* of two sets is that set which contains the elements of the first operand which are not present in the second operand:

$$S_1 - S_2 = \{a, b\}$$
$$e_1 - e_2 = \{x \mid x \in e_1 \land x \notin e_2\}$$

---

[3]If the base set is infinite, this is not the same as the power set which yields the set of all subsets; for finite base sets, set of is identical with power set.

The operators above all yield values which are sets. Other operators yield Boolean results and can be used to test for properties of sets. Membership tests are used above:

$$a \in S_1$$
$$d \notin S_1$$

One set is a *subset* of (or is equal to) another if the second operand contains all elements of the first:

$$\{c\} \subseteq S_1$$
$$S_1 \subseteq S_1$$
$$S_1 \subseteq (S_1 \cup S_2)$$
$$\{\} \subseteq S_1$$
$$S_1 \subseteq (S_1 \cap S_2) \Leftrightarrow S_1 \subseteq S_2$$
$$e_1 \subseteq e_2 \Leftrightarrow (\forall x \in e_1 \cdot x \in e_2)$$

Unqualified use of the word "subset" in this book implies that equality is subsumed. *Proper subset* excludes the case of equality:

$$\{\} \subset S_1$$
$$\{a, b\} \subset S_1$$
$$\neg(S_1 \subset S_1)$$
$$e_1 \subset e_2 \Leftrightarrow e_1 \subseteq e_2 \wedge \neg(e_2 \subseteq e_1)$$

Set equality can be defined:

$$e_1 = e_2 \Leftrightarrow e_1 \subseteq e_2 \wedge e_2 \subseteq e_1$$

These operators are analogous to the ordering operators on numbers ($\leq$, $<$ and $=$). The subset operator is not, however, total: there are S_1 and S_2 such that:

$$\neg(S_1 \subseteq S_2 \vee S_2 \subseteq S_1)$$

The *cardinality* of a (finite) set is the number of elements in the set:

$$\text{card } S_1 = 3$$
$$\text{card } S_2 = 2$$
$$\text{card } \{\} = 0$$

A group of computer scientists who investigated an algebraic view of data types dubbed themselves the "ADJ group". They used a graphical notation for describing the signatures of operators and an *ADJ diagram* of the set operators is shown in Figure 4.2. In such diagrams, the ovals denote data types; the arcs linking ovals to operators show the types of the operands; and those arcs linking operators to ovals show the type of the result. Thus Figure 4.2 shows that:

$$\_ \in \_: X \times \text{set of } X \to \mathbf{B}$$

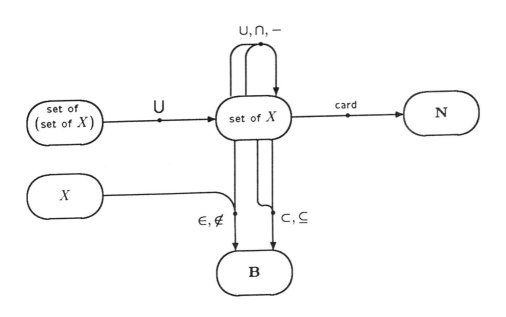

Figure 4.2: ADJ Diagram of Set Operators

Priorities were placed on the logical operators in order to minimize the parentheses required in complex expressions. There is an obvious argument for mirroring the priority of $\wedge/\vee$ by making $\cap$ higher priority than $\cup$—thus:

$$S_1 \cap S_2 \cup S_3$$

means:

$$(S_1 \cap S_2) \cup S_3$$

There is less agreement in textbooks about what should be done beyond this. The problem, which can be seen on the ADJ diagram, is that the operators yield results of different types. In general below, parentheses are used to make expressions like:

$$(A \cup B) \subseteq C$$
$$x \in (A \cup B)$$

clear. The set (or arithmetic) operators are assumed to be of higher priority than the logical operators.

Exercises

1. Write down the values of:

   (a) $\{a, c\} \cap \{c, d, a\}$

   (b) $\{a, c\} - \{c, d, a\}$

   (c) card $\{x^2 \mid x \in \{-1, \ldots, +1\}\}$

   (d) $5 \in \{3, \ldots, 7\}$

   (e) $\{7, \ldots, 3\}$

   (f) $\{i \in \mathbf{N} \mid i^2 \in \{4, 9\}\}$

   (g) $\{i \in \mathbf{Z} \mid i^2 = i\}$

   (h) $\bigcup\{\{a, b\}, \{\}, \{b, c\}, \{d\}\}$

   (i) $\bigcup\{\}$

2. Write set comprehension expressions for:

   (a) the set of integers greater than 100 and less than 200 which are exactly divisible by 9;

   (b) the set of prime numbers in the same range.

   Show the subset relationships between $\mathbf{N}$, $\mathbf{Z}$ and $\mathbf{N}_1$

3. Complete the following by replacing the question mark:

   (a) $e \cup e = ?$

   (b) $e \cap \{\} = ?$

(c) $(e_1 \subseteq e_2) \Leftrightarrow (e_1 - e_2 = ?\,)$

(d) $e \cap e = ?$

(e) $e \cup \{\} = ?$

(f) $e_1 \subseteq e_2 \wedge e_2 \subseteq e_3 \Rightarrow e_1 ? e_3$

(g) $\{\} ? e$

(h) $\mathsf{card}\,(e_1 ? e_2) = \mathsf{card}\,e_1 + \mathsf{card}\,e_2 - \mathsf{card}\,(e_1 \cap e_2)$

(i) $(e_1 - e_2) \cap e_3 = (e_1 ? e_3) - e_2$

(j) $e_1 - (e_1 - e_2) = e_1 ? e_2$

(k) $\bigcup\{\bigcup es\} = ?\ es$

4. Write out:

   (a) Commutative law for intersection.

   (b) Associative law for intersection.

   (c) Distributive laws for intersection over union.

5. Define a predicate:

$$\textit{is-disj}: \mathsf{set\ of}\ X \times \mathsf{set\ of}\ X \to \mathbf{B}$$

   which yields true if the two sets have no common elements (i.e. they are disjoint).

6. Define a distributed intersection operator—is a pre-condition required?

7. * A symmetric difference operator can be defined:

$$S_1 \diamond S_2 = (S_1 \cup S_2) - (S_1 \cap S_2)$$

   Complete the following expressions:

   (a) $S_1 \diamond S_2 = \{\} \Rightarrow S_1 ? S_2$

   (b) $S_1 \diamond S_1 = ?$

   (c) $S_1 ? S_2 \subseteq S_1 \diamond S_2$

   (d) $S_1 \diamond S_2 = S_2 ? S_1$

   (e) $S_1 \diamond S_2 = (S_1 - S_2) ? (S_2 - S_1)$

   (f) $S_1 \diamond (S_1 \diamond S_2) = ?$

4.3   Reasoning about Sets

Given the intuitive understanding of set operators from the preceding section, the next step is to be able to construct proofs about sets. In this section, the proofs contain less formal detail than in Section 3.2. A number of ideas are introduced which leave the proofs rigorous without being completely formal.

Inductive proofs about the natural numbers are based on the generators (i.e. 0, *succ*). Proofs about finite sets can be based on very similar inductive rules[4]. Here again the crucial step is to recognize the generators for sets—these are the empty set:

$$\{\} : \text{set of } X$$

and an insertion operator ($\oplus$) which adds an element to a set:

$$\_ \oplus \_ : X \times \text{set of } X \rightarrow \text{set of } X$$

This insertion operator is only used in the construction of the inductive structure of sets—one would normally use set union with a unit set. The intuition behind these generators is that any finite set can be represented by an expression of the form:

$$e_1 \oplus \left(e_2 \oplus \left(\ldots \oplus \{\} \right) \right)$$

The fact that the elements of a set are unordered is reflected by the following commutativity property of insertion:

$\oplus$-comm
$$\frac{e_1, e_2 \in X; \ s \in \text{set of } X}{e_1 \oplus \left(e_2 \oplus s \right) = e_2 \oplus \left(e_1 \oplus s \right)}$$

Similarly, the fact that sets do not contain duplicate elements is reflected by the property of absorption:

$\oplus$-abs
$$\frac{e \in X; \ s \in \text{set of } X}{e \oplus \left(e \oplus s \right) = e \oplus s}$$

---

[4]It is possible to prove many properties of sets by induction on their cardinality. This reduces induction on sets to induction on the natural numbers. The consistent approach of studying the generators for each data type results in clearer proofs.

Notice that these two properties imply that the intuitive representations of sets are not unique[5].

The induction rule which is suggested by the generators is:

set-ind $\qquad \dfrac{p(\{\}); \ e \in X, s \in \text{set of } X, p(s) \vdash p(e \oplus s)}{s \in \text{set of } X \vdash p(s)}$

Just as with the natural numbers, set operators can be defined over the generators. Thus:

$$\_ \cup \_ : \text{set of } X \times \text{set of } X \to \text{set of } X$$

could be defined as a recursive function. One way of making the proofs about sets slightly less formal than those about natural numbers is to give the information about the operators directly in terms of inference rules. This avoids the need for $\underline{\triangle}$-subs etc. For union, a basis ($\cup$-b) and an inductive ($\cup$-i) rule are given:

$\cup$-b $\qquad \dfrac{s \in \text{set of } X}{\{\} \cup s = s}$

$\cup$-i $\qquad \dfrac{e \in X, \ s_1, s_2 \in \text{set of } X}{(e \oplus s_1) \cup s_2 = e \oplus (s_1 \cup s_2)}$

The rule $\cup$-b shows that *union* absorbs empty sets as left operand; a proof must be given that the same happens on the right (Lemma $\cup$abs$\{\}$):

from $s \in \text{set of } X$

1	$\{\} \cup \{\} = \{\}$	$\cup$-b
2	from $s_1 \in \text{set of } X, \ s_1 \cup \{\} = s_1$	
2.1	$(e \oplus s_1) \cup \{\} = e \oplus (s_1 \cup \{\})$	$\cup$-i
	infer $(e \oplus s_1) \cup \{\} = e \oplus s_1$	=-subs(h2)
	infer $s \cup \{\} = s$	set-ind(1,2)

Detail is being omitted in these proofs by abbreviating the justifications: line numbers, and references to lines which provide type information, are dropped. Clearly, the writer of a proof should have checked the steps and a reviewer who is in doubt can ask for the details to be provided. Just as with the proofs in Section 3.2, the presentation here is given in the order for reading. This proof is actually best found by writing:

---

[5]Strictly, the set operators are parameterized on the type of the set elements—this point is not treated formally here.

- the outer from/infer.

- line 1 and the inner from/infer (2) are generated by the induction rule; this now permits the final justification to be given.

- the justification of line 1.

- completion of the inner from/infer (i.e. line 2.1 and the justification).

This way of generating proofs becomes essential for larger tasks. It is not, however, always obvious which variable to use in the induction.

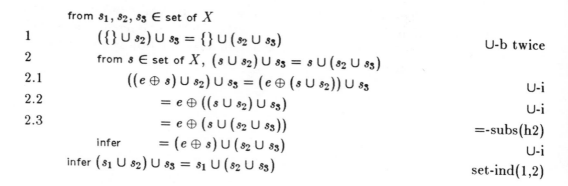

$$\text{from } s_1, s_2, s_3 \in \text{set of } X$$

1	$(\{\} \cup s_2) \cup s_3 = \{\} \cup (s_2 \cup s_3)$	∪-b twice
2	from $s \in$ set of X, $(s \cup s_2) \cup s_3 = s \cup (s_2 \cup s_3)$	
2.1	$((e \oplus s) \cup s_2) \cup s_3 = (e \oplus (s \cup s_2)) \cup s_3$	∪-i
2.2	$= e \oplus ((s \cup s_2) \cup s_3)$	∪-i
2.3	$= e \oplus (s \cup (s_2 \cup s_3))$	=-subs(h2)
infer	$= (e \oplus s) \cup (s_2 \cup s_3)$	∪-i
infer	$(s_1 \cup s_2) \cup s_3 = s_1 \cup (s_2 \cup s_3)$	set-ind(1,2)

Figure 4.3: Proof that Set Union is Associative

A proof that *union* is associative is given (by induction on s_1) in Figure 4.3. Here again, the induction rule has been used to generate the sub-goals (1 and 2). What is more difficult here is to choose the variable over which induction is performed. Often it is necessary to make a few experiments before it becomes clear which of the possible choices best decomposes the proof task.

Using the commutative and absorptive properties of $\oplus$, it is possible to prove that *union* is commutative. A preliminary lemma and the main proof are given in Figure 4.4. The separation of the lemma avoids the need for a nested induction—this point is discussed further in Chapter 7.

The idempotence of union is proved in Figure 4.5.

With the natural numbers, another form of the induction rule is available once subtraction has been introduced (N-indp). The rule has an inductive step which shows that p inherits from $n-1$ to n. It is not the intention here

from $e \in X$, $s_1, s_2 \in$ set of X

1	$e \oplus (\{\} \cup s_2) = e \oplus s_2$	$\cup$-b
2	$= \{\} \cup (e \oplus s_2)$	$\cup$-b
3	from $s \in$ set of X, $e \oplus (s \cup s_2) = s \cup (e \oplus s_2)$	
3.1	$e \oplus ((e_2 \oplus s) \cup s_2) = e \oplus (e_2 \oplus (s \cup s_2))$	$\cup$-i
3.2	$= e_2 \oplus (e \oplus (s \cup s_2))$	$\oplus$-comm
3.3	$= e_2 \oplus (s \cup (e \oplus s_2))$	h3
infer	$= (e_2 \oplus s) \cup (e \oplus s_2)$	$\cup$-i
infer	$e \oplus (s_1 \cup s_2) = s_1 \cup (e \oplus s_2)$	set-ind(2,3)

from $s_1, s_2 \in$ set of X

1	$\{\} \cup s_2 = s_2 \cup \{\}$	$\cup$-b, $\cup$abs$\{\}$
2	from $s \in$ set of X, $s \cup s_2 = s_2 \cup s$	
2.1	$(e \oplus s) \cup s_2 = e \oplus (s \cup s_2)$	$\cup$-i
2.2	$= e \oplus (s_2 \cup s)$	h2
infer	$= s_2 \cup (e \oplus s)$	$\oplus\cup$-comm
infer	$s_1 \cup s_2 = s_2 \cup s_1$	set-ind(1,2)

Figure 4.4: Proof that Set Union is Commutative

from $s \in$ set of X

1	$\{\} \cup \{\} = \{\}$	$\cup$-b
2	from $s \in$ set of X, $s \cup s = s$	
2.1	$(e \oplus s) \cup (e \oplus s) = e \oplus (s \cup (e \oplus s))$	$\cup$-i
2.2	$= e \oplus ((e \oplus s) \cup s)$	$\cup$-comm
2.3	$= e \oplus (e \oplus (s \cup s))$	$\cup$-i
2.4	$= e \oplus (s \cup s)$	$\oplus$-abs
infer	$= e \oplus s$	h2
infer	$s \cup s = s$	set-ind(1,2)

Figure 4.5: Proof that Set Union is Idempotent

to develop the whole of the set notation formally, but—once set difference
has been covered—the following induction rule can be used.

set-ind2
$$\frac{p(\{\});\ s \in \text{set of } X, e \in s, p(s - \{e\}) \vdash p(s)}{s \in \text{set of } X \vdash p(s)}$$

It is possible to characterize the set membership operator by inference
rules and thus provide the basis for formal proofs which include this operator. The basic facts about membership are:

∈-b
$$\frac{}{\neg \exists e \in X \cdot e \in \{\}}$$

∈-i
$$\frac{e_1, e_2 \in X,\ s \in \text{set of } X}{e_1 \in (e_2 \oplus s)\ \Leftrightarrow\ e_1 = e_2 \lor e_1 \in s}$$

For sets defined by comprehension:

$$\frac{}{e \in \{x \in X \mid p(x)\}\ \Leftrightarrow\ e \in X \land p(e)}$$

It is now possible to prove properties like:

$$\frac{x \in (s_1 \cup s_2)}{x \in s_1 \lor x \in s_2}$$

Below, it is necessary to prove properties of the form:

$$\forall e \in \{x \in X \mid p(x)\} \cdot q(x)$$

It should be clear that this is equivalent to:

$$\forall x \in X \cdot p(x)\ \Rightarrow\ q(x)$$

Similarly:

$$\exists e \in \{x \in X \mid p(x)\} \cdot q(x)$$

is equivalent to:

$$\exists x \in X \cdot p(x) \land q(x)$$

When a new class of objects arises, it is normally worth investigating its properties. In effect, a *theory* of the new objects is created which gathers together useful results about the objects. Of course, for the well-known basic types, like sets standard mathematical texts may be consulted. The advantage of building such a theory for other types, as they arise, is that the collection of results is then available for any use of that type. Several authors (see Bibliography) have recognized the crucial role that the development of theories will play in making more widespread use of formal methods.

As an example of such a theory, the remainder of this section outlines some results about the concept of *Partition*. This theory is used in a specification in the next section; there, a motivation for the specific example is given. In this section, the theory is developed abstractly. If this makes the material too difficult to absorb, the reader should skim it now and then return when the results are needed in Section 4.4.

A set can be partitioned by splitting it into (a set of) disjoint subsets whose union is the whole set. Thus:

$$Partition(X) \subseteq \text{set of } (\text{set of } X)$$

providing the property *invp* holds:

$$invp: \text{set of } (\text{set of } X) \to \mathbf{B}$$
$$invp(p) \quad \triangleq \quad \{\} \notin p \wedge \bigcup p = X \wedge is\text{-}prdisj(p)$$

where pairwise disjointness is defined by:

$$is\text{-}prdisj(ss) \quad \triangleq \quad \forall s_1, s_2 \in ss \cdot s_1 = s_2 \vee is\text{-}disj(s_1, s_2)$$

Thus the set of *Partitions* is:

$$\{p \in \text{set of } (\text{set of } X) \mid invp(p)\}$$

Notice that elements of *Partition* are sets of sets—the collection of all partitions is, of course, a set of such objects! To provide a trivial example:

$$Partition(\{a, b\}) = \{\{\{a\}, \{b\}\}, \{\{a, b\}\}\}$$

Here there are exactly two partitions: in the first—fine—partition, each element is in a unit set; in the second, all elements are in the same set. Although:

$$\{\{a, b\}, \{a\}\} \in \text{set of } (\text{set of } X)$$

this is not a partition because it fails to satisfy *invp*. Similarly, nor are:

$$\{\{a\}\}$$
$$\{\{a\}, \{b\}, \{\}\}$$

valid partitions. Notice that, even with the empty set:

$$\{\} \notin Partition(\{\})$$

An example of a *Partition* is pictured in Figure 4.6, where:

$$\bigcup p = X$$
$$\textit{is-prdisj}(p)$$
$$\{\} \notin p$$

The finest partition is the set which contains unit sets for each element of the base set. The following argument shows that such a decomposition matches all of the properties in *invp*. The proof is no more than an outline, but this is a realistic level of detail for this task.

from *defns*

1 $\qquad s \in \{\{x\} \mid x \in X\} \;\Leftrightarrow\; \exists x \in X \cdot s = \{x\}$

2 $\qquad \{\} \notin \{\{x\} \mid x \in X\}$

$\qquad since\{x\} \neq \{\}$

3 $\qquad \bigcup\{\{x\} \mid x \in X\} = \{x \mid x \in X\}$

4 $\qquad\qquad\qquad = X$

5 $\qquad \textit{is-prdisj}(\{\{x\} \mid x \in X\})$

Infer $\textit{invp}(\{\{x\} \mid x \in X\})$ $\qquad\qquad\qquad\qquad\qquad$ 2,4,5

Partitions can be generated from one another by combining sets which satisfy truth-valued functions:

$\qquad tvf: \text{set of } X \to \mathbf{B}$

$\qquad combine: Partition(X) \to Partition(X)$

$\qquad combine(p) \;\overset{\Delta}{=}\; \{s \in p \mid \neg tvf(s)\} \cup \{\bigcup\{s \in p \mid tvf(s)\}\}$

So, for example, if:

$\qquad tvf(s) \;\overset{\Delta}{=}\; \neg\textit{is-disj}(s, \{b, e\})$

then:

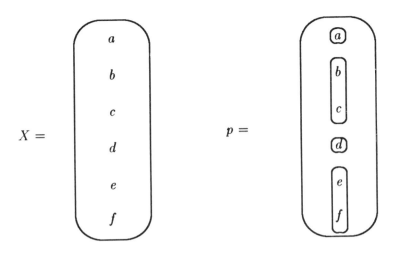

$$p \in Partition(X) \subseteq \text{set of } (\text{set of } X)$$

Figure 4.6: An Example of a *Partition*

$$combine(\{\{a\}, \{b, c\}, \{d\}, \{e, f\}\})$$
$$= \{\{a\}, \{d\}\} \cup \{\bigcup\{\{b, c\}, \{e, f\}\}\}$$
$$= \{\{a\}, \{d\}\} \cup \{\{b, c, e, f\}\}$$
$$= \{\{a\}, \{d\}, \{b, c, e, f\}\}$$

It is, first, important to notice that the types are correct—that is, if:

$$p \in \text{set of } (\text{set of } X)$$

then:

$$combine(p) \in \text{set of } (\text{set of } X)$$

It is now necessary to show that *combine* also preserves *invp*. Firstly, it should be clear that *combine* can only create coarser partitions—that is:

$$\forall s' \in combine(p) \cdot \exists s \in p \cdot s \subseteq s'$$

This is used below to show the empty set is not created. Furthermore (from properties of $\bigcup$):

$$\bigcup combine(p)$$
$$= \bigcup\{s \in p \mid \neg tvf(s)\} \cup \bigcup\{\bigcup\{s \in p \mid tvf(s)\}\}$$
$$= \bigcup\{s \in p \mid \neg tvf(s)\} \cup \bigcup\{s \in p \mid tvf(s)\}$$
$$= \bigcup(\{s \in p \mid \neg tvf(s)\} \cup \{s \in p \mid tvf(s)\})$$
$$= \bigcup p$$

The final step in the argument concerns the pairwise disjointness. Consulting the definition of *combine*; certain sets are copied without change:

$$\{s \in p \mid \neg tvf(p)\} \subseteq combine(p)$$

Clearly, if these sets were pairwise disjoint in p, they are pairwise disjoint in $combine(p)$; also:

$$\{\bigcup\{s \in p \mid tvf(p)\}\}$$

is a unit set and therefore must—itself—satisfy *is-prdisj*; the only remaining danger is that this unit set has some element in common with the copied sets—this also cannot occur since all elements of p were pairwise disjoint.

Then the Lemma (*Partition*-combine) that *combine* preserves *invp* follows since:

- empty sets cannot be introduced by *combine* since sets always get larger;

- the distributed union is unchanged by *combine*;

- pairwise disjointness is preserved.

Exercises

1. Define (over the generators—as with union above) set intersection and prove:

   (a) $s \cap \{\} = \{\}$

   (b) associativity

   (c) commutativity

   (d) idempotence

   (e) distribution of union over intersection and *vice versa*.

2. Define the distributed union operator and prove:

    (a) $\bigcup(es_1 \cup es_2) = \bigcup es_1 \cup \bigcup es_2$

    (b) $\bigcup\{\bigcup es\} = \bigcup es$

3. Define set difference and prove:

$$(S_1 - S_2) \cap S_3 = (S_1 \cap S_3) - S_2$$

4. * Define and develop a useful theory of the symmetric difference operator for sets (cf. Exercise 7 of Section 4.2).

5. * This exercise concerns the theory $Partition(X)$.

    (a) Specify a function which, given a set of objects from X, will return a set containing a partition of the input set into two sets whose sizes differ by at most one.

    (b) Show that the coarsest partition of X satisfies:

    $invp(\{X\})$

    (c) Argue informally that an equivalent formulation of $invp$ is:

    $$\{\} \notin p \wedge \forall x \in X \cdot \exists! s \in p \cdot x \in s$$

    (d) Define a function which can split sets of a partition and show that it preserves $invp$.

4.4 Specifications

The reader should now have a thorough grasp of set notation and some facility with its manipulation in proofs. It would be worth looking back at the specification of the spelling checker in Section 4.2 to ensure that its details are fully understood.

Another simple specification which uses only sets is for a resource manager program. Suppose that the resource is a pool of buffers. Each buffer might be identified by a buffer identifier which could, in the actual implementation, be an address. This information is not, however, needed in the specification and the buffer identifiers are shown as a set Bid. Again, in the likely representation, the free buffers might be organized into a free list. The specification can ignore such representation details and uses a free set (fs). An operation which resets the collection of free buffers is:

$SETUP(s: \text{set of } Bid)$

ext wr $fs: \text{set of } Bid$

post $fs = s$

A free buffer can be obtained by the operation:

$OBTAIN()\ r: Bid$

ext wr $fs: \text{set of } Bid$

pre $fs \neq \{\}$

post $r \in \overleftarrow{fs} \wedge fs = \overleftarrow{fs} - \{r\}$

Notice that this post-condition does not determine which buffer is to be allocated: the specification is non-deterministic. The operation which releases a buffer is:

$RELEASE(b: Bid)$

ext wr $fs: \text{set of } Bid$

pre $b \notin fs$

post $fs = \overleftarrow{fs} \cup \{b\}$

The next example illustrates how properties of the operations become important in understanding specifications. A database is to be set up which classifies people depending on sex and marital status. One possible way of modelling the information is to have three sets: one each for male, female and married names. (*Name* is used as a primitive set—in a real system some form of unique identifier would be used. Thus, no name change is shown on marriage.) In the initial state, all three sets would be empty. An interrogation operation is:

$MARMALE()\ rs: \text{set of } Name$

ext rd $male: \text{set of } Name,$ rd $married: \text{set of } Name$

post $rs = \overleftarrow{male} \cap \overleftarrow{married}$

Two operations which update the database are:

$NEWFEM\,(f\colon Name)$

ext wr $female$: set of $Name$, rd $male$: set of $Name$

pre $f \notin (female \cup male)$

post $female = \overline{female} \cup \{f\}$

$MARRIAGE(m\colon Name, f\colon Name)$

ext rd $male$: set of $Name$,

   rd $female$: set of $Name$,

   wr $married$: set of $Name$

pre $m \in (male - married) \wedge f \in (female - married)$

post $married = \overline{married} \cup \{m, f\}$

In all of these operations, external variables are marked as "read only" where they cannot be changed.

There are certain properties of the operations in this model. For example, the *married* set is always a subset of the union of the other two sets—the *male* and *female* sets are always disjoint. Such properties are "invariants" on the state and are discussed in Section 5.2. The formal proofs of such properties use the methods of the preceding section.

Another point which is taken up in subsequent chapters is the choice of the most appropriate model for a particular specification. That given above is chosen for pedagogic reasons—the notation of Chapter 6 makes it possible to provide a model with simpler invariants. Even with the set notation alone, other models could be employed—one such is suggested in Exercise 4 below.

An interesting example which can be handled with sets (alone) concerns the creation and interrogation of a database which records equivalence relations. Before discussing this as a mathematical concept, some motivation is offered.

Compilers for high-level languages of the ALGOL family have to map programs with many variables onto machines in which some store access times (i.e. for registers) are much faster than others. Storing variables in registers can considerably improve the performance of the created object programs. There is, however, a trap which must be carefully avoided. Distinct variable names can be made to refer to the same location in store. This happens when variables are passed by location in Pascal (i.e. to *var* parameters) or by name in ALGOL. Any change made to one variable must

be reflected in that variable's surrogates. A compiler writer therefore might
need to keep track of a relation between variables which might be known as
"could share storage" and to ensure that appropriate register-to-store operations follow updates. The use of "could" indicates that this check should
be fail-safe. Now, if both pairs A/B and B/C could share storage then
clearly, also, A/C could share storage. This is one of the properties of an
equivalence relation.

There are very many applications of such relations in computing including, for example, codebreaking. The applications in graph processing involve
relations over very large sets.

The form of relation being considered here records connections over elements of a set[6]. If R is a relation, and if the pair of elements x/y stand in
the relation, this can be written[7]:

xRy

There are some important properties of relations. A relation is said to be
transitive if when x/y and y/z stand in the relation, x/z necessarily also
stand in the relation. Figure 4.7 shows which relations over the integers possess the properties being discussed. The reader should use these to confirm
the intuition of the properties (note, in particular, that inequality is not
transitive). A relation is *symmetric* if whenever x/y stand in the relation,
so must y/x. A relation is *reflexive* if for all elements x, the pair x/x stand
in the relation. A relation is an *equivalence relation* if it is reflexive, symmetric and transitive. Referring to Figure 4.7, it can be seen that equality
is the only equivalence relation shown there. The reader should be able to
see that the "could share storage" relation over variables is an equivalence
relation.

The compiler example might involve relatively small sets but the implementation problems become interesting for very large sets. The reader
should spend some time thinking about how to represent the relation so
that it can be queried and updated efficiently. An ingenious solution to the
problem is presented in Chapter 6 and is proved in Chapter 8 to satisfy the
specification given here. For now, the concern is to obtain a clear specification which defines exactly what the system does without getting involved in
the implementation problems.

---

[6]Mathematically, such a relation is a subset of the Cartesian product of two instances of
the set.

[7]Other styles for doing this include $(x, y) \in R$ and $R: x \mapsto y$.

Property	Definition	Example
Reflexive	xRx	$=, \leq, \geq$
Symmetric	$xRy \Rightarrow yRx$	$=, \neq$
Transitive	$xRy \wedge yRz \Rightarrow xRz$	$=, <, \leq, >, \geq$

Figure 4.7: Properties of Relations over Integers

Two operations are to be specified—as well as a starting state. One operation is to $EQUATE$ two elements; the other is to $TEST$ whether two elements are equivalent—the result of the $TEST$ must reflect all pairs which have been $EQUATE$d and the reflexive, symmetric and transitive consequences. If the underlying set is X, then the natural model is to use $Partition(X)$ as defined in the preceding section. One set is allocated to each group of equivalent elements. The initial state is simply the finest partition:

$$p_0 = \{\{e\} \mid e \in X\}$$

The $TEST$ operation establishes whether the two elements are contained in the same group:

$TEST(e_1: X, e_2: X)\ r: \mathbf{B}$
ext rd $p: Partition(X)$
post $r \Leftrightarrow (\exists s \in p \cdot e_1 \in s \wedge e_2 \in s)$

The operation to $EQUATE$ two elements has to merge (union) the sets containing the elements and to leave the other sets unchanged:

$EQUATE(e_1: X, e_2: X)$
ext wr $p: Partition(X)$
post $p = \{s \in \overleftarrow{p} \mid e_1 \notin s \wedge e_2 \notin s\} \cup \{\bigcup\{s \in \overleftarrow{p} \mid e_1 \in s \vee e_2 \in s\}\}$

For some applications of equivalence relations, it might be useful to be able to retrieve the group which contains a stated element. This operation can be specified:

$GROUP(e: X)\ r: \text{set of } X$
ext rd $p: Partition(X)$
post $r \in p \wedge e \in r$

One virtue of this set-based specification is that it is much more succinct than a description based on an implementation. But a more important property is that, because the algebra of sets is established, it is possible to make deductions about this specification more readily than reasoning about contorted details of a particular representation. It is a consequence of the following Lemmas that these operations preserve the property that p is a partition (*invp* of Section 4.3).

- the (initial) finest partition is a partition;

- *TEST* has read only access to p and must, therefore, preserve *invp*;

- the Lemma *Partition*-combine shows that *EQUATE* preserves *invp*;

- *GROUP* has read only access to p.

This is where the development of the theory pays off. Other properties can also be proved. For example, it is easy to show that performing *EQUATE* with the same element as both arguments does not change the database. Some of these properties are considered in exercises below.

Exercises

1. The spell checking program of Section 4.2 would probably need an operation which inserted many words into a dictionary at once. Specify an operation which takes a set of words as arguments, adds all new ones to the dictionary and returns all duplicates as result.

2. A system is to be specified which keeps track of which students are in a room at any point in time—ignore how the operations are invoked (badge reader?) and assume that no two students have the same name. Specify operations for *ENTER, EXIT, ISPRESENT*. Also show the initial state.

3. A system is to be specified which keeps track of which students have done an example class. Specify operations which can be used to:

   (a) record the enrollment of a student (only enrolled students can have the next operation performed);

   (b) record the fact that a student has successfully completed the examples;

    (c) output the names of those students who have, so far, completed
        the examples.

Also show the initial state.

4. Respecify the three operations in the text relating to the recording of
   people based on a model:

$$singfem: \text{set of } Name$$
$$marfem: \text{set of } Name$$
$$singmale: \text{set of } Name$$
$$marmale: \text{set of } Name$$

What invariants hold over these sets?

5. * These results establish useful properties about the equivalence relation specification. State in English and prove:

    (a) $\forall e \in X \cdot \exists s \in p \cdot e \in s \wedge e \in s$

    (b) $(\exists s \in p \cdot e_1 \in s \wedge e_2 \in s) \Leftrightarrow (\exists s \in p \cdot e_2 \in s \wedge e_1 \in s)$

    (c) $(\exists s \in p \cdot e_1 \in s \wedge e_2 \in s) \wedge (\exists s \in p \cdot e_2 \in s \wedge e_3 \in s) \Rightarrow$
$$(\exists s \in p \cdot e_1 \in s \wedge e_3 \in s)$$

    (d) $(\exists s \in \overleftarrow{p} \cdot e_1 \in s \wedge e_2 \in s) \Rightarrow$
$$\{s \in \overleftarrow{p} \mid e_1 \notin s \wedge e_2 \notin s\} \cup$$
$$\{\bigcup\{s \in \overleftarrow{p} \mid e_1 \in s \vee e_2 \in s\}\} = \overleftarrow{p}$$

6. * Respecify the equivalence relation problem so that the $EQUATE$
   and $TEST$ operations take a set of elements as input.

Chapter 5

Composite Objects and Invariants

> We always require an outside point to stand on. in
> order to apply the lever of criticism.
> *C. G. Jung*

Sets are only one item in the toolkit from which abstract descriptions of objects, like states, can be built. Chapters 6 and 7 introduce further familiar mathematical constructs. In this chapter, a way of forming multi-component objects is described; in many respects these composite objects are like the records of Pascal or the structures of PL/I; since, however, the properties of composite objects are not exactly the same as for records, a syntax is chosen which differs from that used in programming languages.

As with the objects discussed above, an (inductive) proof method is given which facilitates proofs about composite objects. In Section 5.2, data type invariants—which are mentioned above—are discussed in detail. Section 5.3 provides amplification of the concept of states and some related proof obligations. Section 5.4 shows that collections of operations can be grouped into a (state based) data type and explains how the operations of one data type can be used in specifying another.

5.1 Notation

Instances of set objects are written using braces; they can be presented either by enumerating the values between the braces or by defining a set by comprehension. The composite values considered in this chapter are created by so-called "make-functions". A *composite object* has a number of fields; each such field has a value. A *make-function*, when applied to appropriate values for the fields, yields a value of the composite type. The notation to define composite types is explained below. Suppose, for now, that some composite type has been defined such that each object contains a form of date. The type is called *Datec*; the first field contains a day and the second the year; the relevant make-function might be:

$$mk\text{-}Datec: \{1, \ldots, 366\} \times \{1583, \ldots, 2599\} \rightarrow Datec$$

Notice that the make-function is specific to a type. Its name is formed by prefixing *mk-* to the name of the type.

A useful property of make-functions is that they yield a tagged value such that no two different make-functions can ever yield the same value. Thus if two sorts of temperature measurements are to be manipulated, one might have:

$$mk\text{-}Fahrenheit: \mathbf{R} \rightarrow Fahrenheit$$

$$mk\text{-}Celsius: \mathbf{R} \rightarrow Celsius$$

Even though each of these types has one field, and the field contains a real number in each case, the types (when viewed as sets) *Fahrenheit* and *Celsius* are disjoint. A single make-function yields distinct results (composite values) for different arguments.

The objects created by make-functions have a number of properties. One way of decomposing such composite values is by selectors. The definitions of such selectors are described below with the notation for defining the composite type itself. For now, assume that the selectors *day* and *year* have been associated with the two fields of *Datec*—then:

$$day(mk\text{-}Datec(7, 1979)) = 7$$

$$year(mk\text{-}Datec(117, 1989)) = 1989$$

Such *selectors*[1] are functions which can be applied to composite values to yield the component values. Thus the signatures are:

$$day: Datec \rightarrow \{1, \ldots, 366\}$$

$$year: Datec \rightarrow \{1583, \ldots, 2599\}$$

---

[1]The selectors serve as projection functions and make-functions as injections.

There are several other ways of decomposing composite values; each essentially uses the name of the make-function in a context which enables it to associate names with the sub-components of a value. A notation used above for defining values is:

$$\text{let } i = \dots$$
$$\text{in } \dots i \dots$$

The expression to the right of the equality sign is evaluated and its value is associated with i, this value of i is used in evaluating the expression to the right of in; the let construct provides a binding for free occurrences of i in the final expression. This notation can be extended in an obvious way to decompose composite values. Suppose that a function is to be defined whose domain is *Datec* and the definition of the function manipulates the values of the components:

$$inv\text{-}Datec \colon Datec \to \mathbf{B}$$

The function could be defined, using selectors:

$$inv\text{-}Datec(dt) \quad \triangleq \quad is\text{-}leapyr(year(dt)) \vee day(dt) \le 365$$

Using the extension of let, this can be written:

$$inv\text{-}Datec(dt) \quad \triangleq \quad \text{let } mk\text{-}Datec(d, y) = dt$$
$$\text{in } is\text{-}leapyr(y) \vee d \le 365$$

The let construct, in a sense, decomposes dt by associating names with the values of its fields. The frequency with which such decompositions occur on parameters of functions prompts the use of the make-functions directly in the parameter list. Thus an equivalent effect can be achieved by writing:

$$inv\text{-}Datec(mk\text{-}Datec(d, y)) \quad \triangleq \quad is\text{-}leapyr(y) \vee d \le 365$$

The tagging property of make functions can be used to support a useful cases construct. A function which reduces either form of temperature to a *Celsius* value might be written:

$$c(t) \quad \triangleq \quad \text{if } t \in Fahrenheit$$
$$\text{then} \quad \text{let } mk\text{-}Fahrenheit(v) = t$$
$$\text{in } mk\text{-}Celsius((v - 32) * 5/9)$$
$$\text{else} \quad t$$

This is rather cumbersome and an obvious cases notation can be used which also has the effect of decomposing the composite objects:

$$c(t) \quad \triangleq \quad \text{cases } t \text{ of}$$

$$mk\text{-}Fahrenheit(v) \rightarrow mk\text{-}Celsius((v-32)*5/9)$$

$$mk\text{-}Celsius(v) \quad \rightarrow t$$

end

At first meeting, the choice of ways for decomposing composite objects might appear excessive. However, it is normally easy to choose, for example, between using selector functions and decomposing an object with let: if only a few fields of a multi-component object are referred to within the function, the use of selectors is more compact; if, on the other hand, all fields are referred to, it is simpler to name them all at once in a let. If no reference is made in the body of a function to the value of the entire object, such a let can be avoided and the decomposition made in the parameter list. Decomposition via the cases construct is obviously of use when several options are to be resolved. Although the notations can be used interchangeably, brevity and clarity result from careful selection.

Classes of values of type set are defined by the set of constructor . It is now necessary to introduce the way in which composite types are defined. For the *Datec* example above the *composite type* is defined:

compose *Datec* of
    $day: \{1, \ldots, 366\},$
    $year: \{1583, \ldots, 2599\}$
end

In general, the name of the type (and thus of its make-function) is written between the compose and of; after the of is written the information about fields—for each field, the name of its selector is followed by the type of value. Similarly:

compose *Fahrenheit* of $v: \mathbf{R}$ end

compose *Celsius* of $v: \mathbf{R}$ end

If it is clear that values in a composite type are never going to be decomposed by selectors, the selector names can be omitted altogether in the definition. Thus, it is possible to write:

compose *Celsius* of $\mathbf{R}$ end

The corresponding sets of objects defined are:

$$\{mk\text{-}Datec(d,y) \mid d \in \{1,\ldots,366\} \wedge y \in \{1583,\ldots,2599\}\}$$
$$\{mk\text{-}Fahrenheit(v) \mid v \in \mathbf{R}\}$$
$$\{mk\text{-}Celsius(v) \mid v \in \mathbf{R}\}$$

From the properties of make-functions, it follows that:

$$is\text{-}disj(Fahrenheit, Celsius)$$

Definitions of composite types can be used in any suitable context. Thus, one could write:

set of (compose $Datec$ of ... end)

However, the most common context is just to associate a name with the set:

$Datec$ = compose $Datec$ of ... end

This name is often the same as the constructor name. The frequency of this special case justifies an abbreviation. The above definition can be written:

$$Datec :: \quad day\text{:}\{1,\ldots,366\}$$
$$year\text{:}\{1583,\ldots,2599\}$$

The :: symbol can be read as "is composed of ...". In general the following two definitions are equivalent:

$$Name :: \quad s_1\text{:} T_1$$
$$\cdots$$
$$s_n\text{:} T_n$$

$Name =$
    compose $Name$ of
        $s_1\text{:} T_1,$
        $\cdots$
        $s_n\text{:} T_n$
    end

New names can be introduced in definitions to add clarity or to provide convenient names for sets. For example, the definition given above could be written:

$$Datec \quad :: \quad day \colon Day$$
$$year \colon Year$$

$$Day = \{1, \ldots, 366\}$$
$$Year = \{1583, \ldots, 2599\}$$

Since these are simple set equalities, the definitions of *Day* and *Year* have not, however, been tagged by constructors—thus:

$$7 \in (Day \cap Year)$$

The functions associated with composite objects (make-functions and selectors so far) are unlike the operators on sets in that the latter are general whereas those for composite objects are specific to a type. Thus the ADJ diagram given in Figure 5.1 relates solely to the *Datec* example. Only one other function is defined for composite objects: the μ function provides a way of creating a composite value, which differs only in one field, from another; thus:

$$dt = mk\text{-}Datec(17, 1927)$$

$$\mu(dt, day \mapsto 29) = mk\text{-}Datec(29, 1927)$$
$$\mu(dt, year \mapsto 1937) = mk\text{-}Datec(17, 1937)$$

The μ function could be generalized[2] to change more than one field at a time. This is not needed in the current book.

The reader will be aware of concrete syntax notations (e.g. BNF) which can be used to define the set of strings of a language. An *abstract syntax* defines a set of objects which contain information but do not retain the syntactic marks (e.g. $\colon =$, ;) which play a part in parsing strings. In fact, one of the reasons that the uniqueness property of make-functions had to be adopted was to simplify the description of the abstract syntax of programming languages. Both the set of and compose of constructs are used in describing abstract syntax and many examples occur below. Certain aspects of concrete syntax notation carry over naturally to the description of abstract syntax.

The [...] notation for marking things as optional is taken over from concrete syntax along with the idea of distinguishing elementary values by fount change. Thus:

---

[2]Strictly, there is a whole family of μ functions—one for each composite type. However, since a μ function cannot change the type of a composite object, no confusion arises if μ is used as a generic name.

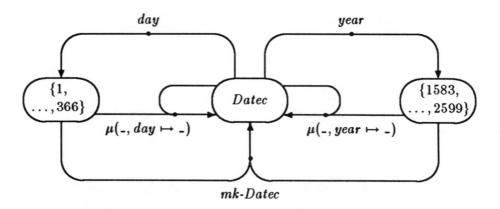

Figure 5.1: ADJ Diagram of *Datec* Operators

$$Month = \{\text{JAN}, \text{FEB}, \ldots, \text{DEC}\}$$

$$Record \; :: \quad day : \{1, \ldots, 366\}$$
$$year : \{1583, \ldots, 2599\}$$
$$valid : [\text{ERROR}]$$

The brackets denoting optional items can be read as:

$$[Set] = Set \cup \{\text{nil}\}$$

Thus, an omitted field is marked by the nil value and:

$$mk\text{-}Record(366, 1984, \text{nil}) \in Record$$

$$mk\text{-}Record(366, 1983, \text{ERROR}) \in Record$$

A number of naming conventions are being followed here—although not strictly part of the notation, conformance to some stated set of conventions can significantly aid the readability of large specifications. The conventions are:

- Names of sets are printed in italics and have their first letter in upper case and the rest of the name in lower case (e.g. *Datec*)—exceptions are standard names for certain mathematical sets (e.g. **N**) which are distinguished by being in bold fount.

- Names of functions (and thus selectors) are in all lower case italic letters.

- Names of operations are in all upper case italic letters.

- Elementary values (e.g. ERROR) are in a *sans serif* fount.

The topic of data type invariants, which is touched upon above, is now explored more formally. The *day* field of *Datec* is restricted to show that, for instance, 399 can never be a value. This sub-range concept is useful but does not solve the problem of restricting values of composite objects. In several places above (and very many below) it is necessary to show that certain combinations of field values cannot arise. *Data type invariants* are truth-valued functions which can be used to record such restrictions. The function *inv-Datec* above is an obvious invariant on dates. It is convenient to write such restrictions as part of the type definition—thus:

$$Datec :: \quad day\!: Day$$
$$year\!: Year$$
$$\text{where}$$
$$inv\text{-}Datec(mk\text{-}Datec(d,y)) \quad \triangleq \quad is\text{-}leapyr(y) \lor d \leq 365$$

defines the set:

$$\{mk\text{-}Datec(d,y) \mid$$
$$d \in \{1,\ldots,366\} \land y \in \{1583,\ldots,2599\} \land$$
$$inv\text{-}Datec(mk\text{-}Datec(d,y))\}$$

The *valid* objects of *Datec* are those which, as well as belonging to the composite type, also satisfy *inv-Datec*. Thus:

$$d \in Datec$$

is taken to imply that the invariant is satisfied[3].

The *Datec* example is typical of the way in which data type invariants arise. The mathematical abstractions tend to fit regular situations; some objects which are to be modelled are ragged and do not immediately fit such an abstraction. The truth-valued function which is used as the data

---

[3]This has a profound consequence for the type mechanism of the notation. In programming languages, it is normal to associate type checking with a simple compiler algorithm. The inclusion of truth-valued functions forces the type checking here to rely on proofs. The next section shows how such proof obligations are generated and discharged.

type invariant cuts out those elements which do not arise in reality. Section 5.3 explains how invariants are also useful on composite objects used as states.

Interesting data types can be defined with the aid of recursion. It is possible to write *recursive abstract syntax definitions* such as:

$$Llist = [Llistel]$$

$$Llistel \ :: \ hd: \mathbf{N}$$
$$tl: Llist$$

These objects are reminiscent of the simplest lists in the Lisp programming language; elements of *Llist* can be nil; non-nil elements are of type *Llistel* and contain a head and a tail where the latter is a (nil or non-nil element of) *Llist*. Just as with sets, there is a clear argument for restricting attention to finite objects. It is assumed that all objects satisfying a recursive composite object definition are finite. It can be useful to think of such objects as trees; Figure 5.2 pictures some elements of *Llist*.

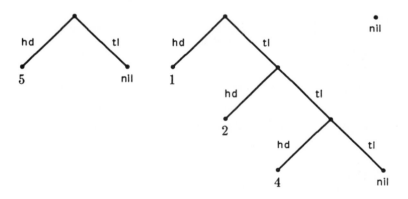

Figure 5.2: Elements of *Llist*

A function which sums the elements of such a list can be written:

$$lsum: Llist \rightarrow \mathbf{N}$$

$lsum(t)$ $\triangleq$ cases t of

nil $\longrightarrow 0$

$mk\text{-}Llistel(hd, tl) \longrightarrow hd + lsum(tl)$

end

Notice that this recursive function is well-defined (i.e. it terminates) only because all elements of $Llist$ are finite.

Further examples of recursive definitions are given in the next section; these are presented with their invariants and a discussion of the relevant proof methods.

Exercises

1. Given:

$$Date \quad :: \quad \begin{aligned} &year: \{1583, \ldots, 2599\} \\ &month: \{\text{JAN}, \ldots, \text{DEC}\} \\ &day: \{1, \ldots, 31\} \end{aligned}$$

   (a) Write the signature of $mk\text{-}Date$ and of the selectors.

   (b) Use $mk\text{-}Date$ to construct an object with an interesting date.

   (c) Define a truth-valued function which determines whether the first of two $Dates$ is earlier than a second. Three versions should be given using, respectively, selectors, let, $mk\text{-}Date$ in the parameter list.

   (d) Write a data type invariant for $Date$.

   (e) Use a μ function to modify the object constructed in (b).

2. Define a composite object which could be used to store the time of day to the nearest second. Why is no data type invariant required? Give the signature of a μ function which modifies the minute field of $Time$.

3. Given a specification of traffic lights:

   $Light = $ set of $Colour$

   $Colour = \{\text{RED}, \text{GREEN}, \text{AMBER}\}$

   limit the possible values with a data type invariant.

4. Suppose a hotel requires a system which stores information about room numbers. Floors are numbered 1 to 25 and rooms are numbered 0 to 63. Define a composite object *Roomno* and an invariant to reflect the facts that:

   - there is no floor number 13;

   - level 1 is an open area and has only room number 0;

   - the top five floors consist of large suites and these are numbered with even integers.

5. Write expressions corresponding to the elements of *Llist* pictured in Figure 5.2. Use a μ function to insert a new tail (*tl*) into the second of these objects. Define a (recursive) function *ljoin* which places one list at the end of (i.e. in the nil position) of another.

6. This exercise develops the form of lists known in pure Lisp. Define a set of objects (*Pllist*) which have fields named *car* and *cdr*; these fields can contain either integers or lists. Define one function which gathers the set of numbers in such an object and another function which sums all of the numbers.

7. * Given

   $$S = T$$
   where
   $$inv\text{-}S(s) \quad \triangleq \quad \ldots$$

   then:

   $$(\forall s \in S \cdot p(s)) \quad \Leftrightarrow \quad (\forall s \in T \cdot inv\text{-}s(s) \Rightarrow p(s))$$
   $$(\exists s \in S \cdot p(s)) \quad \Leftrightarrow \quad (\exists s \in T \cdot inv\text{-}s(s) \wedge p(s))$$

   Explain this using de Morgan's law.

5.2   Structural Induction and Invariants

Induction rules are given above for natural numbers and sets. The situation is similar with composite objects but, in contrast, there is no single induction rule for composite objects. Instead, it is necessary to have an induction rule for each recursively defined class of objects. *Structural induction* provides a way of generating the appropriate induction rules.

The fact that such induction rules exist depends on the finiteness of objects which satisfy recursive type definitions. As with the other induction rules, those for structural induction relate to the ways in which objects are generated. For *Llist* of the preceding section the appropriate induction rule is:

$$Llist\text{-ind} \quad \frac{p(\text{nil});\quad hd \in \mathbf{N}, tl \in Llist, p(tl) \vdash p(mk\text{-}Llistel(hd, tl))}{l \in Llist \vdash p(l)}$$

From this example, it should be clear how induction rules are generated for recursively defined objects. The basis comes from the non-recursive (e.g. nil) case(s) and the induction step from the recursive case(s).

A simple property to prove is that the *lsum* (see preceding section) of a list is half of the *lsum* of the list resulting from:

$$ldbl: Llist \rightarrow Llist$$
$$ldbl(t) \quad \triangle$$

> cases t of
>
> nil $\rightarrow$ nil
>
> $mk\text{-}Llistel(hd, tl) \rightarrow mk\text{-}Llistel(2 * hd, ldbl(tl))$
>
> end

The proof is shown in Figure 5.3

In order to present more interesting examples of proofs, invariants are now added to recursive definitions.

Chapter 8 addresses the problem of finding representations of abstract objects like sets and maps (see Chapter 6). It is necessary to create such representations either because the abstractions are unavailable in the implementation language or to enhance the efficiency of an implementation. One example is finding representations of sets. The sets of *Words* required in the spelling-checking application is a particular example studied below. Here, the problem of representing a set of natural numbers is considered. A large set of numbers can be stored in a binary tree to facilitate efficient updating and checking. Such a *binary tree*:

- has two (possibly nil) branches and a number at each node;

- is arranged so that all numbers in the left branch of a node are less than (and all numbers in the right branch are greater than) the number in the node;

from $l \in Llist$

1	$2 * lsum(\text{nil}) = 0$	$lsum$
2	$lsum(ldbl(\text{nil})) = lsum(\text{nil})$	$ldbl$
3	$= 0$	$lsum$
4	$2 * lsum(\text{nil}) = lsum(ldbl(\text{nil}))$	=-trans(1,3)
5	from $hd \in \mathbf{N},\ tl \in Llist,\ 2 * lsum(tl) = lsum(ldbl(tl))$	
5.1	$2 * lsum(mk\text{-}Llistel(hd, tl)) = 2 * hd + 2 * lsum(tl)$	$lsum, \mathbf{N}$
5.2	$lsum(ldbl(mk\text{-}Llistel(hd, tl)))$	$ldbl$
	$= lsum(mk\text{-}Llistel(2 * hd, ldbl(tl)))$	
5.3	$= 2 * hd + lsum(ldbl(tl))$	$lsum$
5.4	$= 2 * hd + 2 * lsum(tl)$	=-subs,ih5
	Infer $2 * lsum(mk\text{-}Llistel(hd, tl)) =$	=-trans(5.1,5.4)
	$lsum(ldbl(mk\text{-}Llistel(hd, tl)))$	
	Infer $2 * lsum(l) = lsum(ldbl(l))$	$Llist$-ind(4,5)

Figure 5.3: Proof of $lsum$ Property

- is balanced to increase efficiency.

The relevant data structure is defined:

$$Setrep = [Node]$$

$$Node ::\quad lt\!:Setrep$$
$$mv\!:\mathbf{N}$$
$$rt\!:Setrep$$

where
$$inv\text{-}Node(mk\text{-}Node(lt, mv, rt)) \quad \triangleq$$
$$(\forall lv \in retrns(lt) \cdot lv < mv) \land (\forall rv \in retrns(rt) \cdot mv < rv)$$

A function which retrieves the set of numbers in a tree is:

$retrns: Setrep \rightarrow$ set of $\mathbf{N}$

$retrns(sr) \quad \triangleq$

    cases sr of

    nil $\rightarrow \{\}$

    $mk\text{-}Node(lt, mv, rt) \rightarrow retrns(lt) \cup \{mv\} \cup retrns(rt)$

    end

The invariant captures the second requirement above; the third requirement is discussed in Exercise 4 below. Notice that writing the invariant with *Node* requires that it applies to all occurrences within the *Setrep*. If this were not done the invariant would have to be a recursive function; moreover, proofs involving *Nodes* would be more complicated.

The invariant results in the following simple Lemmas about *Nodes*:

$$\forall i \in retrns(mk\text{-}Node(lt, mv, rt)) \cdot i < mv \Rightarrow i \in retrns(lt)$$

$$\forall i \in retrns(mk\text{-}Node(lt, mv, rt)) \cdot mv < i \Rightarrow i \in retrns(rt)$$

One of the proofs is shown in Figure 5.4. Notice how, in order to prove that the implication holds, the definedness of the antecedent is used. A function which checks whether a number is in such a set representation can be defined. Direct definitions are being used here rather than implicit specifications. This is often the case as design steps tackle implementation details.

	from $i \in retrns(mk\text{-}Node(lt, mv, rt))$	
1	from $i < mv$	
1.1	$retrns(mk\text{-}Node(lt, mv, rt)) =$	*retrns*
	$retrns(lt) \cup \{mv\} \cup retrns(rt)$	
1.2	$i \neq mv$	h1
1.3	$i \notin retrns(rt)$	h,*inv-Node*,h1
	Infer $i \in retrns(lt)$	1.1,1.2,1.3
2	$i < mv \in \mathbf{B}$	
	Infer $i < mv \Rightarrow i \in retrns(lt)$	$\Rightarrow\text{-}I(2,1)$

Figure 5.4: Proof of a Lemma on *Node*

Assuming *inv-Node* is true:

$isin: \mathbf{N} \times Setrep \rightarrow \mathbf{B}$

$isin(i, sr) \quad \underline{\Delta}$

    cases sr of

    nil $\rightarrow$ false

    $mk\text{-}Node(lt, mv, rt) \rightarrow$ If $i = mv$

                          then   true

                          else   If $i < mv$

                                    then $isin(i, lt)$

                                    else $isin(i, rt)$

    end

The induction rule for $Setrep$ is:

$Setrep$-ind
$$\frac{\begin{array}{l} p(\text{nil}); \\ mv \in \mathbf{N}, lt, rt \in Setrep, \\ inv\text{-}Node(mk\text{-}Node(lt, mv, rt)), p(lt), p(rt) \vdash \\ \qquad\qquad\qquad p(mk\text{-}Node(lt, mv, rt)) \end{array}}{sr \in Setrep \vdash p(sr)}$$

This can be used to prove:

$$sr \in Setrep \vdash isin(i, sr) \iff i \in retrns(sr)$$

as shown in Figure 5.5.

Exercises

1. Using the definitions above (including Exercise 5 of Section 5.1), prove (by induction):

$$l_1, l_2 \in Llist \vdash lsum(ljoin(l_1, l_2)) = lsum(l_1) + lsum(l_2)$$

2. Give an induction rule for $Pllist$ (as in Exercise 6 of Section 5.1).

   (a) Define a function $flatten$ which places the elements of a $Pllist$ into a $Llist$.

   (b) Prove:

   $$ll \in Pllist \vdash sumll(ll) = lsum(flatten(ll))$$

   where $sumll$ is the function defined in the referenced exercise.

	from $sr \in Setrep$	
1	$\neg isin(i, \text{nil})$	$isin$
2	$retrns(\text{nil}) = \{\}$	$retrns$
3	$i \notin retrns(\text{nil})$	set,2
4	$isin(i, \text{nil}) \Leftrightarrow i \in retrns(\text{nil})$	$\Leftrightarrow$-I(1,3)
5	from $mv \in \mathbf{N}, lt, rt \in Setrep,$	
	$\quad inv\text{-}Node(mk\text{-}Node(lt, mv, rt)),$	
	$\quad (isin(i, lt) \Leftrightarrow i \in retrns(lt)),$	
	$\quad (isin(i, rt) \Leftrightarrow i \in retrns(rt))$	
5.1	$i < mv \lor i = mv \lor i > mv$	$\mathbf{N}$
5.2	from $i = mv$	
5.2.1	$isin(i, mk\text{-}Node(lt, mv, rt))$	$isin$,h5.2
5.2.2	$i \in retrns(mk\text{-}Node(lt, mv, rt))$	$retrns$,h5.2
	infer $isin(i, mk\text{-}Node(lt, mv, rt)) \Leftrightarrow$	$\Leftrightarrow$-I(5.2.1,5.2.2)
	$\quad i \in retrns(mk\text{-}Node(lt, mv, rt))$	
5.3	from $i < mv$	
5.3.1	$isin(i, mk\text{-}Node(lt, mv, rt)) \Leftrightarrow isin(i, lt)$	h5.3,$isin$
5.3.2	$i \in retrns(lt) \Leftrightarrow$	$Lemma$,h5,h5.3
	$\quad i \in retrns(mk\text{-}Node(lt, mv, rt))$	
	infer $isin(i, mk\text{-}Node(lt, mv, rt)) \Leftrightarrow$	$\Leftrightarrow$-trans(5.3.1,h5,5.3.2)
	$\quad i \in retrns(mk\text{-}Node(lt, mv, rt))$	
5.4	from $i > mv$	
	$\quad similar$	
	infer ...	
	infer $isin(i, mk\text{-}Node(lt, mv, rt)) \Leftrightarrow$	$\lor$-E(5.1,5.2,5.3,5.4)
	$\quad i \in retrns(mk\text{-}Node(lt, mv, rt))$	
	infer $isin(i, sr) \Leftrightarrow i \in retrns(sr)$	$Setrep$-ind(4,5)

Figure 5.5: Proof of a Lemma on $Setrep$

3. Define a function which inserts an number into a *Setrep* and prove that the function preserves the invariant (it will be necessary to conjoin a property about the result in order to make the induction work). Do not attempt to preserve the "balanced tree" property.

4. * Define a function which deletes a number from a *Setrep* and show that the function preserves the invariant and has the expected effect on the set of numbers. (Deletion is significantly harder than insertion.) Do not attempt to preserve the "balanced tree" property.

The property of a tree being (height) balanced has not been formalized yet. Write a suitable invariant. What is the problem with defining this at the *Nnode* level? Use this to give an implicit specification of a delete function which does preserve the property.

5.3   States and Proof Obligations

The process of design proceeds, normally in several stages, from specification to implementation. At each stage of design, a claim is being made that the design coincides, in some way, with what has gone before—for example some piece of code satisfies a module specification. In an informal development method, such claims are often only implicit; they are not capable of formalization since the specifications, etc., are informal. In the rigorous approach, such claims are made explicit: they give rise to *proof obligations*. Such proof obligations are in the form of sequents to be proved. The formality of the specification makes proof obligations quite precise. The level of detail to be employed in a particular proof depends on judgement—thus the method is rigorous rather than completely formal. The virtue of recognizing proof obligations is to ensure consideration and to provide a clear hook for extra formality if required.

Even when specifications alone are concerned, there are proof obligations. It is possible to write implicit specifications which cannot be satisfied. For example, a post-condition can be written which requires a number such that it and its successor are even, or a function can be specified to produce the "largest prime number". The proof obligation of *implementability* requires that, for any function or operation, some result exist. For example, for:

$$f(i:D)d:R$$
$$pre\text{-}f:D \to \mathbf{B}$$
$$post\text{-}f:D \times R \to \mathbf{B}$$

the condition is:

$$\forall d \in D \cdot pre\text{-}f(d) \implies \exists r \in R \cdot post\text{-}f(d,r)$$

The need to establish implementability can frequently be discharged with a minimum of work. For example, the appropriate sequent for the pi function of Section 3.2 is:

$$\forall x \in \mathbf{R} \cdot \exists r \in \mathbf{R} \cdot abs(\pi - r) \leq 10^{-2}$$

This expression is obviously true. Since, however, this is the first proof which requires $\exists$-I, its form is shown:

from *defns*

1	from $x \in \mathbf{R}$	
1.1	$3.141 \in \mathbf{R}$	**R**
1.2	$abs(\pi - 3.141) \leq 10^{-2}$	**R**
	infer $\exists r \in \mathbf{R} \cdot abs(\pi - r) \leq 10^{-2}$	$\exists$-I(1.2)
	infer $\forall x \in \mathbf{R} \cdot \exists r \in R \cdot abs(\pi - r) \leq 10^{-2}$	$\forall$-I(1)

Notice how the bound variable r is substituted[4] for the 3.141.

Even in the case of some of the more complex explicit function definitions given above, the implementability proof obligation is straightforward. For example, the square function requires:

$$\forall i \in \mathbf{N} \cdot \exists r \in \mathbf{N} \cdot r = i^2$$

which is obviously true from knowledge of the natural numbers.

Some appreciation of the need for implementability can be seen from an example where it does not hold. Suppose that square root were specified so as to require:

---

[4]It is interesting to note how the actual implementation provides, in this case, the existence proof that an implementation is possible. This has prompted some computer scientists to follow the idea of creating programs by constructively proving the existence of a result. Notable in this area is the work at Cornell on PL/CV2 (see Bibliography).

$$\forall i \in \mathbf{N} \cdot \exists rt \in \mathbf{N} \cdot rt^2 = i$$

This is obviously not true, as can be shown by a simple counter example:

$$\neg \exists rt \in \mathbf{N} \cdot rt^2 = 2$$

There are other cases where the implementability proof obligation is no easier than simply creating the implementation. In such cases, the proof obligation should be used as an item on a check-list and—given a strong feeling that it is satisfied—work on the implementation should proceed.

Type information interacts with the pre- and post-conditions when considering implementability. Thus:

pre $x < 2$
post $x = \overleftarrow{x} - 2$

is implementable for integers (or reals) but not where x is constrained to be a natural number.

Such implementability constraints carry over in an obvious way from functions to operations. The only necessity is to fix an order for the parameters of the pre- and post-conditions when they are taken out of their context. This is done in Section 4.1.

Invariants also play a part in implementability. An operation which has write access to a variable of type *Datec*, must not generate a value like:

$$mk\text{-}Datec(366, 1923)$$

A specification must not be written which rules out all valid elements of *Datec*. Thus:

$OP\ (i\!:\!D)\ o\!:\!\mathbf{R}$
ext wr $dt\!:\!Datec$
pre $p(i, dt)$
post $q(i, \overleftarrow{dt}, o, dt)$

must satisfy:

$$\forall i \in D, \overleftarrow{dt} \in Datec \cdot$$
$$pre\text{-}OP(i, \overleftarrow{dt}) \Rightarrow \exists o \in R, dt \in Datec \cdot post\text{-}OP(i, \overleftarrow{dt}, o, dt)$$

Examples involving *Setrep* or *Partition* behave in exactly the same way and it should now be clear why emphasis was placed on invariant preservation lemmas when these objects were introduced. The concept of implementability provides a way of identifying rules for different contexts. In each case, the requirement is to see that a specification does not preclude all possible implementations.

The idea of recording the external variables of an operation makes it possible to avoid mentioning any irrelevant variables. There is a clear way in which an operation can be used in a state which has, at least, all of the required external variables. (There is, of course, also a requirement that the types match.) A state can be defined as a composite object and can have an invariant. The implementability proof obligation for an operation which is to be used in such a state must reflect the invariant. Consider the example, from Section 4.4, which controls information about people. The state could be:

$$World \ :: \quad male: \text{set of } Name$$
$$female: \text{set of } Name$$
$$married: \text{set of } Name$$

where
$$inv\text{-}World(mk\text{-}World(m, f, e)) \quad \triangleq \quad is\text{-}disj(m, f) \land e \subseteq (m \cup f)$$

No operation which has only read access to the state can disturb the invariant. However, the operation:

$$BIRTHM \ (n: Name)$$

ext wr *male*: set of $Name$, rd *female*: set of $Name$

pre $n \notin (male \cup female)$

post $male = \overleftarrow{male} \cup \{n\}$

poses a non-trivial implementability proof obligation. The basic form is:

$$\forall \overleftarrow{w} \in World \ \cdot$$
$$pre\text{-}BIRTHM(n, male(\overleftarrow{w}), female(\overleftarrow{w})) \ \Rightarrow$$
$$\exists w \in World \ \cdot$$
$$post\text{-}BIRTHM(n, male(\overleftarrow{w}), female(\overleftarrow{w}), male(w)) \land$$
$$female(w) = female(\overleftarrow{w}) \land married(w) = married(\overleftarrow{w})$$

The two final conjuncts come from the fact that the externals show that *BIRTHM* cannot change these values. The set *World* is constrained by *inv-World* such that:

$$World = \{mk\text{-}World(m, f, e) \mid$$
$$m, f, e \in \text{set of } Name \land inv\text{-}World(mk\text{-}World(m, f, e))\}$$

Proofs about quantifiers ranging over such set comprehensions are discussed in Exercise 7 of Section 5.1. From the equivalences there, it can be seen that the proof obligation becomes:

$$\forall n \in Name, \overleftarrow{m}, \overleftarrow{f}, \overleftarrow{e} \in \text{set of } Name \cdot$$
$$inv\text{-}World(mk\text{-}World(\overleftarrow{m}, \overleftarrow{f}, \overleftarrow{e})) \Rightarrow$$
$$(pre\text{-}BIRTHM(n, \overleftarrow{m}, \overleftarrow{f}) \Rightarrow$$
$$\exists m \in \text{set of } Name \cdot$$
$$inv\text{-}World(mk\text{-}World(m, \overleftarrow{f}, \overleftarrow{e})) \land$$
$$post\text{-}BIRTHM(n, \overleftarrow{m}, \overleftarrow{f}, m))$$

Using the fact that:

$$\frac{E_1 \Rightarrow (E_2 \Rightarrow E_3)}{E_1 \land E_2 \Rightarrow E_3}$$

and the usual translation into a sequent, the proof is shown in Figure 5.6. Clearly, it is not normally necessary to produce such formal versions of implementability proofs. It is done here by way of illustration.

The role of invariants on states can perhaps best be visualized by considering them as some form of global (or "meta") pre- and post-condition: an invariant on a state is an assertion which can be thought of as having been conjoined to the pre- and post-conditions of all operations on that state.

This raises the question of why it is thought worth separating data type invariants. There are three main arguments:

- for consistency checking;

- to guide subsequent revisions;

- to ease implementation.

It is not possible to prove formally that a specification matches a user's wishes since these latter are inherently informal. The more that can be done to postulate and prove theorems about a specification, the greater is the chance of discovering any undesirable properties. Thus the obligation to prove results about invariants can be seen as an opportunity to increase confidence in the consistency of a specification.

from $n \in Name, \overleftarrow{m}, \overleftarrow{f}, \overleftarrow{e} \in$ set of $Name$

1   from $is\text{-}disj(\overleftarrow{m}, \overleftarrow{f}) \wedge \overleftarrow{e} \subseteq (\overleftarrow{m} \cup \overleftarrow{f}) \wedge n \notin (\overleftarrow{m} \cup \overleftarrow{f})$

1.1 $\overleftarrow{m} \cup \{n\} \in$ set of $Name$ h,$\cup$

1.2 $is\text{-}disj(\overleftarrow{m} \cup \{n\}, \overleftarrow{f})$ h1,h1,$is\text{-}disj$

1.3 $\overleftarrow{e} \subseteq (\overleftarrow{m} \cup \{n\} \cup \overleftarrow{f})$ h1,$\cup$

1.4 $\overleftarrow{m} \cup \{n\} = \overleftarrow{m} \cup \{n\}$ =-term

infer $\exists m \in$ set of $Name \cdot$ $\exists$-I($\wedge$-I(1.2,1.3,1.4),1.1)

$is\text{-}disj(m, \overleftarrow{f}) \wedge \overleftarrow{e} \subseteq (\overleftarrow{m} \cup \overleftarrow{f}) \wedge m = \overleftarrow{m} \cup \{n\}$ $\Rightarrow$-I

infer $is\text{-}disj(\overleftarrow{m}, \overleftarrow{f}) \wedge \overleftarrow{e} \subset (\overleftarrow{m} \cup \overleftarrow{f}) \wedge n \notin (\overleftarrow{m} \cup \overleftarrow{f}) \Rightarrow$

$\exists m \in$ set of $Name \cdot$

$is\text{-}disj(m, \overleftarrow{f}) \wedge \overleftarrow{e} \subseteq (m \cup \overleftarrow{f}) \wedge m = \overleftarrow{m} \cup \{n\}$

Figure 5.6: Proof of Invariant Preservation

The techniques described in this book were developed in an industrial environment. The sort of application considered was rarely stable; specifications often had to be updated. Recording data type invariants is one way in which the authors of a specification can record assumptions about the state on which their operations work. An explicit assumption, and its attendant proof obligation, are likely to alert someone making a revision to an error which could be missed if the reliance were left implicit.

The task of showing that representations are adequate for abstractions used in specifications is addressed in Section 8.1. It should, however, be intuitively clear that assumptions which limit the abstraction facilitate the search for representations.

Although there are these advantages in recording invariants, it is also true that their presence—or complexity—can provide a hint that a simpler model might be more appropriate. This point is pursued below when other data-structuring mechanisms are available. But it is generally true that a state with a simpler invariant is to be preferred in a specification to one with a complex invariant.

The process of designing representations frequently forces the inclusion of redundancy—for example to make some operation efficient. Such redundancy (e.g. a doubly-linked list) gives rise to invariants. Thus, as in the *Setrep* example above, more complex invariants do tend to arise in the design process.

As can be seen, data type invariants provide information about any single state which can arise. They do not provide information about the way in which states change (e.g. a constraint that a variable does not increase in value). Knowledge about single states (e.g. $fn = t!$ in the factorial example used in Exercise 4 of Section 4.1) and between states (e.g. the greatest common divisor of i and j is the same in each succeeding state) both have parts to play in the implementation proofs of Chapter 10. In specifications themselves, it is data type invariants which are most useful.

Exercises

1. Write out the implementability proof obligation (without proof) for:

   (a) double (cf. Exercise 1 of Section 3.2);
   (b) choose (cf. Exercise 3 of Section 3.2);
   (c) mult (cf. Exercise 6 of Section 3.2)

2. Outline the proof of Exercise 1(a)—this is very simple but shows the overall structure.

3. Exercise 3 of Section 4.4 can be specified in (at least) two ways. The different models are distinguished by their invariants.

   Document the invariant used in answering that exercise and prove that the operations are implementable with respect to it. Then find another model and record its invariant.

5.4 Data Types

The notion of data type is very important. The view taken in this book is that a *data type* is characterized by its behaviour. The *behaviour* is the relationship between the results of the operators of the data type. Thus:

$$x \in (S \cup T) \iff x \in S \lor x \in T$$

provides information about the set-union operator by relating it to the set-membership operator. The importance of this inter-relationship is that a value is exposed in another, more basic, data type. In the example, the set membership operator yields a Boolean result. The Boolean data type is, here, taken as given.

Clearly, if one knows all about the behaviour of a data type, one need know nothing else in order to use the data type. The fact that it is realized (or implemented) in some particular way is unimportant. This focusses the discussion on how data types can be specified. For interesting data types, the behaviours would be infinite and it is clear that the behaviours have to be specified other than by enumeration. Section 9.2 shows how the properties themselves can be used to form a specification. The approach followed in the body of this book is to specify data types via models. Thus, the map objects in the next chapter can be modelled by sets of pairs. This *model-oriented* approach appears to be appropriate for the specification of larger computer systems. There are some dangers in the approach and these are discussed in Section 9.1. Essentially, the model must be seen as a way of describing the behaviour and nothing more.

Data types like sets or integers have operators which are purely functional in the sense that their results depend only on their arguments. In contrast, the results of operations (in an example like the calculator of Section 4.1) depend on the state. This distinction is made here by referring to *functional data types* and *state-based data types*. In the main, the specifications of computer systems are state-based data types. In the model-oriented approach to specifications, the states themselves are built using functional data types (e.g. sets).

A model-oriented specification of a state-based data type comprises:

- a definition of the set of states (possibly including invariants);

- a definition of possible initial states (normally, exactly one);

- a collection of operations whose external variables are parts of the state; these operations must be implementable.

It would be possible to construct some fixed concrete syntax for presenting a whole data-type specification. This is not done in this book because of the wish to focus on concepts rather than details of syntax. The place for fixing such a syntax is in the design of support tools for handling specifications.

In a state-based data type, the history of the operations plays a part in governing the behaviour. Even so, the behaviour can be seen as the essence of the data type. The model is a convenient way of defining the behaviour. To a user of the data type, internal details of the state are important only in so far as they effect the behaviour. Those details which are not made visible by operations should be ignored.

Section 4.1 explains why one operation cannot, as such, be used in the specification of another. It is, however, clear that the separation provided by data types is very useful in structuring specifications. There is, therefore, a need to be able to use, in some way, even state-based data types in the specifications of others.

The use of operations from another state-based data type is facilitated by *quoting* their pre- and post-conditions. Suppose the equivalence relation specification of Section 4.4 is taken as a state-based data type and named *Qrel*. It would be possible to define a new data type whose specification used two instances of *Qrel*. The state might be:

$$Db \; :: \; dba: Qrel$$
$$dbb: Qrel$$

The initial object in *Db* is the composite object formed from two instances of the initial objects of *Qrel*. In order to quote the operations of *Qrel*, remember that the implied types of their pre- and post-conditions are:

$$pre\text{-}TEST: X \times X \times Qrel \rightarrow \mathbf{B}$$
$$post\text{-}TEST: X \times X \times Qrel \times \mathbf{B} \rightarrow \mathbf{B}$$
$$pre\text{-}EQUATE: X \times X \times Qrel \rightarrow \mathbf{B}$$
$$post\text{-}EQUATE: X \times X \times Qrel \times Qrel \rightarrow \mathbf{B}$$

The use of *Qrel* rather than *Partition*(X) is to emphasize that the internal details of the state of *Qrel* are not being exposed. It is now possible to define operations on *Db*. Suppose an operation is required which tests whether two elements are equivalent in both parts of *Db*:

$TESTB \; (e_1: X, e_2: X) \; r: \mathbf{B}$

ext rd $d: Db$

pre $pre\text{-}TEST(e_1, e_2, dba(d)) \land pre\text{-}TEST(e_1, e_2, dbb(d))$

post $\exists r_1, r_2 \in \mathbf{B} \; \cdot$

$\qquad post\text{-}TEST(e_1, e_2, dba(d), r_1) \land$

$\qquad post\text{-}TEST(e_1, e_2, dbb(d), r_2) \land$

$\qquad (r \; \Leftrightarrow \; r_1 \land r_2)$

Since *pre-TEST* is true, these references are included solely for illustration. The references to *post-TEST* should themselves be clear; the need to insert

the existential quantifier is to provide a binding for the "results" of the
TEST operation. The quotes in the last sentence provide a reminder that
this is not an invocation of *TEST*. The post-condition of an operation is a
logical expression; here, *post-TESTB* has been formed by using the truth-
valued function *post-TEST*.

An example of quoting an operation, which brings about a change of
state, is provided by specifying an operation on *Db* which records an equate
on *dbb* if the elements are equivalent in *dba*:

$$CEQUATE \ (e_1 \colon X, e_2 \colon X)$$

ext wr $d \colon Db$

post $\exists r \in \mathbf{B} \cdot post\text{-}TEST(e_1, e_2, dba(d), r) \ \wedge$

$$(r \ \Rightarrow$$

$$\exists db \in Qrel \ \cdot$$

$$post\text{-}EQUATE(e_1, e_2, dbb(\overleftarrow{d}), db) \ \wedge$$

$$d = \mu(\overleftarrow{d}, dbb \mapsto db)) \ \wedge$$

$$(\neg r \ \Rightarrow \ d = \overleftarrow{d})$$

Here, the vacuous pre-condition is omitted. Furthermore, the μ function is
used to place the result of *EQUATE* into the overall state.

This example uses multiple instances of the known data type in a composite object. Although this illustrates the essential points of operation
quotation, more telling examples are presented below when known data
types can be used in maps or sequences. It would be possible, even with the
(functional) data types covered so far, to provide an example which creates
a set of instances of a known data type whose state is specified in terms of a
composite object. Most such specifications appear contrived when compared
with the realistic examples of the subsequent chapters.

One important property of data types is the possibility which they offer
to "close off" one piece of work and use it in another. One manifestation
of this property—in the case of state-based data types—is the ability to
change the details of the quoted operation without having to change the
quoting operation. This can be achieved only if the meaning of the quoted
operation remains the same: insulation is given only against changes to
internal details. But providing the change is to an equivalent specification,
it is true that an operation using it will not have to be changed.

The insulation provided by data types is a valuable property, but it does not justify making every set into a separate data type. Taste in the selection of data types comes from consideration of their likely re-use. Extensive use would prompt the need for a stricter syntactic framework than is necessary (or desirable) in a book like this. Such a syntax would include ways of referring to initial states (possibly via a truth-valued function) and could define mechanisms which allow the same operation name to be used in more than one data type.

It is important to understand that the concept of quoting operations in specifications is intended to help form a specification; it is not intended to provide a guide to the implementations. There are several reasons for this caveat. The most obvious one is that the implementation might need to adopt a different structuring in order to achieve acceptable performance[5].

Exercises

1. Use the available specification of *Qrel* to specify operations on *Db* which:

   (a) test whether three elements are such that the first and second are equivalent in *dba* and the second and third are equivalent in *dbb*;

   (b) equate three elements (as in (a)).

2. Consider the example of a binary tree representation of a set (cf. Section 5.2). The obvious way to define an *INSERT* operation on *Setrep* is to use the recursive function of Exercise 3 of Section 5.2. As an exercise in quoting operations, use the idea to simulate recursion of the *INSERT* operation.

---

[5]Technically, it would be necessary to show that the quoting contexts were such that they would accept any implementation of the specification. This monotonicity (with respect to the satisfaction ordering) holds for normal programming language constructs but does not hold for arbitrary formulae of the predicate calculus.

Chapter 6

Map Notation

> Just as everybody must strive to learn language and writing before he can use them freely for the expression of his thoughts, here too there is only one way to escape the weight of formulae. It is to acquire such power over the tool ... that, unhampered by formal technique, one can turn to the true problems.
>
> *H. Weyl*

Functions provide a mapping between their domain and range sets—a result can be computed by evaluating the expression in the direct definition with particular arguments substituted for the parameter names. Function definition uses powerful concepts, of which the most difficult is recursion. Because of this, it is not—in general—possible to answer even simple questions about functions such as whether they are defined for some value. In writing specifications it is often sufficient to construct a finite map; the virtue of the restriction is that more general operators can be defined. The maps which are described in this chapter are, however, similar to functions in many respects and the terminology and notation reflects the similarities. The differences result from the fact that the argument/result relationship is explicitly constructed for maps. Building a map is like building a table of pairs; application of a map requires table look-up rather than evaluation of a defining expression. Whereas functions are defined by a fixed rule, maps are often dynamically created.

Access to information by keys is very common in computer applications

and poses significant implementation problems. A powerful abstract notation for maps from key to data provides a crucial tool for the construction of
concise specifications. Consequently, maps are the most common structure
used in large specifications.

6.1   Notation

In order to provide an introduction to the notation for maps, a specification is constructed—in terms of maps—which is equivalent to that for the
equivalence relation problem in Chapter 4. It should be remembered that
elements of some set X have to be separated into partitions but that partitions can be merged by an $EQUATE$ operation; another operation makes it
possible to $TEST$ whether two elements are in the same partition. Here, the
property of being in the same partition is governed by a map: equivalent
elements are mapped to the same partition identifier (the set of which is
Pid). The required map type is defined:

$$Partrep(X) = \mathsf{map}\ X\ \mathsf{to}\ Pid$$

Thus the partition:

$$\{\{a, b, c\}, \{d\}, \{e, f\}, \ldots\}$$

might be represented by a table of X/Pid values:

(a, pid_1)
(b, pid_1)
(c, pid_1)
(d, pid_7)
(e, pid_4)
(f, pid_4)
$\ldots$

A linear presentation of *map* values can be used: individual pairs are known
as *maplets* and the elements are separated by an arrow ($\mapsto$); the collection
of pairs is contained in set braces. Thus:

$$\{a \mapsto pid_1, b \mapsto pid_1, c \mapsto pid_1, d \mapsto pid_7, e \mapsto pid_4, f \mapsto pid_4, \ldots\}$$

The map is shown as a set of maplets or element pairs. Their order is
unimportant and a natural model for finite maps is a finite set of ordered

pairs. Arbitrary sets of such pairs would, however, be too general. In order for maps to be used with a function style of notation, they must satisfy the restriction that no two pairs have the same left-hand value. In other words, a map represents a many-to-one mapping.

The information about variables, etc., for the *TEST* operation can be rewritten:

$TEST\ (e_1\!:X, e_2\!:X)\ r\!:\mathbf{B}$

ext rd $m\!:Partrep(X)$

post ...

The post-condition must state that r is true if and only if e_1 and e_2 are mapped to the same Pid value. Application of maps is just like functions and the same notation is used. Thus:

post $r\ \Leftrightarrow\ (m(e_1) = m(e_2))$

The post-condition of the *EQUATE* operation must describe how m changes. There is a mapping overwrite operator (†) which enables pairs from its second operand to take precedence over any pairs from its first operand for the same key—thus:

$$\{a \mapsto 1, b \mapsto 2\}\dagger\{a \mapsto 3, c \mapsto 4\} = \{a \mapsto 3, b \mapsto 2, c \mapsto 4\}$$

Thus it would be possible to write in *post-EQUATE*:

$$m = \overleftarrow{m}\dagger\{e_1 \mapsto \overleftarrow{m}(e_2)\}$$

but this would be wrong! By changing only one key, other members of the e_1 partition would not be updated (and the transitivity property would be lost). A comprehension notation, like that for sets, can be used for maps. The correct specification of *EQUATE* is:

$EQUATE\ (e_1\!:X, e_2\!:X)$

ext wr $m\!:Partrep(X)$

post $m = \overleftarrow{m}\dagger\{e \mapsto \overleftarrow{m}(e_2) \mid \overleftarrow{m}(e) = \overleftarrow{m}(e_1)\}$

The second operand of the overwrite contains all pairs from the old value of m which have the same key as e_1 did in the old value of m. How is the initial value of $Partrep(X)$ to be defined? It should be clear that, to represent the finest partition, each element of X must be mapped to a different element of

Pid: the mapping must be one-to-one. This can be defined in a number of ways. One possibility is to say that the domain and range of the map must have the same number of elements. Since the domain and range operators for maps yield sets, this can be written:

$$is\text{-}oneone(m_0)$$

$$is\text{-}oneone\colon (\text{map } X \text{ to } Y) \rightarrow \mathbf{B}$$

$$is\text{-}oneone(m) \quad \overset{\Delta}{=} \quad \text{card rng } m = \text{card dom } m$$

Notice that this leaves it completely arbitrary which elements of *Pid* are used—the only requirement is that no two elements of X have the same *Pid* (and thus that *Pid* has enough elements). This is a case where there is a set of possible initial states (of a state-based data type). There are now two specifications of the equivalence relation problem. Chapter 8 shows how one can be shown to model the other.

Now that the toolkit of data type constructors is larger, it is necessary to spend more time considering which model best suits the task to be specified and this is taken up in Section 7.4.

The remainder of this section takes a closer look at the notation for maps. Maps are associations between two sets of values; within a pair (maplet), the key and value are separated by $\mapsto$; a map value contains a collection of such pairs where no two pairs have the same first element. For example:

$$\{1 \mapsto 1, 2 \mapsto 4, -1 \mapsto 1, 0 \mapsto 0\}$$

The pairs can be written in any order within the braces:

$$\{1 \mapsto 1, 2 \mapsto 4, -1 \mapsto 1, 0 \mapsto 0\} = \{-1 \mapsto 1, 0 \mapsto 0, 1 \mapsto 1, 2 \mapsto 4\}$$

Map values can also be defined by a notation like that for set comprehension. Thus:

$$\{i \mapsto i^2 \mid i \in \{-1, \ldots, 2\}\}$$

is the same map value as above. The general form is:

$$\{x \mapsto f(x) \mid p(x)\}$$

Such expressions must be written so as to generate only finite maps. With care, one can also write map comprehension as:

$$\{x \mapsto y \mid q(x, y)\}$$

but, in order to be able to look up values, it is essential that q does not associate two different y values with the same x value.

The examples which follow use the values:

$$m_1 = \{a \mapsto 1, c \mapsto 3, d \mapsto 1\}, \qquad m_2 = \{b \mapsto 4, c \mapsto 5\}$$

The domain operator yields, when applied to a map value, the set of first elements of the pairs in that map value. Thus:

$$\text{dom } m_1 = \{a, c, d\}$$
$$\text{dom } m_2 = \{b, c\}$$

and for the empty map:

$$\text{dom } \{\} = \{\}$$

A map value can be applied to a value for which it is defined (in the set given by dom)—thus:

$$m_1(a) = 1$$
$$m_2(c) = 5$$

and for maps defined by comprehension:

$$m = \{x \mapsto f(x) \mid p(x)\}, p(x_0) \vdash m(x_0) = f(x_0)$$

Given an understanding of these operators, all other map operators (cf. Figure 6.1) can be defined.

The set of values on the right of the pairs contained in a map can be determined by the range operator:

$$\text{rng } m_1 = \{1, 3\}$$
$$\text{rng } m_2 = \{4, 5\}$$
$$\text{rng } \{\} = \{\}$$

which is defined:

$$\text{rng } m = \{m(d) \mid d \in \text{dom } m\}$$

Notice that for any map value m:

$$\text{card rng } m \leq \text{card dom } m$$

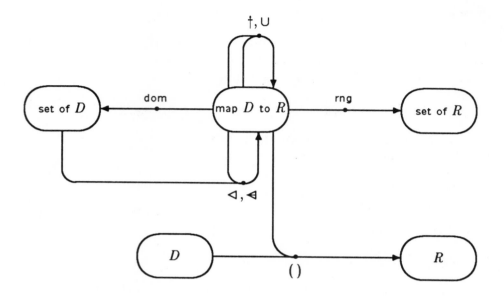

Figure 6.1: ADJ Diagram of Map Operators

The map overwrite operator yields a map value which contains all of the pairs from the second (map) operand and those pairs of the first (map) operand whose first elements are not in the domain of the second operand. Thus:

$$m_1 \dagger m_2 = \{a \mapsto 1, b \mapsto 4, c \mapsto 5, d \mapsto 1\}$$
$$m_2 \dagger m_1 = \{a \mapsto 1, b \mapsto 4, c \mapsto 3, d \mapsto 1\}$$
$$m \dagger \{\} = m \dagger \{\} = \{\} \dagger m$$

The types of all of the map operators can be read from Figure 6.1; map overwrite is defined:

$$ma \dagger mb \quad \triangleq$$
$$\{d \mapsto (\text{if } d \in \text{dom } mb \text{ then } mb(d) \text{ else } ma(d)) \mid$$
$$d \in (\text{dom } ma \cup \text{dom } mb)\}$$

Notice that the domain of the second operand can contain elements which are not in the domain of the first operand.

The overwrite operator is not commutative. When the domains of two map values are disjoint, the values can be combined by a union operator:

$$m_2 \cup \{a \mapsto 7\} = \{a \mapsto 7, b \mapsto 4, c \mapsto 5\}$$

for which:

$$\textit{is-disj}(\operatorname{dom} ma, \operatorname{dom} mb) \vdash ma \cup mb = mb \cup ma$$

The definition of map union is the same as for overwrite:

$$\textit{is-disj}(\operatorname{dom} ma, \operatorname{dom} mb) \vdash ma \cup mb = ma \dagger mb$$

The advantage of identifying this special case is that the commutativity property can be used in proofs. Remember, however, that the union operator is undefined if the domains of the operands overlap.

The union symbol is used in two distinct contexts. Strictly, set union and map union are two different operators. The same symbol is used because of their similarity. Such overloading is familiar both in mathematics and in programming languages. For example, Pascal uses the same plus operator for integer and real numbers (as well as for set union!).

A restriction operator is defined with a first operand which is a set value and a second operand which is a map value; the result is all of those pairs in the map value whose first element is in the set value. Thus:

$$\{a, d, e\} \triangleleft m_1 = \{a \mapsto 1, d \mapsto 1\}$$
$$\{\} \triangleleft m_1 = \{\}$$
$$s \triangleleft \{\} = \{\}$$

Map restriction is defined:

$$s \triangleleft m \;\triangleq\; \{d \mapsto m(d) \mid d \in (\operatorname{dom} m \cap s)\}$$

and for any map:

$$(\operatorname{dom} m) \triangleleft m = m$$

Similarly, a deletion operator with the same type yields those pairs whose first elements are not in the set:

$$\{a, d, e\} \triangleleft\!\!\!\!- m_1 = \{c \mapsto 3\}$$

Map deletion is defined:

$$s \triangleleft m \quad \triangleq \quad \{ d \mapsto m(d) \mid d \in (\text{dom } m - s) \}$$

and for any map values:

$$\{\} \triangleleft m = m$$
$$ma \dagger mb = (\text{dom } mb \triangleleft ma) \cup mb$$

The set of all maps with domains which are a subset of D and ranges a subset of R is defined by:

$$T = \text{map } D \text{ to } R$$

Any value of type T is a (finite) map whose domain is a subset of D and whose range is a subset of R. Thus:

$$\text{map } \{a, b\} \text{ to } \{1, 2\}$$

denotes a set of maps:

$$\{\{\},$$
$$\{a \mapsto 1\}, \{a \mapsto 2\},$$
$$\{b \mapsto 1\}, \{b \mapsto 2\},$$
$$\{a \mapsto 1, b \mapsto 1\}, \{a \mapsto 1, b \mapsto 2\},$$
$$\{a \mapsto 2, b \mapsto 1\}, \{a \mapsto 2, b \mapsto 2\}\}$$

Thus:

$$\{a \mapsto 1, b \mapsto 2\} \in (\text{map } \{a, b\} \text{ to } \{1, 2\})$$

It should be clear from this example that the type (given by map) defines the maximum domain for a map. The domain operator determines the domain set of a particular map value. Thus:

$$\text{dom } \{b \mapsto 2\} = \{b\} \subseteq \{a, b\}$$
$$\text{dom } \{\} = \{\} \subseteq \{a, b\}$$

Because of the restriction that maps be many-to-one, the inverse of a map is not—in general—a map. Only if a map is one-to-one is its inverse also a map. Although it is needed less, this can be shown by:

$$\text{map } D \text{ into } R$$

where:

$$(\text{map } D \text{ into } R) = \{ m \in (\text{map } D \text{ to } R) \mid \textit{is-oneone}(m) \}$$

If:

$$m \in \text{map } D \text{ into } R$$

then the inverse, which is defined:

$$m^{-1} = \{r \mapsto d \mid d \in \text{dom } m \wedge r = m(d)\}$$

is of type:

$$m^{-1} \in \text{map } R \text{ into } D$$

In the description of the notation given above, all of the operators are defined formally except dom and application. In fact, the other operators are defined in terms of these two. The reliance on examples can also be eliminated for these basic operators. The general style of specification in this book is to provide a model for any new data type; the model being defined using data types which are already understood. Maps can be defined in this way. The essence of the definition is to find a model for ordered pairs. If a pair is formed by the function pr and $first$ and $second$ are functions which decompose a pair, the key properties are:

$$first(pr(a, b)) = a$$
$$second(pr(a, b)) = b$$
$$(pr(a, b) = pr(c, d)) \Leftrightarrow (a = c \wedge b = d)$$

Either of the data type constructors from the preceding chapters can be used to construct a suitable model. Using composite objects:

$$Pair :: \quad first: D$$
$$second: R$$

This satisfies the required properties with:

$$pr(a, b) \quad \triangleq \quad mk\text{-}Pair(a, b)$$

Notice that, by choosing the selectors appropriately, the decomposition functions come for free!

It is also possible to model pairs solely in terms of sets—though this takes some thought. In order to be able to decompose the pair and to obtain the uniqueness property, it is necessary to define:

$$pr(a, b) \quad \triangleq \quad \{\{a\}, \{a, b\}\}$$

There is a problem with naming the results of the decomposition functions. This is overcome here by writing implicit specifications:

$first\ (p\colon Pair)\ v\colon D$

$\text{post}\ \{v\} \in p$

$second\ (p\colon Pair)\ v\colon R$

$\text{post}\ \exists u \in \bigcup p \cdot p = \{\{u\}, \{u, v\}\}$

If the reader finds these definitions complicated, a few moments should be spared trying out values like:

$pr(1, 1)$

Either model suffices and only the properties of pairs are important. A map can be modelled by a set of pairs in which no two elements have the same *first* value:

$\text{map } D \text{ to } R \quad \triangleq \quad \text{set of } Pair$

where

$inv\text{-}Map(s) \quad \triangleq \quad \forall p_1, p_2 \in s \cdot p_1 = p_2 \lor first(p_1) \neq first(p_2)$

It is then straightforward to define:

$\text{dom } m = \{first(p) \mid p \in m\}$

Application is again defined implicitly but, because it is an infix operator, this is written:

$m(v) = r \;\Rightarrow\; \exists p \in m \cdot v = first(p) \land r = second(p)$

All of the map notation has now been defined and thus, in some sense, it could be avoided by writing everything in terms of one of the models of *Pair*. As subsequent examples show, however, the map notation is one of the main tools for achieving concise specifications.

Exercises

1. Given:

$$m_1 = \{a \mapsto x, b \mapsto y, c \mapsto x\}$$
$$m_2 = \{b \mapsto x, d \mapsto x\}$$

what is the value of:

(a) $m_1(c)$

(b)   dom m_1

(c)   rng m_2

(d) $m_1(x)$

(e) $m_1 \dagger m_2$

(f) $m_2 \dagger m_1$

(g) $m_1 \cup m_2$

(h) $\{a, e\} \lhd m_1$

(i) $\{d, e\} \lhd m_2$

2. Complete the following expressions (m_i are arbitrary maps):

(a) $m \dagger \{\} = ?$

(b) $\{\} \dagger m = ?$

(c) $m_1 \dagger (m_2 \dagger m_3) = (m_1 \dagger m_2) \; ? \; m_3$

(d)   dom $(m_1 \dagger m_2) = ? \; m_1 \; ? \; ? \; m_2$

(e)   rng $(m_1 \dagger m_2) = ?$

(f)   dom $\{x \mapsto f(x) \mid p(x)\} = ?$

(g)   rng $(m_1 \dagger m_2) \; ? \; (\text{rng } m_1 \cup \text{rng } m_2)$

3. As for Exercise 4 of Section 5.1, sketch a mapping which shows which rooms are on which floors:

    map *Floor* to (set of *Roomno*)

4. In the text of the chapter, operators like rng and $\cup$ are defined in terms of dom and application. Redefine all of the map operators directly in terms of sets of pairs (use the composite object model of *Pair*).

5. The reader should now look back at the introductory example of the equivalence relation specification built on *Partrep*(X). To check the understanding of the way maps are used:

(a) Write a different definition of *is-oneone*.

(b) Specify, on *Partrep*, the *GROUP* operation of Section 4.4.

(c) Reformulate *post-EQUATE* in a way which leaves open the choice of whether the key of e_1 or e_2 is used in the update.

(d) Respecify the *TEST* and *EQUATE* operations (as in Exercise 6 of Section 4.4) to take sets as arguments.

6.2   Reasoning about Maps

As with other data types, the interesting proofs about maps require induction. It would be possible to conduct such proofs by using set induction on the domain of the map. Rather than do this, specific induction rules are given for maps. As above, these rules rely on the operators which generate maps. The ones chosen are very like those for sets. The empty map is a map:

$$\{\} : \mathsf{map}\ D\ \mathsf{to}\ R$$

and an operator is defined which inserts one new pair into a map:

$$\{\_ \mapsto \_\} \oplus \_ : D \times R \times (\mathsf{map}\ D\ \mathsf{to}\ R) \to (\mathsf{map}\ D\ \mathsf{to}\ R)$$

The specification in Section 6.3 and subsequent chapters use the normal operators which are introduced in the previous section. These operators can be defined in terms of the generators but the insertion operator ($\oplus$) is used only in the definitions of—and proofs about—the normal map operators.

The generators provide an intuitive representation for any (finite) map:

$$\{d_1 \mapsto r_1\} \oplus (\dots \oplus \{\})$$

Of two insertions for the same key value, only the outer one has effect, thus:

$$\{d \mapsto r_1\} \oplus (\{d \mapsto r_2\} \oplus m) = \{d \mapsto r_1\} \oplus m$$

However, for different keys, insertions can be commuted:

$$\begin{aligned}
d_1 \neq d_2 \Rightarrow \\
\{d_1 \mapsto r_1\} \oplus (\{d_2 \mapsto r_2\} \oplus m) = \\
\{d_2 \mapsto r_2\} \oplus (\{d_1 \mapsto r_1\} \oplus m)
\end{aligned}$$

The intuitive representations given above are, therefore, not unique.

More important for the current purpose is the fact that the full induction rule reflects the absorption:

map-ind $$\frac{p(\{\}); \; p(m), d \notin \text{dom } m \vdash p(\{d \mapsto r\} \oplus m)}{m \in \text{map } D \text{ to } R \vdash p(m)}$$

Thus it is necessary to prove that a property holds for the empty map and that it inherits over insertion in order to conclude that the property holds for any map. The second hypothesis of the induction step shows that any map can be generated with no key occurring more than once. However, one of the operators whose properties are discussed below is the domain operator; in this case the second hypothesis is not used.

The definition of the domain operator can be given in terms of the generators. The rules are given here less formally than for sets (i.e. types are not shown as antecedents in the inference rules—they are suggested by the choice of identifiers). Thus:

$\text{dom } \{\} = \{\}$

$\text{dom } (\{d \mapsto r\} \oplus m) = \{d\} \cup \text{dom } m$

Notice how the insert case relies on the absorption property of set union. Similarly, application is defined over the generators.

$(\{d \mapsto r\} \oplus m)(d) = r$

$d_2 \in \text{dom } m \vdash d_1 \neq d_2 \;\Rightarrow\; (\{d_1 \mapsto r\} \oplus m)(d_2) = m(d_2)$

These rules do not permit the empty map to be applied to any value.

The overwrite operator can also be defined ($\dagger$-b, $\dagger$-i) in terms of the generators:

$m \dagger \{\} = m$

$m \dagger (\{d \mapsto r\} \oplus m_1) = \{d \mapsto r\} \oplus (m \dagger m_1)$

In the case of set union, the first operand is the one which is analyzed by the cases of the definition. Here, it is necessary to analyze the second argument because of the priority given to values of the second operand. The second case essentially decomposes the second operand and generates a series of inserts around the first operand. This process could generate a string of insertions with duplicate keys (one instance coming from each operand). In conjunction with the—limited—commutativity of insertion, these can be eliminated by the absorption rule for keys given above.

The first proof about maps (cf. Figure 6.2) shows that the empty map is absorbed also when used as left operand of overwrite. The associativity of overwrite is proved in Figure 6.3.

from $m \in (\text{map } D \text{ to } R)$

1	$\{\} \dagger \{\} = \{\}$	$\dagger$-b
2	from $\{\} \dagger m = m$	
2.1	$\{\} \dagger (\{d \mapsto r\} \oplus m) = \{d \mapsto r\} \oplus (\{\} \dagger m)$	$\dagger$-i
	infer $\qquad = \{d \mapsto r\} \oplus m$	=-subs(2.1,h2)
	infer $\{\} \dagger m = m$	map-ind(1,2)

Figure 6.2: Proof of Absorption of Empty Set by Overwrite

from $m_1, m_2, m_3 \in (\text{map } D \text{ to } R)$

1	$m_1 \dagger (m_2 \dagger \{\}) = m_1 \dagger m_2$	$\dagger$-b
2	$m_1 \dagger (m_2 \dagger \{\}) = (m_1 \dagger m_2) \dagger \{\}$	$\dagger$-b,1
3	from $m \in (\text{map } D \text{ to } R), m_1 \dagger (m_2 \dagger m) = (m_1 \dagger m_2) \dagger m$	
3.1	$m_1 \dagger (m_2 \dagger (\{d \mapsto r\} \oplus m)) = m_1 \dagger (\{d \mapsto r\} \oplus (m_2 \dagger m))$	$\dagger$-i
3.2	$= \{d \mapsto r\} \oplus (m_1 \dagger (m_2 \dagger m))$	$\dagger$-i
3.3	$= \{d \mapsto r\} \oplus ((m_1 \dagger m_2) \dagger m)$	h3
	infer $\quad = (m_1 \dagger m_2) \dagger (\{d \mapsto r\} \oplus m)$	$\dagger$-i
	infer $m_1 \dagger (m_2 \dagger m_3) = (m_1 \dagger m_2) \dagger m_3$	map-ind(2,3)

Figure 6.3: Proof that Overwrite is Associative

From the development of sets, the next property to consider is commutativity. It is made clear in the preceding section that overwrite is not commutative. Consulting the proof of the property for set union (cf. Figure 4.4), it can be seen that the lack of this property for overwrite results from the restriction placed on the commutativity of insert ($\oplus$).

The relationship between the domain and overwrite operators is proved in Figure 6.4.

The development of the results for maps is—given an understanding of the proofs about sets—routine. A number of further results are given as exercises.

from $m_1, m_2 \in (\text{map } D \text{ to } R)$

1	$\text{dom}\,(m_1 \dagger \{\}) = \text{dom}\, m_1$	$\dagger$-b
2	$= \text{dom}\, m_1 \cup \{\}$	set
3	$= \text{dom}\, m_1 \cup \text{dom}\, \{\}$	dom
4	from $m \in (\text{map } D \text{ to } R), \text{dom}\,(m_1 \dagger m) = \text{dom}\, m_1 \cup \text{dom}\, m$	
4.1	$\text{dom}\,(m_1 \dagger (\{d \mapsto r\} \oplus m)) = \text{dom}\,(\{d \mapsto r\} \oplus (m_1 \dagger m))$	$\dagger$-i
4.2	$= \text{dom}\,(m_1 \dagger m) \cup \{d\}$	dom
4.3	$= \text{dom}\, m_1 \cup \text{dom}\, m \cup \{d\}$	h4
infer	$= \text{dom}\, m_1 \cup \text{dom}\,(\{d \mapsto r\} \oplus m)$	dom
infer	$\text{dom}\,(m_1 \dagger m_2) = \text{dom}\, m_1 \cup \text{dom}\, m_2$	map-ind(3,4)

Figure 6.4: Relationship between Domain and Overwrite Operators

Exercises

1. Define, in terms of the generators for maps, the map operators:

    (a) $\lhd$

    (b) $\lhd\!\!\!-$

    (c) $\cup$

    (it will prove convenient for Exercise 2 to analyze the first operand in writing the last definition).

2. Prove (with appropriate assumptions):

    (a) $\{\} \lhd m = \{\}$

    (b) $m \cup \{\} = m$

    (c) $(m_1 \cup m_2) \cup m_3 = m_1 \cup (m_2 \cup m_3)$

    (d) $\{d \mapsto r\} \oplus (m_1 \cup m_2) = m_1 \cup (\{d \mapsto r\} \oplus m_2)$

    (This splits out the equivalent of the lemma used in set union.)

    (e) $m_1 \cup m_2 = m_2 \cup m_1$

    (f) $m_1 \dagger m_2 = m_2 \cup m_1$

3. * Develop further results about map operators including links to application.

6.3 Specifications

It is claimed above that maps are the most ubiquitous of the basic data types. In order to show why this is so, a simple bank system is considered. The need to locate information by keys is typical of many computing applications. The example is also (just) complicated enough to rehearse some arguments which must be considered when choosing a model to underlie a specification.

The customers of the bank to be modelled are identified by customer numbers (Cno); accounts are also identified by numbers ($Acno$). One customer may have several accounts whose balances must be kept separately. A customer has an overdraft limit which applies to each account—a credit in one account cannot be set against a debit elsewhere.

There are, then, two sorts of information to be stored for each customer: the relevant overdraft and the balance information. Both pieces of information can be located by maps whose domains are customer numbers. But is there to be one map or two? There are advantages in either solution. Separating the maps into:

odm: map Cno to $Overdraft$

acm: map Cno to $\ldots$

makes it possible for some operations to reference only one of the maps. There is, however, the need to define a data type invariant that the domains of the two maps are always equal. The need for this invariant is avoided by using one map to composite objects:

$Bank$ = map Cno to $Acinf$

$Acinf$ :: od: $Overdraft$
$\qquad\quad ac$: map $Acno$ to $Balance$

where
$inv\text{-}Acinf(mk\text{-}Acinf(od, m)) \quad \triangleq \quad \forall acno \in \text{dom } m \cdot -od \leq m(acno)$

$Overdraft = \mathbf{N}$

$Balance = \mathbf{Z}$

Invariants, as seen above, introduce proof obligations. It is therefore worth avoiding gratuitous complexity and the second model is used here[1].

Before considering other general issues raised by this specification, some minor points about interpretation should be cleared up. Both *Overdraft* and *Balance* concern sums of money. The temptation to treat these as real numbers should be resisted. Although most currencies do have fractional parts, π is an unusual balance! The fractions are there for human use and a whole number of the lowest denomination is clearly appropriate in a computer system. *Balances* can be negative—it is necessary to choose how to show overdrafts. The decision here can be seen clearly from the invariant on *Acinf*; representing the overdraft information as a minimum balance would be a possibility which would avoid a minus sign.

A larger and more general point surrounds the uniqueness of account numbers. Most banks make account numbers unique to a customer. An invariant can be used to show that no two different customers can have the same account number:

$$Bank = \text{map } Cno \text{ to } Acinf$$
$$\textsf{where}$$
$$inv\text{-}Bank(m) \quad \triangleq$$
$$\quad \forall cno_1, cno_2 \in \text{dom } m \cdot$$
$$\quad\quad cno_1 \neq cno_2 \Rightarrow$$
$$\quad\quad\quad is\text{-}disj(\text{dom } ac(m(cno_1)), \text{dom } ac(m(cno_2)))$$

However, this suggests that the account information could be organized in a totally different way. Consider:

$$Bank \ :: \ acm: \text{map } Acno \text{ to } Acdata$$
$$\quad\quad\quad\ odm: \text{map } Cno \text{ to } Overdraft$$

$$\textsf{where}$$
$$inv\text{-}Bank(mk\text{-}Bank(acm, odm)) \quad \triangleq$$
$$\quad \forall mk\text{-}Acdata(cno, bal) \in \text{rng } acm \cdot$$
$$\quad\quad cno \in \text{dom } odm \wedge bal \geq -odm(cno)$$

$$Acdata \ :: \ own: Cno$$
$$\quad\quad\quad\quad\ bal: Balance$$

---

[1] Once the material in Chapter 8 on relating models is understood, it is possible to work with more than one model.

The invariant is not too complex and the many-to-one relationship between accounts and customers has been fitted naturally onto a map. This model looks plausible enough to justify attempting some operation specifications. To introduce a new customer into the system:

$NEWC$ $(od\colon Overdraft)$ $r\colon Cno$

ext wr $odm\colon$ map Cno to $Overdraft$

post $r \notin$ dom $\overleftarrow{odm} \land odm = \overleftarrow{odm} \cup \{r \mapsto od\}$

Notice that this operation allocates the new customer number. It is also worth observing that both *post-NEWC* and *inv-Bank* rely on the LPF. Since many map operators are partial, the reliance on the non-strict propositional operators is greater.

An operation to introduce a new account is:

$NEWAC$ $(cu\colon Cno)$ $r\colon Acno$

ext rd $odm\colon$ map Cno to $Overdraft$,

    wr $acm\colon$ map $Acno$ to $Acdata$

pre $cu \in$ dom odm

post $r \notin$ dom $\overleftarrow{acm} \land acm = \overleftarrow{acm} \cup \{r \mapsto mk\text{-}Acdata(cu, 0)\}$

Both of the foregoing operations trivially preserve the invariants. A simple enquiry operation is:

$ACINF$ $(cu\colon Cno)$ $r\colon$ map $Acno$ to $Balance$

ext rd $acm\colon$ map $Acno$ to $Acdata$

post $r = \{acno \mapsto bal(acm(acno)) \mid$

        $acno \in$ dom $acm \land own(acm(acno)) = cu\}$

The model stands up to the test of defining these operations. Things are rarely so easy and it is only the restriction to a very simplified system which gives this slightly unrealistic outcome. In large specifications, the writer must be prepared to revise the underlying model. Time spent in ensuring that the state matches the problem can lead to a vastly clearer specification than results from simply using one's first guess.

The next specification is of a different type. The preceding section showed that maps can be modelled on other types. Here, another type is modelled on maps. A *bag* (or *multiset*) can contain multiple elements but the order of elements is not preserved. Bags thus share properties with both sequences and sets. The model of a bag is:

$$Bag(X) = \text{map } X \text{ to } \mathbf{N_1}$$

This can be viewed as associating the multiplicity with each element which has a non-zero multiplicity. The initial object—the empty bag—is:

$$b_0 = \{\}$$

The operation which shows how many occurrences of an element are in a bag is $COUNT$. Clarity can be heightened in this specification if an auxiliary function (mpc) is identified to compute (possibly zero) multiplicities:

$COUNT \ (e{:}\,X) \ c{:}\,\mathbf{N}$
ext rd $b{:}\,Bag(X)$
post $c = mpc(e, b)$

$mpc{:}\, X \times Bag(X) \to \mathbf{N}$
$mpc(e, m) \ \triangleq \ \text{if } e \in \text{dom } m \text{ then } m(e) \text{ else } 0$

An operation to update a bag is:

$ADD \ (e{:}\,X)$
ext wr $b{:}\,Bag(X)$
post $b = \overleftarrow{b} \dagger \{e \mapsto mpc(e, \overleftarrow{b}) + 1\}$

Suppose that it were now necessary to have a collection of such bags. The bags might be conveniently stored in a map:

$$Mbag = \text{map } D \text{ to } Bag(X)$$

where they are indexed by elements of D. The initial object of $Mbag$ might be the empty map:

$$m_0 = \{\}$$

And the collection of bags could be enlarged by:

$MNEW \ (w{:}\,D)$
ext wr $m{:}\,Mbag$
pre $w \notin \text{dom } m$
post $m = \overleftarrow{m} \cup \{w \mapsto init\text{-}Bag()\}$

Here, the first need to quote information from the bag specification is the reference to the initial bag object. This is done in a way which assumes:

$$init\text{-}Bag() \quad \triangleq \quad b_0 = \{\}$$

An operation which returns the count of some element in a particular bag can be defined by quoting $COUNT$:

> $MCOUNT\ (w\colon D, e\colon X)\ c\colon \mathbf{N}$
>
> ext rd $m\colon Mbag$
>
> post $post\text{-}COUNT(e, m(w), c)$

This operation does not change the state. In contrast, an operation which adds an element to a stated element of the collection bags is:

> $MADD\ (w\colon D, e\colon X)$
>
> ext wr $m\colon Mbag$
>
> post $\exists b \in Bag(X) \cdot post\text{-}ADD(e, \overleftarrow{m}(w), b) \wedge m = \overleftarrow{m} \dagger \{w \mapsto b\}$

Notice that the specification of these three operations is insulated from any reformulation of the specification of $Bag(X)$ itself.

The equivalence relation example can be used to illustrate an interesting use of the specification notation in the description of an implementation. The description in Section 6.1 uses $Partrep(X)$. Viewed as a specification, there is no worry about efficiency. But, as an implementation, the searching implied in $post\text{-}EQUATE$ would be unacceptable for large collections of elements. The map provides fast response to $TEST$ operations but not to $EQUATE$.

The need to implement equivalence relations over very large collections of data has given rise to considerable research. The aim is to find a way of implementing both $TEST$ and $EQUATE$ efficiently. The technique, known after its authors as the Fischer/Galler algorithm, employs a clever data structure in order to achieve efficiency. The basic idea is that equivalent elements should be collected into trees. These trees can be searched from any element to find a root. Two elements are equivalent if, and only if, they have the same roots[2].

---

[2]Notice that these trees (cf. Figure 6.5) are unlike those formed from recursive abstract syntax definitions: there, the essential operations are to break up the trees into their sub-components.

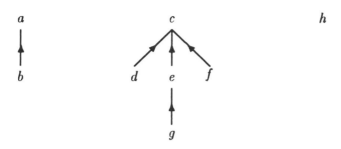

Figure 6.5: Fischer/Galler Trees

The other operation is, of course, to *EQUATE* two elements: it is necessary only to "graft" the root of one element onto some point in the tree of the other element. Notice that it is essential that the grafted tree is taken by the root so that all equivalent elements are carried over.

Formally, a model for the collection of trees can be based on:

$Forest(X) = \text{map } X \text{ to } X$
where . . .

In this model, each link in the tree is represented by one pair in the map; roots are represented by not occurring in the domain of the map. The basic (reflexive) map could be used to represent many different structures including circular ones. The task of the invariant is to rule out such circularities.

The concept required is well known in mathematics. The map represents a relation which must be *well founded* in the sense that links cannot be followed forever. Any loop would contain a series of links which could be traced indefinitely[3]. The restriction to finite maps makes it possible to express the invariant as:

$Forest(X) = \text{map } X \text{ to } X$
where
$inv\text{-}Forest(m) \quad \triangleq \quad \forall s \subseteq \text{dom } m \cdot s \neq \{\} \Rightarrow \exists e \in s \cdot m(e) \notin s$

Thus, providing each non-empty subset of X has an element which is mapped to an element outside that set, then there are no loops. Were there a loop,

---

[3]The normal way of capturing this constraint for some function $f\colon X \to X$ is to say that there must not exist a function $g\colon \mathbf{N} \to X$ such that $f(g(i)) = g(i+1)$ for all i.

the elements touched by the loop would constitute a set s for which there were no element outside the set.

For well-founded maps, a recursive function can be defined which locates the root of any element:

$$root\colon X \times Forest(X) \rightarrow X$$

$$root(e,f) \quad \triangleq \quad \text{if } e \notin \text{dom} f \text{ then } e \text{ else } root(f(e),f)$$

This function is used in both of the main operations. Before coming to these operations, some properties of forests are investigated.

Given a root element r, the *collect* function yields all elements with that root:

$$collect\colon X \times Forest(X) \rightarrow \text{set of } X$$

$$\text{pre } r \notin \text{dom} f$$

$$collect(r,f) \quad \triangleq \quad \{e \in X \mid root(e,f) = r\}$$

One useful property is that two different roots collect disjoint sets of elements:

$$r_1, r_2 \notin \text{dom} f \wedge r_1 \neq r_2 \;\Rightarrow\; \textit{is-disj}(collect(r_1,f) collect(r_2,f))$$

This property relies on the fact that maps are many-to-one (or single-valued).

The essential Lemma for the implementability of the $EQUATE$ operation is that grafting preserves the forest property. Thus:

$$\forall \overline{f} \in \text{map } X \text{ to } X, e_1, e_2 \in X \cdot$$
$$\textit{inv-Forest}(\overline{f}) \;\Rightarrow\;$$
$$\textit{inv-Forest}(\overline{f} \dagger \{root(e_1, \overline{f}) \mapsto root(e_2, \overline{f})\})$$

This result follows from the definition of *inv-Forest*.

The definitions of the operations are as follows:

$$f_0 = \{\}$$

$$TEST\ (e_1\colon X, e_2\colon X)\ r\colon \mathbf{B}$$

$$\text{ext rd } f\colon Forest(X)$$

$$\text{post } r \;\Leftrightarrow\; (root(e_1,f) = root(e_2,f))$$

$EQUATE\ (e_1\!:X, e_2\!:X)$

ext wr $f\!: Forest(X)$

post $f = $ if $root(e_1, \overleftarrow{f}\,) = root(e_2, \overleftarrow{f}\,)$

    then $\overleftarrow{f}$

    else $\overleftarrow{f} \dagger \{root(e_1, \overleftarrow{f}\,) \mapsto root(e_2, \overleftarrow{f}\,)\}$

In order to show that the $EQUATE$ specification satisfies the implementability proof obligation, it is necessary to prove:

$$\forall \overleftarrow{f} \in Forest(X), e_1, e_2 \in X \cdot$$
$$\exists f \in Forest(X) \cdot post\text{-}EQUATE(e_1, e_2, \overleftarrow{f}, f)$$

which follows from the earlier Lemma. The $TEST$ operation has read only access to the state and its implementability is straightforward.

The definition of $post\text{-}EQUATE$ is over-specific in that it would be possible to graft the trees in the other order. A non-deterministic specification could be constructed in order to avoid this commitment. It would even be possible to graft the root of one tree onto some arbitrary point in the other.

There is, however, a considerable incentive to keep the trees as short as possible. That is, the depth of any branch of the tree must be kept as low as possible. This follows from the use of the *root* function in both of the main operations. It would be ideal if trees could be kept to a maximum depth of one. Irrespectively of the order in which $EQUATE$ is made to graft the trees, they can become deeper than this ideal. The overall efficiency of the Fischer/Galler algorithm is, however, very good. The search time is proportional to the average depth of a tree—rather than the number of elements in X.

This description of the Fisher/Galler algorithm is of an implementation (the actual code is developed in Chapter 10). It is shown, in Chapter 8, to satisfy the specifications given above (cf. Sections 6.1, 4.4). Thus it can be seen that the specification notation can be used at different stages of design.

As a final example of the use of maps, the concept known as "virtual store" is considered. A virtual store is one which provides multiple users each with an apparent addressing space larger than the real store which is actually available to the user—perhaps even larger than the real store of the whole machine. This is achieved by paging inactive portions of store onto a backing store with slower access. The penalty is, of course, that a reference to a page which is not in fast store must be delayed while the page fault is handled.

This specification provides a good example of how abstraction can be used to explain concepts in an orderly way. The first step is to obtain a clear understanding of the basic role of store. This has nothing, as yet, to do with virtual store. The following should be easily understood by the reader:

$Store$ = map $Addr$ to Val

$RD\ (a\colon Addr)\ v\colon Val$

ext rd $s\colon Store$

pre $a \in$ dom s

post $v = s(a)$

There is an overhead in a virtual store system: the current position (i.e. in fast or slow store) of each addressable value has to be tracked. In order to reduce this overhead, addresses are grouped into pages which are always moved between levels of store as a unit. The $Addr$ set has not so far been defined. It is now assumed to contain a page number and an offset (i.e. position within its page):

$Addr$ :: $p\colon Pageno$
$o\colon Offset$

A page can now be defined:

$Page$ = map $Offset$ to Val
where
$inv\text{-}Page(m)\ \ \overset{\Delta}{=}\ \ $ dom $m = Offset$

The virtual store system can now be defined to have front and backing stores, each of which contain pages:

$Vstore$ :: $fs\colon$ map $Pageno$ to $Page$
$bs\colon$ map $Pageno$ to $Page$
where
$inv\text{-}Vstore(mk\text{-}Vstore(fs, bs))\ \ \overset{\Delta}{=}\ \ is\text{-}disj(\text{dom } fs, \text{dom } bs)$

The read operation can be respecified on $Vstore$. At this level, the concept of page faulting is introduced by showing that the relevant page must be in fs after the read operation. Any consideration of a specific algorithm (e.g. least recently used) to choose which page to move out is deferred. The post-condition only shows that no pages are lost and leaves open how much paging activity occurs. This non-determinism is being used to postpone design decisions.

$RDVS\ (a\!:\!Addr)\ v\!:\!Val$

ext wr fs: map $Pageno$ to $Page$,

wr bs: map $Pageno$ to $Page$

pre $p(a) \in (\text{dom}\ fs \cup \text{dom}\ bs)$

post $fs \cup bs = \overleftarrow{fs} \cup \overleftarrow{bs} \wedge is\text{-}disj(\text{dom}\ fs, \text{dom}\ bs) \wedge$
$\qquad p(a) \in \text{dom}\ fs \wedge v = fs(p(a))(o(a))$

Exercises

1. Specify, for the banking system discussed above, operations which:

   (a) close an account;
   (b) remove a customer;
   (c) transfer money between accounts;
   (d) change an overdraft limit.

   What changes need to be made if each account has a separate overdraft limit? Each of these operations can be interpreted in different ways—record any assumptions which are made in formalizing the specification.

2. Specify an operation to remove an occurrence of an element from a bag and show that it is implementable (Hint: notice the range of $Bag(X)$).

3. Repeat Exercise 3 of Section 4.4 using a map as a state:

   $Studx = $ map $Studnm$ to $\{\text{Y}, \text{N}\}$

   What is the advantage of this state?

4. Write the specification of a system which keeps track of which rooms people at a conference are in. Assume that operations $ARRIVE$, $MOVE$ and WHO (giving all names in a given room) are automatically triggered.

5. * It is explained in Section 5.4 how operations which work on a sub-
state can be quoted (via their pre-/post-conditions) in the specification
of other operations. This idea has been shown in this section to extend
in an obvious way to mappings. Repeat the preceding exercise using
(trivial) operations which work on a single room.

6. Assume that a state is available for a hotel system which shows the
set of possible room numbers and the current occupancy:

$$Shotel :: \quad rooms: \text{set of } Roomno$$
$$occupancy: \text{map } Roomno \text{ to } Name$$
$$\text{where}$$
$$inv\text{-}Shotel(mk\text{-}Shotel(rms, occ)) \quad \triangleq \quad \text{dom } occ \subseteq rms$$

Specify some useful operations such as allocating a room, checking out
and determining if there are empty rooms.

7. Repeat part (d) of Exercise 5 of Section 6.1 on a state using $Forest(X)$;
also specify $GROUP$ (cf. part b) but comment on the implementation
problem with this operation.

8. A simple "bill of materials" system uses a database which, for each
assembly, keeps track of the immediate components or sub-assemblies
required in its construction. In this first—simplified—system, no attempt is made to record the number of each component required. Some
way is needed of distinguishing basic components (no sub-assemblies).
An "explosion" can trace recursively from some assembly down to its
basic components.

   (a) Define a suitable data type (with invariant) for the bill of materials.

   (b) Define a function which shows all sub-assemblies and components
   required to produce some given assembly.

   (c) Define a function similar to (b) which yields only the basic components required.

   (d) Specify an operation (say, $WHEREUSED$) which looks up in the
   database all of the assemblies which need a given part number as
   an immediate component.

9. * Write a specification for a bill of materials system which counts
the number of required components. Obviously, the basic data type
must include the number of components per part. Furthermore, the
required number of parts must be computed by multiplying the number
of assemblies required by the number of components. This, and the
requirement to sum such counts, will best be achieved by developing
some theory of such maps.

10. * Specify some operations relating to a database for an employment
agency. The database should record people and their skills (more
than one per person) as well as the required skills for available jobs.
Operations should include showing people suitable for jobs and various
updates.

Chapter 7

Sequence Notation

> Various models of the same objects are possible,
> and these may differ in various respects. We should
> at once denote as inadmissible all models which
> contradict our laws of thought. We shall denote
> as incorrect any permissible models, if their essen-
> tial relations contradict the relations of the external
> things. But two permissible and correct models of
> the same external objects may yet differ in respect
> of appropriateness. Of two models of the same ob-
> ject that is the more appropriate which includes in
> it more of the essential relations of the object ...
> the more appropriate is the one which contains the
> smaller number of superfluous or empty relations:
> the simpler of the two.
> *Heinrich Hertz*

The concept of a sequence is both familiar to programmers and something
whose manipulation is very intuitive—almost tactile. The notation developed in this chapter is abstract in the sense that useful mathematical properties, rather than implementation efficiency, are taken as guidance to the
operator definitions. As a consequence, a specification written in terms of
this sequence notation will need to be subjected to design steps (i.e. data
reification) before it can be used as the basis for a program.

Sequences can be viewed as maps with a restricted domain. The advantage in recognizing sequences as a special case is that operators, such as

concatenation, which are natural for sequences can be defined.

The basic collection of specification notation (sets, composite objects, maps and sequences) is completed by this chapter. It is possible to specify large systems with its help; on the other hand, careful thought has to be given to the choice of an appropriate model for an application since the range of choices is now wide. Section 7.4 explores such choices on some interesting examples.

7.1 Notation

The description of the notation itself is, as in previous chapters, preceded by an introductory example. This specification concerns queues. Operations are to be defined, for this first-in-first-out data structure, which enqueue, dequeue, and test whether a queue is empty. The state must record the collection of elements which are in the queue. It is possible for multiple occurrences of a Qel to be present and the order of elements is clearly important. These are exactly the properties of sequences. Thus:

$$Queue = \text{seq of } Qel$$

where the queue elements (Qel) are not further defined. The initial queue object is an empty sequence; sequence brackets are square—thus:

$$q_0 = [\,]$$

The operator for forming larger sequences from smaller ones is concatenation ($\frown$). The operands of a concatenation operator must both be sequences so the enqueue operation has to create a unit-sequence from the new element:

$ENQUEUE\ (e\colon Qel)$

ext wr $q\colon Queue$

post $q = \overleftarrow{q} \frown [e]$

This operation requires no pre-condition; in contrast, it is only possible to remove an element from a non-empty queue. A pleasing symmetry with $post\text{-}ENQUEUE$ is shown by the following specification:

$DEQUEUE\ ()\ e\colon Qel$

ext wr $q\colon Queue$

pre $q \neq [\,]$

post $\overleftarrow{q} = [e] \frown q$

Alternatively, the post-condition could be written:

post $q =$ tl $\overleftarrow{q} \wedge e =$ hd $\overleftarrow{q}$

This shows the operators which yield the first element—or head—of a sequence (hd) and the rest of a sequence—or tail—after its head is removed(tl).

The operation which can be used to check whether a queue is empty is specified:

ISEMPTY () *r*: **B**

ext rd q: *Queue*

post $r \iff (\text{len } q = 0)$

The operator which yields the length of a sequence (len) is used in a comparison to check for an empty sequence.

The first topic to be considered in the more formal treatment of sequence notation is the creation of sequence values. As is indicated above, these are written in square brackets. With sequences, both the position of values and the occurrence of duplicate values is important, thus:

$$[b, a] \neq [a, b]$$
$$[a, b] \neq [a, b, b]$$

The examples which follow use the following sequences:

$$s_1 = [b, b, c]$$
$$s_2 = [a]$$

The length operator counts the number of (occurrences of) elements in a sequence, thus:

len $s_2 = 1$
len $s_1 = 3$

and for the empty sequence:

len $[\,] = 0$

The signatures of the sequence operators are shown in Figure 7.1.

Sequences can be applied to valid indices—the validity of indices can be determined via the length operator—*indexing* has the properties:

$s \in$ seq of $X \vdash 1 \leq i \leq$ len $s \implies s(i) \in X$
$s_1(1) = s_1(2) = b$

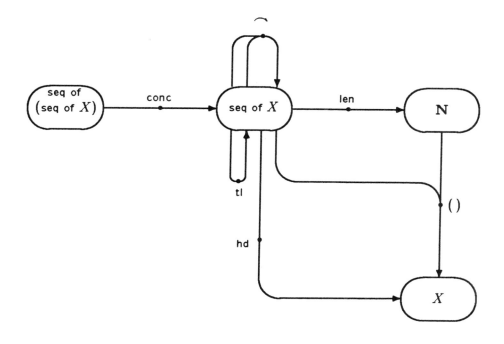

Figure 7.1: ADJ Diagram of Sequence Operators

All of the other sequence operators can be defined in terms of len and application. These two basic sequence operators can be defined if the sequence type is viewed as a particular form of map:

seq of X = map $\mathbf{N}_1$ to X
where
dom s = $\{1, \ldots, n\}$

Thus:

len s = card dom s

and sequence indexing is simply map application.

The set of valid indices to a sequence is given by its domain:

$\text{dom } s = \{1, \ldots, \text{len } s\}$

$\text{dom } s_1 = \{1, 2, 3\}$

$\text{dom } s_2 = \{1\}$

$\text{dom } [\,] = \{\}$

The collection of elements contained in a sequence can be determined by the rng operator. The set which results from this operator obviously loses any duplications of elements:

$\text{rng } s = \{s(i) \mid i \in \text{dom } s\}$

$\text{rng } s_2 = \{a\}$

$\text{rng } s_1 = \{b, c\}$

$\text{rng } [\,] = \{\}$

Sequence equality must take account of the position and duplications of elements and cannot, therefore, be defined in terms of the rng operator. Instead:

$\_ = \_ : \text{seq of } X \times \text{seq of } X \to \mathbf{B}$

$s_1 = s_2 \iff \text{len } s_1 = \text{len } s_2 \land \forall i \in \text{dom } s_1 \cdot s_1(i) = s_2(i)$

Sequence values can be *concatenated* (i.e. joined together) by:

$\_ \frown \_ \; (s_1 : \text{seq of } X, s_2 : \text{seq of } X) \; rs : \text{seq of } X$

$\text{post len } rs = \text{len } s_1 + \text{len } s_2 \land$

$\quad \forall i \in \text{dom } s_1 \cdot rs(i) = s_1(i) \land$

$\quad \forall i \in \text{dom } s_2 \cdot rs(i + \text{len } s_1) = s_2(i)$

Thus:

$s_1 \frown s_2 = [b, b, c, a]$

$s_2 \frown s_1 = [a, b, b, c]$

$s_2 \frown s_2 = [a, a]$

$s_2 \frown [\,] = s_2$

Notice that concatenation is neither commutative nor absorptive.

A distributed concatenation operator is also available which concatenates all of the sequences within a sequence of sequences. This is defined by a recursive function:

$\text{conc } \_ : \text{seq of } (\text{seq of } X) \to \text{seq of } X$

$\text{conc } ss \quad \overset{\Delta}{=} \quad \text{if } ss = [\,] \text{ then } [\,] \text{ else } (\text{hd } ss) \frown \text{conc } (\text{tl } ss)$

$$\mathsf{conc}\,[s_1, [\,], s_2, s_2] = [b, b, c, a, a]$$

The head of a non-empty sequence is given by:

$\mathsf{hd}\,\_\,(s\colon \mathsf{seq}\ \mathsf{of}\ X)\ r\colon X$

$\mathsf{pre}\ s \neq [\,]$

$\mathsf{post}\ r = s(1)$

Thus:

$\mathsf{hd}\ s_1 = b$

$\mathsf{hd}\ s_2 = a$

Notice that this operator yields the first element of a sequence whereas the tail operator yields a sequence:

$\mathsf{tl}\,\_\,(s\colon \mathsf{seq}\ \mathsf{of}\ X)\ rs\colon \mathsf{seq}\ \mathsf{of}\ X$

$\mathsf{pre}\ s \neq [\,]$

$\mathsf{post}\ s = [\mathsf{hd}\ s]\frown rs$

A useful operator for extracting sub-sequences of sequences is:

$\_(\_, \ldots, \_)\,(s\colon \mathsf{seq}\ \mathsf{of}\ X, i\colon \mathbf{N}_1, j\colon \mathbf{N})\ rs\colon \mathsf{seq}\ \mathsf{of}\ X$

$\mathsf{pre}\ i \leq j + 1 \wedge i \leq \mathsf{len}\ s + 1 \wedge j \leq \mathsf{len}\ s$

$\mathsf{post}\ \exists s_1, s_2 \in \mathsf{seq}\ \mathsf{of}\ X\ \cdot$

$\qquad \mathsf{len}\ s_1 = i - 1 \wedge$

$\qquad \mathsf{len}\ s_2 = \mathsf{len}\ s - j \wedge$

$\qquad s = s_1 \frown rs \frown s_2$

The pre-condition of this operation is chosen to permit the extraction of empty sequences:

$s_1(2, \ldots, 2) = [b]$

$s_1(1, \ldots, 3) = [b, b, c]$

$s_1(1, \ldots, 0) = [\,]$

$s_1(4, \ldots, 3) = [\,]$

Notice that:

$\mathsf{len}\ rs = \mathsf{len}\ s - (i - 1 + (\mathsf{len}\ s - j))$

$\qquad = (j - i) + 1$

A sequence type is defined by:

seq of X

which defines values of the type to be any finite sequence all of whose elements are members of X. Thus members of:

seq of $\{a, b, c\}$

include:

[ ]
s_1
s_2
$[a, a, a, a, a, a]$

Because of the possibility of duplicates, the number of possible sequences is infinite even when the base set is finite.

Exercises

1. Which of the following expressions is true (in general)?

   (a) $\quad s_1 \frown (s_2 \frown s_3) = (s_1 \frown s_2) \frown s_3$

   (b) $\quad s_1 \frown s_2 = s_2 \frown s_1$

   (c) $\quad s_1 \frown [\,] = s_1$

   (d) $\quad s_1 \frown s_1 = s_1$

2. What is the value of each of the following?

   (a) $\quad$ tl $[a, b]$

   (b) $\quad$ len $[[a, b], [a, b]]$

   (c) $\quad$ hd $[a]$

   (d) $\quad$ tl $[a]$

   (e) $\quad$ hd $[[a, b], [c]]$

   (f) $\quad$ rng $[a, b, a]$

   (g) $\quad$ rng $[\{a\}, a, [a], a]$

   (h) $\quad [a] \frown [a]$

   (i) $\quad [a] \frown [[b]]$

3. In each of the following, identify a possible value for a sequence which satisfies the properties:

   (a) $\text{hd } s_1 = [a], \text{hd tl } s_1 = \{1\}, \text{tl tl } s_1 = [a]$

   (b) $\text{tl } s_2 = [\text{hd } s_2]$

   (c) $\text{len } s_3 \neq \text{card} (\text{rng } s_3)$

4. (a) Define a function which determines whether a sequence has only one occurrence of each of its elements.

   (b) Specify a function which, given a set, lays it out in a random order.

5. It is often useful to be able to locate things within sequences (i.e. to determine indices where values are located). Specify functions which:

   (a) show all indices where a value can be found:

   $$alloccs: (\text{seq of } X) \times X \rightarrow (\text{set of } \mathbf{N_1})$$

   (b) gives the first index where a value can be found assuming that it does occur:

   $$firstocc: (\text{seq of } X) \times X \rightarrow \mathbf{N_1}$$

   (c) locate (the first occurrence of) one sequence within another:

   $$locate: (\text{seq of } X) \times (\text{seq of } X) \rightarrow \mathbf{N}$$

   such that:

   $$locate([a, b], [a, a, b, a]) = 2$$
   $$locate([b, b], [a, a, b, a]) = 0$$

6. In the text of this chapter, operators like concatenation and tail are defined via the more basic operators length and application. Redefine all of the sequence operators directly in terms of the map.

7.2   Reasoning about Sequences

The theory of sequences is strongly related to that of sets. As the reader should by now expect, the basis of the theory comes from the generator functions—here:

$[\,]\colon \mathsf{seq\ of}\ X$

$cons\colon X \times \mathsf{seq\ of}\ X \to \mathsf{seq\ of}\ X$

The function to insert an element in a sequence is called *cons* (rather than $\oplus$) because the name is familiar from list-processing languages. Thus sequence values can be created by:

$$cons(e_1, cons(e_2, \ldots, [\,]))$$

Whereas, with both sets and maps, different terms built from the constructors correspond to the same value, the expressions built from sequence constructors stand in one-to-one correspondence with the values. For sets and maps, properties were given which showed that certain terms were equal; no such properties need be given for sequences. The distinction between the theory of sequences and that of sets is that any properties which rely on the commutativity and absorption of $\oplus$ do not carry over to sequences.

The induction rule for sequences is, apart from the changes of symbols, the same as the first one given for sets:

seq-ind $\dfrac{p([\,]);\ e \in X, t \in \mathsf{seq\ of}\ X, p(t) \vdash p(cons(e,t))}{t \in \mathsf{seq\ of}\ X \vdash p(t)}$

The definition of concatenation (over the constructors) is also a translation of that for set union:

$\_ \frown \_ \colon \mathsf{seq\ of}\ X \times \mathsf{seq\ of}\ X \to \mathsf{seq\ of}\ X$

$[\,] \frown s = s$

$cons(e, s_1) \frown s_2 = cons(e, s_1 \frown s_2)$

It should therefore be obvious that:

$\forall s \in \mathsf{seq\ of}\ X \cdot s \frown [\,] = s$

$\forall s_1, s_2, s_3 \in \mathsf{seq\ of}\ X \cdot (s_1 \frown s_2) \frown s_3 = s_1 \frown (s_2 \frown s_3)$

The proofs of these are simple transliterations of the corresponding ones for sets. The next properties which are developed for set union are commutativity and absorption. These proofs rely on the corresponding properties of the insertion operator and do not therefore carry over to concatenation. In general:

$$cons(a, cons(b, s)) \neq cons(b, cons(a, s))$$
$$cons(a, cons(a, s)) \neq cons(a, s)$$

It is useful to define unit sequences as an abbreviation:

$[\_]: X \rightarrow$ seq of X

$[e] \triangleq cons(e, [\,])$

This can be used in the definition of a function which reverses a sequence:

rev: seq of $X \rightarrow$ seq of X

$rev([\,]) = [\,]$
$rev(cons(e, s)) = rev(s) \frown [e]$

An obvious property of rev is that applying it twice to any sequence should yield the original sequence. A frontal attack on this theorem yields a messy proof. The identification of two simple lemmas (cf. Figure 7.2) gives rise to a more readable presentation. The proof of the main result is given in Figure 7.3.

The definitions of the other operators are left to the exercises. Once these are defined, a restatement of the induction rule for sequences is possible. The two forms of the rule correspond to the option of defining induction over the natural numbers in terms of either $succ$ or $pred$.

seq-ind2 $\qquad \dfrac{p([\,]); \ t \in \text{seq of } X, t \neq [\,], p(\text{tl } t) \vdash p(t)}{t \in \text{seq of } X \vdash p(t)}$

Exercises

1. Write out the proofs for:

$\forall s \in \text{seq of } X \cdot s \frown [\,] = s$
$\forall s_1, s_2, s_3 \in \text{seq of } X \cdot (s_1 \frown s_2) \frown s_3 = s_1 \frown (s_2 \frown s_3)$

2. Only concatenation is defined in the text of this section. Define the operators len, application, hd and tl over the constructors. Prove some useful results like:

$\forall s_1, s_2 \in \text{seq of } X \cdot \text{len} (s_1 \frown s_2) = \text{len } s_1 + \text{len } s_2$
$\forall s \in \text{seq of } X \cdot s = [\,] \lor cons(\text{hd } s, \text{tl } s) = s$

from $e \in X$

1	$rev([e]) = rev(cons(e, [\,]))$	unit
2	$= rev([\,]) \frown [e]$	rev
3	$= [\,] \frown [e]$	rev
infer	$= [e]$	$\frown$

from $s_1, s_2 \in$ seq of X

1	$rev([\,] \frown s_2) = rev(s_2)$	$\frown$
2	$= rev(s_2) \frown [\,]$	$\frown$
3	$= rev(s_2) \frown rev([\,])$	rev
4	from $t \in$ seq of X, $rev(t \frown s_2) = rev(s_2) \frown rev(t)$	
4.1	$rev(cons(e, t) \frown s_2) = rev(cons(e, t \frown s_2))$	$\frown$
4.2	$= rev(t \frown s_2) \frown [e]$	rev
4.3	$= (rev(s_2) \frown rev(t)) \frown [e]$	h4
4.4	$= rev(s_2) \frown (rev(t) \frown [e])$	$\frown$-ass
infer	$= rev(s_2) \frown rev(cons(e, t))$	rev
infer $rev(s_1 \frown s_2) = rev(s_2) \frown rev(s_1)$		seq-ind(3,4)

Figure 7.2: Proof of Lemmas on rev

7.3   Specifications

The task of sorting provides an obvious application for the sequence notation. Suppose records are to be sorted whose structure is:

Rec :: k: Key
$\quad\quad\;\; d$: $Data$

For compactness, the ordering relation on keys is written $\leq$. The fact that a sequence of records is ordered in ascending key order can be defined:

$is\text{-}orderedk$: seq of $Rec \rightarrow \mathbf{B}$

$is\text{-}orderedk(t) \quad \triangleq \quad \forall i, j \in$ dom $t \cdot i < j \;\Rightarrow\; k(t(i)) \leq k(t(j))$

Because the ordering relation is transitive, it is equivalent to write:

$is\text{-}orderedk(t) \quad \triangleq \quad \forall i \in \{1, \ldots, $ len $t - 1\} \cdot k(t(i)) \leq k(t(i+1))$

from $t \in$ seq of X

1      $rev(rev([\,])) = rev([\,])$ *rev*

2      $= [\,]$ *rev*

3   from $t \in$ seq of X, $rev(rev(t)) = t$

3.1 $rev(rev(cons(e,t))) = rev(rev(t) \frown [e])$ *rev*

3.2 $= rev([e]) \frown rev(rev(t))$ *rev*lemma

3.3 $= [e] \frown t$ *rev*lemma,h3

     infer $= cons(e,t)$ $\frown$

infer $rev(rev(t)) = t$ seq-ind(2,3)

Figure 7.3: Proof that Two Reversals Cancel

Notice how the rule about universal quantification over an empty set conveniently covers unit and empty sequences. Accepting, for the moment, some intuitive notion of permutation, the specification for the sorting task can be written:

$SORT$

ext wr rl: seq of Rec

post *is-orderedk*$(rl) \land$ *is-permutation*$(rl, \overleftarrow{rl}\,)$

Defining the concept of one sequence being a permutation of another is an interesting exercise. Clearly, if the sequences can contain duplicates, it is not enough to check that their ranges are equal. Nor does it cover all cases to check both len and rng. One possibility is to write *is-permutation* as a recursive function which, in the recursive case, locates and removes the head of one sequence from wherever it is in the other. Such a definition is rather mechanical for a specification and would not be easy to use in subsequent proofs. A direct model of the idea of counting occurrences can be given using bags. Thus:

$bagol$: seq of $X \to Bag(X)$

$bagol(t) \overset{\Delta}{=} \{e \mapsto \text{card}\{i \in \text{dom } t \mid t(i) = e\} \mid e \in \text{rng } t\}$

then:

is-permutation: seq of X × seq of X → **B**

is-permutation(s_1, s_2) $\triangleq$ $bagol(s_1) = bagol(s_2)$

Another possibility is to think of a permutation as inducing a one-to-one map between the two sequences:

is-permutation(s_1, s_2) $\triangleq$

    len $s_1 =$ len $s_2 \wedge$

    $\exists m \in$ map **N** to **N** ·

        dom $m =$ rng $m =$ dom $s_1 \wedge \forall i \in$ dom $s_1 \cdot s_1(i) = s_2(m(i))$

It is not possible to argue convincingly that one of these is better than the other. It is, however, likely that the last one would be of more use in developing a theory of sequences. For the sorting program itself, the only properties of *is-permutation* required for most in-store sorts are reflexivity, transitivity and the fact that swapping two elements creates a permutation. It is clear that these properties follow easily from the latter definition of *is-permutation*.

This specification of *SORT* is non- deterministic in that the final placing of two different records with the same key is not determined. This reflects the fact that the sorting task is described as bringing the records into key order. There are applications where a stable sort is required in which records with the same key preserve their relative order from the starting state. The specification can be made to cover this requirement by adding an extra conjunct to *post-SORT* whose definition is:

is-stable: seq of Rec × seq of Rec → **B**

is-stable(s_1, s_2) $\triangleq$ $\forall k \in extractks(s_1) \cdot sift(s_1, k) = sift(s_2, k)$

The keys required are defined by:

extractks: seq of Rec → set of Key

extractks(s) $\triangleq$ $\{k(r) \mid r \in$ rng $s\}$

The sub-sequence of *Recs* with a given key can be defined:

sift: seq of Rec × Key → seq of Rec

sift(rs, k) $\triangleq$ if $rs = [\,]$

        then $[\,]$

        else   if $k(\text{hd } rs) = k$

            then $[\text{hd } rs]^\frown sift(\text{tl } rs, k)$

            else $sift(\text{tl } rs, k)$

The introductory example in Section 7.1 specified a simple first-in-first-out queue. Another form of queue which is used in computing systems relies on a priority to govern which element is dequeued. This example provides a basis for a discussion of the choices to be made in constructing a model.

Assume that there is some given set *Priority* which, for conciseness, is assumed to be ordered by $\leq$. Then items in the queue might be defined:

$$Qitem \ :: \ p\text{:}\ Priority$$
$$d\text{:}\ Data$$

Perhaps the most obvious model for the queue type itself is:

$$Qtp = \textsf{seq of } Qitem$$

where the data type invariant (say *is-orderedp*) would require that the priority order holds in the sequence. This would permit the operation for adding elements to the queue to be specified:

$ENQ\ (it\text{:}\ Qitem)$

$\textsf{ext wr}\ q\text{:}\ Qtp$

$\textsf{post}\ \exists i \in \textsf{dom}\ q \cdot del(q,i) = \overleftarrow{q} \wedge q(i) = it$

$$del(t,i) \ \triangleq \ t(1,\ldots,i-1) ^\frown t(i+1,\ldots,\textsf{len}\ t)$$

Recall that the invariant can be thought of as being conjoined to the pre- and post-conditions; it is then clear that the post-condition combines two of the techniques used to achieve concise specifications. The existentially quantified expression works back from the result to the starting state—thus providing a simple description of insertion. The implied conjunction of *is-orderedp* with that expression captures the required specification by stating two separate properties.

The specification as it stands does not constrain the placing of queue items with equal priority. Providing this matches the requirements, the next question to ask is whether the sequence model given is the most appropriate. Why are the queue items ordered in the state? Presumably because it makes the dequeuing operation easy to specify! But this is not really a convincing argument. In fact an alternative specification could be based on sets (or, if duplicate records have to be handled, bags). Thus:

$$Qtps = \textsf{set of } Qitem$$

The *ENQ* operations simply adds its argument to the state and the *DEQ* operation locates one of the elements with lowest priority number. With the limited repertoire of operations, it is difficult to say which is the better model, but the set model is more abstract and might be preferred.

If, however, it is required to preserve the arrival order of queue items with the same priority, it is clear that the set model cannot support the intended semantics. It is easy to see how to extend the post-condition of *ENQ*, as defined on sequences, to ensure correct placement. The sequence model is, however, not the only one which would cover these requirements. The *ENQ* operation is easier to specify if the queues for each priority are separated:

$$Qtpm = \text{map } Priority \text{ to } (\text{seq of } Data)$$

Some decisions have to be made in this model about whether each priority always has a (possibly empty) sequence associated with it. But, on balance, the map model is the best fit to the operations. The complete set of operations would have to be agreed before a final decision were made. (One could envisage operations which force consideration of the queue as a whole—for example, operations which manipulated the priorities.)

Another example in which some thought must be applied to the choice of model is a specification for a cipher machine. Many children play games with coding messages by, for instance, changing letter *a* to *b*, *b* to *c*, etc. Such a cipher is called monoalphabetic and is very susceptible to cryptanalysis (code breaking) by measuring the frequency of letters. A more sophisticated polyalphabetic (or Vigenère) coding is safer. The idea of substituting one letter by another is extended so that different letters of the original message (plain text) are coded under different translations. In order that the enciphered message can be deciphered by friends, the appropriate transliterations must be known, or be computable, by them. One way to achieve this is to have a table of translation columns each headed by a letter; a keyword is then agreed and the *i*th letter of the keyword indicates the column under which the *i*th letter of the message is to be (or was) ciphered; the keyword can be replicated if it is shorter than the message. Thus for the table:

	a	b	c
a	a	c	b
b	b	a	c
c	c	b	a

the plaintext *acab* is coded under keyword *abc* to *abbb*:

plaintext	a	c	a	b
keyword	a	b	c/	a
ciphered text	a	b	b	b

A simple frequency analysis of letters will no longer disclose the coding table since, on the one hand, different letters are translated to the same letter and, on the other hand, the same plaintext letter can be translated to different letters.

How is this polyalphabetic cipher to be specified? The regular appearance of the table above might tempt one to describe the coding by index arithmetic on a sequence of twenty-six letters. There are two reasons to resist this particular temptation: the regular tables are only a sub-class of the possible tables, and anyway the index arithmetic becomes very confusing. The best model of an individual column appears to be a map from letters to letters. As is discussed below, it is necessary that such a map be one-to-one. Thus:

$Mcode = $ map $Letter$ to $Letter$

where

$inv\text{-}Mcode(m) \quad \triangleq \quad is\text{-}oneone(m) \wedge$ dom $m = Letter$

The second conjunct in the invariant ensures that there is a translation for each letter.

The whole (polyalphabetic) table can be defined:

$Pcode = $ map $Letter$ to $Mcode$

where

$inv\text{-}Pcode(m) \quad \triangleq \quad$ dom $m = Letter$

In practice, it is obviously desirable that $Pcode$ stores different $Mcodes$ for each letter—this requirement is not, however, enshrined in the invariant. A function which defines the (polyalphabetic) translation is:

$ptrans: Letter \times Letter \times Pcode \rightarrow Letter$

$ptrans(kl, ml, code) \quad \triangleq \quad (code(kl))(ml)$

The remaining hurdle, before the specification can be written, is to choose a model for the keyword. The obvious model is a sequence of letters. The problem of sufficient replications then becomes a manipulation of indices which is made slightly messy by the fact that the sequences here are indexed from one. (The alternative, to index all sequences from zero, turns out to be just as inconvenient in other cases.) Here, indexing from zero is simulated by:

$$Key = \text{map } \mathbf{N} \text{ to } Letter$$

where

$$inv\text{-}Key(m) \quad \overset{\triangle}{=} \quad \exists n \in \mathbf{N} \cdot \text{dom } m = \{0, \ldots, n\}$$

This ensures that a Key is non-empty. It could be argued that the keyword should be replicated in the state. This is not done here since it appears to make the task of designing representations unnecessarily tiresome. The final specification is then:

$CODE$ (m: seq of $Letter$) t: seq of $Letter$

ext rd c: $Pcode$, rd k: Key

post len t = len m $\wedge$

    let $l = maxs(\text{dom } k) + 1$

    in $\forall i \in \text{dom } t \cdot t(i) = ptrans(k(i \bmod l), m(i), c)$

The specification of $DECODE$ is, of course, possible in the same style. It is, however, more elegant to quote the existing specification:

$DECODE$ (t: seq of $Letter$) m: seq of $Letter$

ext rd c: $Pcode$, rd k: Key

post $post\text{-}CODE(m, c, k, t)$

This shows clearly that the task of $DECODE$ is to recreate the input to $CODE$. It is possible, from this requirement, to deduce the need for the invariant on $Mcode$. The correct decipherment of messages can be stated (omitting all of the quantifiers):

$$post\text{-}CODE(m, c, k, t) \wedge post\text{-}DECODE(t, c, k, n) \;\Rightarrow\; m = n$$

which is equivalent (cf. $post\text{-}DECODE$) to:

$$post\text{-}CODE(m, c, k, t) \wedge post\text{-}CODE(n, c, k, t) \;\Rightarrow\; m = n$$

Inspecting $post\text{-}CODE$ it is clear that the length of m and n must be the same and thus the question is pushed back to whether $ptrans$ is one-to-one. The function $ptrans$ simply selects a (determined) $Mcode$ in either case and thus it can be seen that $Mcode$ must be a one-to-one map in order to prevent, for some i, two different letters $m(i)$ and $m(j)$ from giving the same translation $t(i)$.

The idea of quoting the post-condition of one operation in the specification of another is most often used for applying operations to parts of a state. The following specification is a case where this is used in a way which separates (state-based) data types. A compiler dictionary can be used to record attribute information about identifiers. Many texts on compiler writing use the name "symbol table". Information is added to a local dictionary when the declarations of a block are processed, and this information can be looked up when code is to be generated for the statements in the block. In a block-structured language like ALGOL, the declaration information for different blocks must be kept separately. The attributes of a non-local identifier must be found by looking in the local dictionaries for outer blocks, but the appropriate declaration is always the one in the closest surrounding block. Here, it is assumed that the compiler is one-pass and that entering (and leaving blocks) causes the creation of empty (and the destruction of) local dictionaries. The reader should have no difficulty in specifying each of these operations directly in terms of:

$Cdict = $ seq of $Ldict$

$Ldict = $ map Id to $Attribs$

Here, the specification is presented by first defining operations on the local dictionaries:

$STOREL\ (i\colon Id, a\colon Attribs)$

ext wr $ld\colon Ldict$

pre $i \notin$ dom ld

post $ld = \overleftarrow{ld} \cup \{i \mapsto a\}$

Similarly, an interrogation operation:

$ISINL\ (i\colon Id)\ r\colon \mathbf{B}$

ext rd $ld\colon Ldict$

post $r \Leftrightarrow i \in$ dom ld

Finally:

$LOOKUPL\ (i\colon Id)\ r\colon Attribs$

ext rd $ld\colon Ldict$

pre $i \in$ dom ld

post $r = ld(i)$

The initial local dictionary is an empty map:

$$ld_0 = \{\}$$

The definition *Ldict* can be regarded as a state-based data type which can be used in the definition of the main operations. As explained in Section 5.4, quoting the pre- and post-conditions makes it possible to change the internal detail of *Ldict* without having to change this level of specification.

The *STORE* operation on the entire dictionary is specified:

$STORE\ (i\colon Id, a\colon Attribs)$

ext wr $cd\colon Cdict$

pre $cd \neq [\,] \wedge pre\text{-}STOREL(i, a, \text{hd}\ cd)$

post $\exists ld \in Ldict \cdot post\text{-}STOREL(i, a, \text{hd}\ \overleftarrow{cd}, ld) \wedge cd = [ld]^\frown \text{tl}\ \overleftarrow{cd}$

Then:

$ISLOC\ (i\colon Id)\ r\colon \mathbf{B}$

ext rd $cd\colon Cdict$

pre $cd \neq [\,]$

post $post\text{-}ISINL(i, \text{hd}\ cd, r)$

and:

$LOOKUPC\ (i\colon Id)\ r\colon Attribs$

ext rd $cd\colon Cdict$

pre $\exists j \in \text{dom}\ cd \cdot pre\text{-}LOOKUPL(i, cd(j))$

post let $k = mins\{j \mid pre\text{-}LOOKUPL(i, cd(j))\}$

    in $post\text{-}LOOKUPL(i, cd(k), r)$

The operations on the complete dictionary which correspond to entering and leaving blocks are:

$ENTER$

ext wr $cd\colon Cdict$

post $cd = [ld_0]^\frown \overleftarrow{cd}$

$LEAVE$

ext wr $cd\colon Cdict$

pre $cd \neq [\,]$

post $cd = \text{tl}\ \overleftarrow{cd}$

The initial object of *Cdict* is:

$$cd_0 = [\,]$$

Exercises

1. Complete the operation specifications for en-queuing, de-queuing, and testing for empty for all three of the models discussed in the text for priority queues.

2. A stack is a last-in-first-out storage structure.

   (a) Specify an (unbounded) stack with operations for *PUSH*, *POP* and *ISEMPTY*; also show the initial stack object.

   (b) As above, but assume a bound (say 256) on the contents of a stack; specify an additional operation *ISFULL*.

   (c) As in (b) but, instead of making *PUSH* partial, arrange that pushing an element onto a full stack loses the oldest element!

   (d) Another form of stack which has attracted some interest is known as "Veloso's Traversable Stack". This stack—in addition to the normal operations—can be *READ* from a point indicated by a cursor; the cursor can be *RESET* to the top of the stack or moved *DOWN* one element; the normal *POP* and *PUSH* operations can only be performed with the cursor at the top of the stack but the operations preserve this property. Specify this form of stack.

3. Specify an operation which has access to a set of file names (character strings). Given the prefix of a file name as input, the operation yields the set of matching file names.

4. A formal model of the children's game of snakes and ladders can be based on sequences. Design an appropriate state and specify some operations (e.g. *MOVE*).

5. A very simple diary reminder system can be specified around:

   $$Diary = \mathsf{map}\ Date\ \mathsf{to}\ (\mathsf{seq\ of}\ Task)$$

   Specify an operation which adds a *Task* for a given *Date* (do not assume that the *Date* is already in the *Diary*). This operation should then be quoted in the specification of an operation for a given user in a state:

$$Diarysys = \text{map } Uid \text{ to } Diary$$

6. The German cipher machine, known as "Enigma", was constructed with a reflecting property (i.e. if a was coded as n then n was coded as a. This meant that the operator performed the same operation whether coding or decoding a text. What changes does this make to the specification given above?

7. Specify the function rev by a post-condition using quantifiers and indexing. Sketch the argument that applying rev twice acts as an identity function on sequences. A *palindrome* is a word (e.g. "dad") which is the same when it is reversed. Define a palindrome by properties over the indices and prove that the result of applying rev to a palindrome p is equal to p.

8. * Develop operators, predicates and a theory for sequences which are (not necessarily contiguous) sub-sequences of other sequences in the sense that the former can be found imbeded in the latter (e.g. $[a, b, c]$ is a sub-sequence of $[a, c, a, d, b, c, a, b]$). Refine the notation by writing specifications of a number of tasks (e.g. a function which merges two sequences, a function which finds the "longest ascending sub-sequence" of a sequence of natural numbers).

7.4   Exercises in Abstraction

Some operation specifications in this book have restrictive pre-conditions. It is pointed out, in earlier chapters, that this might well be realistic for operations which are used within a system: essentially, the environment of the operations ensures that the pre-condition is fulfilled. There are, however, operations which might be invoked in a way which makes such restrictive pre-conditions unrealistic. The first part of this section introduces some notational extensions which can be used to record *exceptions*.

It is worth introducing the extended notation by considering the effect of trying to avoid it. Suppose it were wished to make the *DEQUEUE* operation of Section 7.1 total. It would be possible to write:

$DEQUEUE\ ()\ e\colon [Qel]$

ext wr $q\colon Queue$

pre true

post $\overleftarrow{q} \neq [\,]\wedge\overleftarrow{q}=[e]^{\frown}q\ \vee$

$\quad\ \overleftarrow{q}=[\,]\wedge\overleftarrow{q}=q\wedge e=$ nil

Here, the return of the nil value is taken to indicate an error. It would also be possible to base the specification on the signature:

$DEQUEUE()e\colon[Qel]err\colon[QUEUEEMPTY]$

There are several observations about this approach. Perhaps the most obvious problem is that the specification of the normal case can become submerged in detail. But, this may not be the worst problem. This style of specification forces decisions about how errors are to be shown. In some programming languages (e.g. Pascal) it might be necessary to return an extra result, or a distinguished value, in order to indicate an exception; but there are languages (e.g. PL/I, Ada, ML) which contain explicit exception mechanisms. As far as possible, it is worth postponing commitments to implementation languages. It should certainly not be necessary to choose an implementation language in order to record a specification.

The requirements for exception specifications thus include the ability to separate exceptional cases from the normal and an avoidance of commitment as to how exceptions are to be signaled.

One possible notation is to add error clauses to operation specifications. In general, the format becomes:

$OP\ (i\colon Ti)\ r\colon Tr$

ext wr $v\colon Tv$

pre p

errs $COND_1\colon c_1\ \rightarrow\ r_1$

$\quad\ COND_2\colon c_2\ \rightarrow\ r_2$

post r

The condition names can be taken to be the name of the exception: how this is returned is a matter for the implementation. Leaving aside the name, the specification can be explained by its translation to:

$OP\ (i\colon Ti)\ r\colon Tr$

ext wr $v\colon Tv$

pre $p\ \lor\ c_1\ \lor\ c_2$

post $p \land r\ \lor\ c_1 \land r_1\ \lor\ c_1 \land r_2$

Some consequences of this translation should be noted. Firstly, the precondition is effectively widened by the conditions on the error clauses. Secondly, the form of the given post-condition can leave non-determinism on the result. If both c_1 and c_2 are true, either exception can be signaled and the corresponding state transformation can occur. Even if both the normal case and an exception can arise, this translation does not fix the effect. In practice, it is wise to make the normal and exception conditions mutually disjoint, but there are advantages in not determining which of several exceptions should occur, since it leaves an implementation freedom to choose the order in which tests are made. If it is important which exception is signaled, the conditions can again be made mutually exclusive.

The above example could now be written:

$DEQUEUE\ ()\ e\colon [Qel]$

ext wr $q\colon Queue$

pre $q \neq [\ ]$

errs QUEUE EMPTY: $q = [\ ] \rightarrow q = \overleftarrow{q}$

post $\overleftarrow{q} = [e] \frown q$

A very common special case is where the exceptions do not cause a state change. This is, in fact, a very desirable property of a system. It is possible to further economize on notation by recognizing this special case.

One reason for postponing the introduction of the notation for exceptions is that there is a wide variety of different approaches (see Bibliography). The aim of this book being to put over the basic concepts of specifications, it appeared to be wiser to avoid such a contested issue. One particularly interesting approach is to entirely separate error conditions—for example:

$DEQUEUEERR\ ()\ e\colon$ nil

ext wr $q\colon Queue$

pre $q = [\ ]$

post $\overleftarrow{q} = q$

Operators can then be defined between operation specifications which yield some combination of the meanings.

It is a trite observation that formal specifications for large systems are long. The formal description of the PL/I language contains about 120 pages of formulae. Care and preparedness to rewrite parts of such a specification can make the model itelf far easier to understand. The tasteful use of natural language annotations can also make it much easier to begin to understand a formal specification. There are several styles of annotation:

- in-line comments—as in programming languages;

- numbered lines with annotations, after each block of formula, which relate to line numbers;

- careful decomposition into abstract data types with text introducing each such separate concept.

The constraints of a textbook have moved this presentation closest to the third option. It is likely that the development of appropriate machine support will make a form of the second approach much more attractive.

It is possible to discern the architecture of a system without reading the whole description. With experience, the underlying state-like objects of a definition can be understood to define the scope of the architecture. In the PL/I description, the so-called "semantic objects" occupy about five pages. A clear understanding of this material shows many facets of the language without having to read all of the fine detail.

The importance of the state can be shown by the development of a series of vignettes of file systems. Suppose—for all of the definitions—the internal structure of a file is of no interest. A *File* might be an unstructured sequence of bytes or it might have a richer structure. In the latter case, it could be treated as a separate data type. If files are to be accessed, they must be named. Thus the state of the most trivial file system is:

$$Trivfs = \mathsf{map}\ Name\ \mathsf{to}\ File$$

It would be possible to define a range of operations on this state (e.g. *CREATE*, *DELETE*, *COPY*); but it is more interesting to observe what cannot be done. It is obvious from the properties of maps that no two different files can have the same name. If two users wish to have separate name spaces, this file system is not rich enough. This observation can be made without an exhaustive search of operation specifications.

It is not difficult to extend the state in a way which permits nested directories. For example:

$$Nestedfs = Directory$$

$$Directory = \text{map } Name \text{ to } Node$$

$$Node = Directory \cup File$$

This covers the problem of separate users employing the same name in the way that $Unix^{(tm)}$ introduces directories. Here again, operations could be specified on this state; but one can also see what cannot be done in this system. In particular, it is not possible to share the same file via two different name paths. Here sharing is taken to imply that if a user changes the file by one path, the change will appear when the file is accessed via another path.

There is a standard way of establishing such sharing patterns in specifications and that is to introduce some intermediate link (here a file identifier—Fid). Thus:

$$Sharedfs \ :: \quad root: Directory$$
$$filem: \text{map } Fid \text{ to } File$$

$$Directory = \text{map } Name \text{ to } Node$$

$$Node = Directory \cup Fid$$

It is now clear, from the state above, that files can be shared in the sense that different paths can lead to the same file identifier.

Having developed the state, some operations are given. An operation to show the contents of a directory is:

$$Dirstatus = \text{map } Name \text{ to } \{\text{FILE, DIR}\}$$

$$SHOW \ () \ m: Dirstatus$$
$$\text{ext rd } d: Directory$$
$$\text{post } m = \{nm \mapsto$$
$$\qquad\qquad (\text{if } d(nm) \in Directory \text{ then } \text{DIR else } \text{FILE}) \ |$$
$$\qquad\qquad nm \in \text{dom } d\}$$

An operation to create a new directory is:

$MKDIR\ (n\!:Name)$

ext wr $d\!:Directory$

pre $n \notin$ dom d

errs DUPLICATE: $n \in$ dom d

post $d = \overleftarrow{d} \cup \{n \mapsto \{\}\}$

It is then possible to quote these operations in order to form others such as:

$Path =$ seq of $Name$

$SHOWP\ (p\!:Path)\ m\!:Dirstatus$

ext rd $d\!:Node$

pre $d \in Directory\ \wedge$
$\qquad (p = [\,]\ \vee$
$\qquad p \neq [\,]\ \wedge\ hd\ p \in$ dom $d\ \wedge\ pre\text{-}SHOW(tl\ p, d(hd\ p)))$

errs NOTDIR: $d \notin Directory$
$\qquad$INVALIDPATH: $p \neq [\,]\wedge($hd$\ p \notin$ dom $d \vee \neg pre\text{-}SHOW(tl\ p, d(hd\ p)))$
post $p = [\,]\wedge post\text{-}SHOW(d, m)\ \vee$
$\qquad p \neq [\,]\wedge post\text{-}SHOWP(tl\ p, d(hd\ p), m)$

The claim is being made that the state can convey a great deal of information about a system. This is, of course, only true where the state is well chosen. An example of a less appropriate state for the system above is:

$Sharedfs\ ::\ access\!:$ map $Path$ to Fid
$\qquad\qquad\quad filem\!:\ldots$

The most obvious comment is that this would considerably complicate the definition of $SHOW$. It is also clear that there would have to be a complicated invariant on this state. This having been said, it is possible to define all of the operations on such a state. What is left is the observation that this second state conveys a much less clear picture of the intended system than the first state shows.

In specifying even moderately sized systems, one must be prepared to discard possible states as it becomes clear that some operations or invariants become inconvenient. In this way the state comes to be the essence of the specification, and can then provide much insight.

The point about the knowledge derivable from the state can also be made by counter-example. The ECMA/ANSI specification of PL/I is based on a formal model. The state of that definition contains many sequences but no sets. (Perhaps there was some feeling that sets might be too abstract for the standards organization!) But no use is made of the order of some of these sequences. To know which sequences do convey essential order one has to inspect the remaining 300 or more pages of the definition.

The reference to standards activities presents an appropriate point to contrast the terms "specification" and "description". Although the former term has been used in this book, it should be noted that it really relates to an official status; the term "description" is often the more appropriate one. It is, of course, the hope of the author that it will become ever more frequent for standards committees to adopt formal specifications.

A more encouraging story from the world of standards is the evolving work on a "Standardized Generalized Markup Language". This is intended to be a way of describing the structure of a text-book so that the typographical information can be defined separately from the layout. An earlier book by this author was computer typeset in this way. In the terminology of this book, the markup provides an abstract syntax of the text. The appropriateness of the abstraction was ensured in the "GML" system used for the earlier book by working closely to the University of Chicago Press *Manual of Style*.

Chapter 5 introduces various forms of lists as occur in list-processing languages. The most LISP-like of these is shown (cf. Exercise 6 of Section 5.1) as:

$$Pllist = [Node]$$

$$Node :: car: Pllist \cup \mathbf{N}$$
$$ cdr: Pllist \cup \mathbf{N}$$

This fails to reflect the possibility—which exists in most dialects of LISP—that sub-lists are shared. Handling this possibility is another example of the need to introduce an intermediate link. Thus, one model which covers sharing is:

$$Lisp1 :: \quad l: Lisplist$$
$$ nm: \text{map } Nid \text{ to } Node$$
$$Lisplist = [Nid]$$
$$Node :: car: Lisplist \cup \mathbf{N}$$
$$ cdr: Lisplist \cup \mathbf{N}$$

Given the basic idea of intermediate links, there are various ways in which it can be employed. It would, for example, be possible to define:

$Lisp2$ :: $carrel$: map Nid to $(Nid \cup \mathbf{N})$
 :: $cdrrel$: map Nid to $(Nid \cup \mathbf{N})$

Figure 7.4 pictures a structure; its two possible representations are:

$mk\text{-}Lisp1(a, \{$
$\qquad\qquad a \mapsto mk\text{-}Node(b, c),$
$\qquad\qquad b \mapsto mk\text{-}Node(5, d),$
$\qquad\qquad c \mapsto mk\text{-}Node(d, 2),$
$\qquad\qquad d \mapsto mk\text{-}Node(3, 7)\})$

$mk\text{-}Lisp2(\{a \mapsto b, b \mapsto 5, c \mapsto d, d \mapsto 3\},$
$\qquad\qquad \{a \mapsto c, c \mapsto 2, b \mapsto d, d \mapsto 7\})$

The drawback of the second is the need for a relatively complicated invariant.

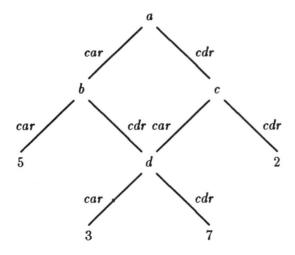

Figure 7.4: LISP list

There are systems in which a very clean abstraction can be given of nearly all of the functionality but where some detail distorts the final model. If one is involved in designing such an architecture, one can use this as a prompt to check whether the complexity could be avoided. If an established architecture is being described, there is no choice but to accept the extra complexity in the final model. The virtual store system which was discussed in Section 6.3 provides a basis for an example. Virtual store systems in actual computers need many extra features: it is often possible to lock pages into fast store; some operations might allow access to values which cross the page boundaries. In such a case, it is good practice to record the simplified versions so as to convey the basic concepts. For some architectures this process of approximating to the final functionality can require several stages.

It is not practical, in such a textbook, to present any really large specifications. The Bibliography provides references to such documents. For various reasons (including the character sets of printers) the VDM notation has evolved somewhat over the last decade or so. An attempt is being made to revise at least some of the larger specifications and to republish them in the *Teacher's Notes* referred to in the Preface.

Exercises

1. Rewrite the specification of Exercise 2 of Section 4.4 using the exception notation.

2. Write the exception specifications (where appropriate) for the stack examples given in question 2 of Section 7.3.

3. * Extend the specification of the file system given in this section. Firstly define other operations on *Sharedfs*. Secondly consider new features (e.g. security/authority, stored path names) and show how these affect the state. In all operation definitions, attempt to use operation quotation to separate the data types.

4. * Exercise 5 of Section 7.3 introduces a trivial diary system. Write down a reasonable list of requirements and then develop (using separate data types and combining them) a specification of a realistic computer-based diary manager.

5. * Develop the state for a relational database system. Unless the reader is an expert in this area, an actual system should be used as a reference point. Focus the work on building a model for the storage of, and the type information for, relations.

6. * Define an abstract syntax for expressions of propositional logic (there are some interesting points to be decided upon). Write a function which determines, in classical two-valued logic, whether an expression is a tautology.

Implication and equivalence operators can be expanded out using their definitions. In Disjunctive Normal Form (DNF) expressions are reduced to a form which is a disjunction of conjunctions of (possibly negated) literals (E_i). Define a function which converts arbitrary propositional expressions into DNF. In terms of this limited structure define an efficient algorithm for tautology checking.

Consider the changes required to handle the LPF used in this book and define a function which checks LPF propositional sequents for validity.

Design an abstract syntax for proofs in the propositional calculus. There is considerable scope for experiment here and it is worth considering the need for relations.

Define an abstract syntax for formulae of the predicate calculus and functions to determine the free variables of a logical expression and to apply systematic substitution.

Chapter 8

Data Reification

It should be clear that the construction of a formal specification can yield greater understanding of a system than is normally possible before implementation is undertaken. On larger examples the process of constructing the formal specification can also prompt consideration of questions whose resolution results in a "cleaner architecture". It is, therefore, possible that the work involved in producing a formal specification would be worthwhile even if the ensuing development were undertaken using informal methods.

The remaining chapters of this book present a more exciting possibility. A formal specification provides a reference point against which a proof can be constructed. A proof can show that a program works for all inputs. Clearly, no real proof could be based on an informal description whose semantics are unclear. The idea that programs can be proved to satisfy formal specifications is now well-documented in scientific papers. More recently it has been shown that a design process can be based on formal specifications.

The essence of such a design process is to record a design step with a series of assumptions about subsequent development (i.e. specifications of sub-components) and then to show that the design step is correct under the given assumptions. Once this has been done, the assumptions (specifications of the sub-components) are tackled. It is a crucial property of the rigorous development method presented here that each step of development is isolated by its specification. Without such a property of isolation, a development method is open to one of the worst risks that currently manifests itself in testing: work based on early mistakes must be discarded when errors are detected. The property of isolation is sometimes called *compositionality*.

There are some respects in which the above description is over-simplified. Firstly, a development hardly ever proceeds strictly top-down. But, even if one is forced to backtrack, the eventual design will be made clearer by documentation presented in a neat hierarchy. (Sub-components can also be developed bottom-up—such sub-components will be used safely only if they are accompanied by their formal specifications.)

Another issue which could be taken with the over-simplified description is the level of formality to be used in the design process. Any design step generates a proof obligation. Such proof obligations can be completely formal and some proofs are shown below in detail. Once one knows how to conduct such proofs, the level of formality can be relaxed for most steps of design. The formal structure provides a way of giving more detail when required. A knowledge of the formal structure will itself minimize the danger of mistakes.

The process of design can be seen as making commitments. The representation chosen is a commitment which the designer makes based on an understanding of the required operations and their relative frequencies of use. The method outlined here is not intended to help make such choices. Design relies on invention. Such invention has been automated only in very narrow areas. What is provided is a notation for recording designs and the proof obligations necessary to establish their correctness (rather than their optimality). Experience has shown that the formal structure does aid designers by clarifying their choices. But the case for the rigorous approach should never be construed as claiming that the design process can be automated.

The style of formal specification proposed in the preceding chapters uses (abstract) models of data types and implicit specification by pre- and post-conditions. High-level design decisions normally involve the representation of data; *data reification*[1] involves the transition from abstract to concrete

---

[1] The term reification is preferred here to the more widely-used word "refinement". Michael Jackson pointed out to the author that the latter term is hardly appropriate for the step from a clean mathematical abstraction to a messy representation dictated by a particular machine architecture. The *Concise Oxford Dictionary* defines the word "reification" as 'convert (person, abstract concept) into thing, materialize'.

data types and the justification of the transition. At the end of this process, the data types are those of the implementation language but the transformations are still defined implicitly (i.e. by pre- and post-conditions). Operation decomposition—described in Chapter 10—is the process of choosing, and justifying, a sequence of transformations which can be expressed in the implementation language.

The examples in Chapters 4 to 7 include descriptions of data types which arise in design. For example, the choice of one form of binary tree is motivated by noting that it can provide a representation of a set. In general, a representation (of one data type) is just another data type—as such it can be described by the toolkit of data structuring devices used above.

In choosing the data types for a specification, the aim is that they should be as abstract as possible. Although this notion is not made precise until Chapter 9, the reader should by now have a general feel for avoidance of unnecessary details in a state. The proof obligations given in Sections 8.1 and 8.2 actually relate to the special case where the "bias" is increasing at each step of reification. This is a very common special case—a more general rule is given in Section 9.1. Designers make commitments—commitments which reflect special properties of the application and of the implementation machine. These commitments give rise to redundancy, complexity (e.g. of invariants) and efficiency! Thus the data types which result from reification tend to require long descriptions and give rise to complex operation specifications.

The key to relating an abstract data type and its representation is a "retrieve" function—this concept, and the first of the proof obligations, is introduced in Section 8.1. The proof obligations which concern the operations are explained in the succeeding section. Section 8.3 discusses the problems of given interfaces and presents some larger examples.

8.1 Retrieve Functions and Adequacy

Given a specification, a designer chooses a representation which reflects implementation constraints. The notion of satisfaction introduced in Section 4.1, provides a criterion by which the correctness of the choice of representation can be judged. The proof obligations, which are explained in this and the following section, reflect an extremely common special case of data reification. (Section 9.1 reviews some alternatives.) In the case being considered, it is possible to separate some questions about the reification of the state itself from consideration of the operations over such states.

Suppose that some specification uses dates (*Date*) as in Exercise 1 of Section 5.1. A representation might be chosen which packs the date into two bytes (5 bits for the day, 4 bits for the month, 7 bits for the year—this last allowing an increment from 0 to 127 to be added to some notional base date). One could fix the relation between elements of *Date* and the bit representation by a relation. The relation would be one-to-one, and this should suggest to the reader that a function could be used to record the relationship. In this simple example, there is no obvious reason to prefer one direction or the other for the function. More guidance comes from considering an example like the use of a binary tree to represent a set. The set might have been chosen in the specification because its properties were appropriate to the application being specified; a binary tree might be chosen as a representation so that the test operation can be performed efficiently for large volumes of data. In this example, each abstract set value has more than one possible represenation as a tree. The relation between abstraction and representation values is one-to-many.

Clearly, a one-to-many relation can be treated as a general relation. But there is also the possibility that it is treated as a function (from the "many" side to the "one"). Is the reverse situation likely to arise? If different abstract values correspond to one concrete value, it is intuitively obvious that such values could have been merged in the abstraction. So, in the situation where the objects used in the specification were abstract enough, the many-to-one situation would not arise. Working with relations can lead to rather heavy notation. Here, the opportunity to avoid this heaviness is taken. The relationship between abstract values and their representations is expressed by a function from the latter to the former (e.g. from binary trees to sets). Because such functions can be thought of as regaining the abstraction from among the implementation details, they are called *retrieve functions*.

The spell-checking specification of Section 4.2 is based on:

$Dict =$ set of *Word*

Assuming that the dictionary is large, the designer is faced with the problem of choosing a representation which makes efficient searching possible. The choice must reflect not only algorithms but also storage usage—wasted store could cause excessive paging and subvert the performance of a representation which was chosen to support some particular algorithm. The designer has to

consider many facets of efficiency. Here, some alternative representations are
considered. The first is chosen for pedagogic, rather than realistic, reasons.
Suppose the dictionary is represented by a sequence without duplicates:

$$Dicta = \text{seq of } Word$$
where
$$inv\text{-}Dicta(wl) \quad \triangleq \quad is\text{-}uniques(wl)$$

The one-to-many situation mentioned above is shown clearly here—to each
abstract set with n words, there correspond $n!$ different possible sequence
representations. The relationship between the representation and abstraction is easily expressed:

$$retr\text{-}Dict: Dicta \rightarrow Dict$$
$$retr\text{-}Dict(wl) \quad \triangleq \quad \text{rng } wl$$

Here, $retr\text{-}Dict$ can be said to be retrieving the abstract set from among the
irrelevant ordering information of the sequence values.

One straightforward property which is required of retrieve functions is
that they be total. In this case there is no doubt about $retr\text{-}Dict$ since the
rng operator is total on sequences. In some cases, however, it is necessary
to tighten an invariant on the representation in order to ensure that the
retrieve function is defined for all values which can arise.

It is intuitively clear that there should be at least one representation
for any abstract value. This property is embodied in the *adequacy* proof
obligation. For the case in hand:

$$\forall d \in Dict \cdot \exists da \in Dicta \cdot retr\text{-}Dict(da) = d$$

This says that there must exist at least one sequence (without duplicates)
which can be retrieved onto any possible set value. The result here is obvious
and the proof (cf. Figure 8.1) is given only for illustration.

In the majority of cases, the adequacy proof obligation can be discharged
by an informal, constructive argument. For example:

given any finite set, its elements can be arranged into a sequence
by taking them in an arbitrary order; choosing each element once
ensures that the representation invariant is not violated

Figure 8.2 illustrates the idea behind the adequacy proof obligation[2]; the
general form is:

---

[2]Strictly, a representation is adequate—or not—with respect to a retrieve function.

from $d \in Dict$

1      $\operatorname{rng}[\,] = \{\}$

2      $\exists da \in Dicta \cdot retr\text{-}Dict(da) = \{\}$ $\exists\text{-I}(retr\text{-}Dict,1)$

3   from $d \in$ set of $Word$, $w \notin d$,

         $\exists da \in Dicta \cdot retr\text{-}Dict(da) = d$

3.1   from $da \in Dicta$, $retr\text{-}Dict(da) = d$

3.1.1 $\operatorname{rng} da = d$ h3.1,$retr\text{-}Dict$

3.1.2 $w \notin \operatorname{rng} da$ h3,3.1.1

3.1.3 $da \frown [w] \in Dicta$ $Dicta$,3.1.2

3.1.4 $\operatorname{rng}(da \frown [w]) = \operatorname{rng} da \cup \{w\}$ rng

3.1.5 $retr\text{-}Dict(da \frown [w]) = d \cup \{w\}$ 3.1.1,3.1.4

     infer $\exists e_1 \in Dicta \cdot retr\text{-}Dict(e_1) = d \cup \{w\}$ $\exists\text{-I}(3.1.5)$

     infer $\exists e_1 \in Dicta \cdot retr\text{-}Dict(e_1) = d \cup \{w\}$ $\exists\text{-E}(h3,3.1)$

     infer $\exists da \in Dicta \cdot retr\text{-}Dict(da) = d$ set-ind(2,3)

Figure 8.1: Example of an Adequacy Proof

$$\forall a \in Abs \cdot \exists r \in Rep \cdot retr(r) = a$$
$$retr\colon Rep \to Abs$$

Pragmatically, a retrieve function can be seen as providing an interpretation of the representation. In the initial example, two bytes are interpreted as a date. In the case of the sequence of words, the retrieve function interprets it as the unordered set of $Dict$—such a sequence could just as well have represented the current book (where the order of the words is believed to be important).

Understanding a proof obligation is often made easier by considering cases where it fails. Clearly, proof obligations are likely to uncover genuine errors only on larger examples—such failures are discussed below. With

---

When the retrieve function in question is clear, the qualification is omitted. Technically, the retrieve function is a homomorphism between the carrier of the representation and that of the abstraction. The retrieve function can also be seen to induce an equivalence relation on the representation: two elements are considered to be equivalent if they are retrieved onto the same abstract value. This is a key concept for the proofs of the operations—the proof obligations in the next section require that the induced equivalence relation is respected.

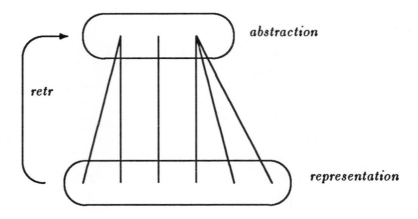

Figure 8.2: Retrieve Function

Dict and *Dicta*, however, a simple illustration can be given. Suppose that the specification had been based on the sequences (*Dicta*) and the implementation on sets (*Dict*). Even with this reversal of roles, a retrieve function could be given:

$$retr\text{-}Dicta\colon Dict \rightarrow Dicta$$

For example, the function could deliver a sequence sorted in alphabetical order. But the representation would not be adequate because there would be elements of the specification state (e.g. unordered sequences) for which there was no corresponding set. Although the example is, in some sense, just a restatement of the need to avoid "bias" in a specification, it should give some feel for why adequacy is a useful check.

In more realistic examples, there are two likely causes of inadequacy. The obvious one is that some combination of values has been overlooked. This is clearly what the proof obligation is intended to uncover, and the situation must be remedied by redesigning the representation. The other way in which adequacy might fail is if the invariant on the abstraction is too loose: abstract values might satisfy it but never arise as a result of a sequence of operations. If such values cannot be represented in the chosen design, the adequacy failure is only a technical issue. The invariant in the specification can be tightened (implementability must be rechecked) and the design can then be pursued.

The basic notions of retrieve functions and adequacy can now be applied to a more realistic design for the spell-checking specification. One way to provide for efficient searching is to split the dictionary into sections by word length; each such section is then stored in alphabetical order. As words are scanned from the text to be checked, their length is computed. The relevant dictionary section can then be located via a table and the word to be tested sought in the selected section. The search can use a technique known as "binary search", which is efficient because it relies on the order. A series of distinct design decisions are embodied in this description. A record of the first design decision can be given in terms of the following objects:

$Dictb = $ seq of $Section$

where

$inv\text{-}Dictb(sl) \quad \triangleq \quad \forall i \in \text{dom } sl \cdot \forall w \in sl(i) \cdot \text{len } w = i$

$Section = $ set of $Word$

$Word = $ seq of $Letter$

Notice that, in order to describe the invariant, it has been necessary to say more about *Words* than in the specification. The retrieve function required here is:

$retr\text{-}Dict\colon Dictb \to Dict$

$retr\text{-}Dict(sl) \quad \triangleq \quad \bigcup \text{rng } sl$

Here again there is no difficulty with totality, and adequacy can be established by a simple constructive argument:

> the empty set can be represented by an empty sequence of sections; the way of representing a new *Word* depends on whether *Words* of the same length already occur in the *Dictb* value; if so, the new word is placed in the set; if not, the *Section* sequence is extended (if necessary) with empty *Sections* and the new *Word* is placed in a unit *Section* at the appropriate place in the *Section* sequence.

The next step of development might again be a reification of each *Section* onto a sequence. The final steps would concern the decomposition of operations specified by post-conditions onto the envisaged binary search algorithms.

The choices of representations are crucial decisions made by a designer. No amount of clever coding can restore performance squandered on ill-conceived data structures. Equally, correctness is vital. Representation decisions are normally made early in design. Errors made at this stage can be eradicated only by repeating the work based on the mistaken decision. It is, then, very important to make careful checks at this stage. The documentation of a retrieve function requires little effort and experience shows that this effort often uncovers errors. Similarly, outlining an adequacy argument for the representation of a state is not onerous and may uncover serious errors.

Here the state alone is being considered; the proof obligations in Section 8.2 must be undertaken for each operation of the data type. It is therefore harder to justify the work of formal proofs for the operation proof obligations. It is, then, fortunate that experience has shown that these proof obligations are less likely (than adequacy) to uncover important errors.

The preceding representation required that a whole word be scanned before any searching could be done. A student project offered a way of using each letter as it is scanned. The initial proposal was to use Pascal arrays indexed by letters; the values stored in such arrays were to be pointers to other arrays; all of the arrays were allocated on the heap; nil pointers were to be used to mark where words ended. Using map notation it is possible to nest maps as follows:

$$Dicte = \text{map } Letter \text{ to } Dicte$$

The word set:

$$\{[a, n, d], [a, n, t]\}$$

can then be represented by:

$$\{a \mapsto \{n \mapsto \{d \mapsto \{\}, t \mapsto \{\}\}\}\}$$

Notice how the lack, for example, of any word beginning with b is shown by the absence of this letter from the domain of the outer map. But one must also notice that this representation is not adequate (with respect to any retrieve function). There is, for example, no way of adding a word, in $Dicte$ which is a prefix of an existing word (consider $[a, n]$). On realizing this, an indicator had to be added to each array (in Pascal, a record is used with a Boolean value and the array of pointers as its fields)—here:

$$Dictc \ :: \ eow : \mathbf{B}$$
$$map : \mathsf{map} \ Letter \ \mathsf{to} \ Dictc$$

The retrieve function required is defined by recursion:

$$retr\text{-}Dict : Dictc \to Dict$$

$$retr\text{-}Dict(mk\text{-}Dictc(eow, m)) \quad \triangleq$$
$$(\mathsf{if} \ eow \ \mathsf{then} \ \{[\,]\} \ \mathsf{else} \ \{\}) \cup$$
$$\bigcup\{\{[l] \frown w \mid w \in retr\text{-}Dict(m(l))\} \mid l \in \mathsf{dom} \ m\}$$

The reader should experiment with this retrieve function in order to understand the distinction in the first case of the set union. From this understanding it is possible to provide an invariant for $Dictc$.

Exercises

1. This exercise continues the spell-checking problem discussed in the text of this section.

   (a) In terms of some particular programming language, discuss the efficiency—especially storage requirements—of $Dictb$ and $Dictc$.

   (b) Define a representation in which all words with the same first letter are collected into a set, each such set is the range element of a map from the first letter. Write a retrieve function and argue the adequacy of the representation.

2. Document the relationship between the state given in Exercise 4 of Section 4.4 and that given in the text of Section 4.4 by writing retrieve functions in both directions.

3. Consider the set of objects $Llist$ described in Section 5.1 and the sequences of Chapter 7. In which directions can retrieve functions be written?

4. Explain the binary trees ($Setrep$) of Section 5.2 as representations of sets by using retrieve functions, and present an adequacy proof.

5. Many encodings are used for integers. A binary numeral can be thought of as a sequence of symbols—show how a (natural number) value can be associated with such a symbol sequence by providing a retrieve function. The sign-and-magnitude representation of integers

used in some computers reserves one bit for the sign and the remaining bits in a word are used as above—again, explain this relation with a retrieve function. The ones-complement representation essentially stores, for negative numbers, the bit-wise complement of the positive number—here again, explain the relation by a retrieve function (remember that all zeros or all ones represent the number zero).

6. Consider the abstract state:

$$State \; :: \; \begin{array}{l} as : \text{set of } \mathbf{N} \\ bs : \text{set of } \mathbf{N} \end{array}$$

and the representation:

$$Rep = \text{seq of } \mathbf{B}$$

Write a retrieve function and either prove Rep to be adequate or show how it fails to be and suggest an invariant on $State$ which ensures that the representation is adequate.

8.2   Operation Modelling Proofs

The preceding section has given some examples of the way in which data reification gives rise to complex data objects. This complexity reflects the move from data objects which are chosen to match the task being specified to representations which can be efficiently implemented. Efficiency might require redundancy (e.g. doubly-linked lists or extra copies) and this results in lengthier invariants.

Turning now to the operations: in general, representation detail forces operation specifications to be more algorithmic; for example, neat post-conditions on the abstraction might give way to recursive functions on the representation. As the examples below illustrate, post-conditions are more concise than code—but the closer the representation is to the data types of programming languages, the more complex will be the specifications. This is, of course, precisely the reason that overall functional specifications should be written in terms of abstract data types. But the time has come to look at the proof obligations associated with the modelling of operations.

The abstract specification consists of a set of states, the initial states, and operations. The preceding section has shown how the states themselves are reified. The next design task is to respecify the operations on the chosen state representation. The format of such operation specifications is standard. Thus the *CHECKWORD* operation of Section 4.2 would be respecified on *Dicta* of the preceding section by:

$CHECKWORDa$ (w: $Word$) b: **B**

ext rd $dict$: $Dicta$

post b ⟺ $\exists i \in$ dom $dict \cdot dict(i) = w$

It is easier to picture the proof obligations which arise in the case of functions than operations. Figure 8.3 shows an (abstract) function f_a over elements of A; an alternative way of performing such a mapping is to find a corresponding element of R (assume, for now, that *retr* is one-to-one) apply a function f_r on R and then map this back to A by applying *retr*. The function f_r models f_a if the alternative mapping is the same as f_a for all values in the domain of f_a.

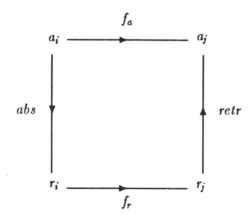

Figure 8.3: Function Modelling

This could be written formally:

$$\forall a \in A \cdot retr(f_r(abs(a))) = f_a(a)$$

where *abs* is the inverse of *retr*.

The proof obligations needed for operations have to cope with two complications. Firstly, operations themselves are partial (cf. pre-condition) and non-deterministic (cf. post-condition); secondly, retrieve functions are normally many-to-one and thus their inverses are not functions. One way of comprehending the resulting proof rules is to think of viewing the operations on the representation via the retrieve function. Thus, the basic proof obligations for *operation modelling* are:

$$\forall r \in R \cdot pre\text{-}A(retr(r)) \;\Rightarrow\; pre\text{-}R(r)$$

$$\forall \overleftarrow{r}, r \in R \cdot$$
$$pre\text{-}A(retr(\overleftarrow{r})) \wedge post\text{-}R(\overleftarrow{r}, r) \;\Rightarrow\; post\text{-}A(retr(\overleftarrow{r}), retr(r))$$

These rules can be extended in an obvious way to cope with inputs and results of operations.

The second of these proof obligations is known as the *result rule*. This can be seen as requiring that any pair of states in the *post-R* relation must—when viewed under the retrieve function—satisfy the *post-A* relation. An implementation should not be rejected for an unnecessarily wide pre-condition, nor should it be forced to perform any particular (e.g. *post-R*) computation outside the required domain. Thus the first conjunct of the antecedent of the implication limits the proof obligation to those states which—when viewed under the retrieve function—satisfy the abstract pre-conditions.

The explanation of the result rule argues against requiring too much of the operations on the representation. It must, however, be remembered that the specification of the operations on the representation consist of two parts. The result rule ensures that the post-condition is not too wide; the *domain rule* (first above) requires that the pre-condition of the operation on the representation is not too narrow[3].

The concept of viewing under the retrieve function can be formalized by requiring that representation operations respect the equivalence relation induced on the representation states by the retrieve function.

For the first example in the preceding section, the domain rule:

$$\forall wl \in Dicta, w \in Word \cdot$$
$$pre\text{-}CHECKWORD(w, retr\text{-}Dict(wl)) \;\Rightarrow\;$$
$$pre\text{-}CHECKWORDa(w, wl)$$

is vacuously true because the operation on the representation is total.

---

[3]The validity of the proof rules given here relies on the adequacy of the representation.

Noting that the pre-condition of the abstract operation is also true, the result rule becomes:

$$\forall wl \in Dicta, w \in Word, b \in \mathbf{B} \cdot$$
$$post\text{-}CHECKWORDa(w, wl, b) \Rightarrow$$
$$post\text{-}CHECKWORD(w, retr\text{-}Dict(wl), b)$$

which follows from:

$$\forall wl \in \text{seq of } Word, w \in Word, b \in \mathbf{B} \cdot$$
$$(b \Leftrightarrow \exists i \in \text{dom } wl \cdot wl(i) = w) \Rightarrow (b \Leftrightarrow w \in \text{rng } wl)$$

Thus, $CHECKWORDa$ can be said to model $CHECKWORD$[4].

The $ADDWORD$ operation changes the state and can be modelled by:

$ADDWORDa$ (w: $Word$)

ext wr $dict$: $Dicta$

pre $\neg \exists i \in \text{dom } dict \cdot dict(i) = w$

post $dict = \overleftarrow{dict} \frown [w]$

The domain rule becomes:

$$\forall wl \in Dicta, w \in Word \cdot$$
$$pre\text{-}ADDWORD(w, retr\text{-}Dict(wl)) \Rightarrow$$
$$pre\text{-}ADDWORDa(w, wl)$$

This is proved in Figure 8.4.

The result rule becomes:

$$\forall \overleftarrow{wl}, wl \in Dicta, w \in Word \cdot$$
$$pre\text{-}ADDWORD(w, retr\text{-}Dict(\overleftarrow{wl})) \wedge$$
$$post\text{-}ADDWORDa(w, \overleftarrow{wl}, wl) \Rightarrow$$
$$post\text{-}ADDWORD(w, retr\text{-}Dict(\overleftarrow{wl}), retr\text{-}Dict(wl))$$

which is, again, straightforward (cf. Figure 8.5). Thus $ADDWORDa$ models $ADDWORD$. If these are the only operations, the reification has been justified and attention can be turned to the next step of development.

---

[4]Strictly, this statement is with respect to $retr\text{-}Dict$ but this qualification can normally be omitted without confusion.

from $wl \in$ seq of $Word, w \in Word$

1   from $w \notin$ rng wl

1.1 $w \notin \{wl(i) \mid i \in$ dom $wl\}$ rng

1.2 $w \notin \{v \mid \exists i \in$ dom $wl \cdot v = wl(i)\}$ set compr

        infer $\neg \exists i \in$ dom $wl \cdot w = wl(i)$ $\in$

2      $(w \notin$ rng $wl) \in \mathbf{B}$ h

3      $w \notin$ rng $wl \Rightarrow \neg \exists i \in$ dom $wl \cdot w = wl(i)$ $\Rightarrow$-I(2,1)

infer $pre\text{-}ADD\,WORD(w, retr\text{-}Dict(wl)) \Rightarrow pre\text{-}ADD\,WORDa(w, wl)$

Figure 8.4: Example of Proving the Domain Rule

from $\overleftarrow{wl}, wl \in$ seq of $Word, w \in Word$

1   from $wl = \overleftarrow{wl} \frown [w]$

1.1   rng $wl =$ rng $\overleftarrow{wl} \cup$ rng $[w]$

        infer $=$ rng $\overleftarrow{wl} \cup \{w\}$

2      $(wl = \overleftarrow{wl} \frown [w]) \in \mathbf{B}$

3      $wl = \overleftarrow{wl} \frown [w] \Rightarrow$ rng $wl =$ rng $\overleftarrow{wl} \cup \{w\}$ $\Rightarrow$-I(2,1)

infer $post\text{-}ADD\,WORDa(w, \overleftarrow{wl}, wl) \Rightarrow$

        $post\text{-}ADD\,WORD(w, retr\text{-}Dict(\overleftarrow{wl}), retr\text{-}Dict(wl))$

Figure 8.5: Example of Proving the Result Rule

It is also necessary to show that the initial states correspond—with resect to the retrieve function. The proof is straightforward in this case and is shown explicitly only on examples where the initial states are less obvious.

In large applications of the rigorous approach, there are likely to be several steps of data reification: when the data objects have been refined to the level of the machine or language constructs, operation decomposition is carried out. In either case, the compositionality property of the development method requires that the next step of development relies only on the result (e.g. *Dicta*, etc.) of this stage of development and not on the original specification.

The operations on the second dictionary representation are addressed in Exercise 3 below. The third dictionary representation given above is more interesting. In this case, the initial state is worth special consideration. The proof obligation for initial states is:

$$retr(dictc_0) = dict_0$$

This can be satisfied with:

$$mk\text{-}Dictc(\mathsf{false}, \{\})$$

The specification of *CHECKWORDc* must be written in terms of *Dictc*. A specification which used the retrieve function would make little real progress in design. To avoid such insipid steps of development, one could use a function:

$$is\text{-}inc\colon Word \times Dictc \to \mathbf{B}$$
$$is\text{-}inc(w, mk\text{-}Dictc(eow, m)) \quad \triangleq$$
$$\qquad w = [\,] \land eow \ \lor$$
$$\qquad w \neq [\,] \land \mathsf{hd}\, w \in \mathsf{dom}\, m \land is\text{-}inc(\mathsf{tl}\, w, m(\mathsf{hd}\, w))$$

The modelling proof relies on the lemma:

$$\forall w \in Word, d \in Dictc \cdot is\text{-}inc(w, d) \ \Leftrightarrow \ w \in retr\text{-}Dict(d)$$

which can be proved by structural induction. In fact, a theory of *Dictc* can be developed. A function which inserts words is:

$insc$: $Word \times Dictc \rightarrow Dictc$

$insc(w, mk\text{-}Dictc(e, m))$ $\triangleq$
if $w = [\,]$
then $mk\text{-}Dictc(\text{true}, m)$
else   if hd $w \in$ dom m
        then $mk\text{-}Dictc(e, m \dagger [\text{hd } w \mapsto insc(\text{tl } w, m(\text{hd } w))])$
        else $mk\text{-}Dictc(e, m \cup [\text{hd } w \mapsto insc(\text{tl } w, mk\text{-}Dictc(\text{false}, \{\})])$

The relevant lemma here is:

$$retr\text{-}Dict(insc(w, d)) = retr\text{-}Dict(d) \cup \{w\}$$

In the spell-checking example, all of the operations are deterministic. The buffer pool example of Section 4.4 exhibits non-determinism. The abstract buffer pool is shown as:

set of Bid

Suppose this is modelled by:

$Bufl = $ seq of Bid
where
$inv\text{-}Bufl(l)$ $\triangleq$ $is\text{-}uniques(l)$

Clearly this is an adequate representation with respect to the retrieve function:

$retr\text{-}BUF$: $Bufl \rightarrow$ set of Bid

$retr\text{-}BUF(bidl)$ $\triangleq$ rng $bidl$

The model of $OBTAIN$ can be specified:

$OBTAIN1$ () res: Bid
ext wr fl: $Bufl$
pre $fl \neq [\,]$
post $\overleftarrow{fl} = [res] \frown fl$

The domain proof obligation is straightforward—that for the result becomes:

$\forall \overleftarrow{fl}, fl \in Bufl, res \in \mathbf{B} \cdot$
    $pre\text{-}OBTAIN(retr\text{-}Buf(\overleftarrow{fl})) \wedge$
    $post\text{-}OBTAIN_1(\overleftarrow{fl}, fl, res) \Rightarrow$
        $post\text{-}OBTAIN(retr\text{-}Buf(\overleftarrow{fl}), retr\text{-}Buf(fl), res)$

Notice that a proof of this result relies on the invariant of *Bufl*.

Two models are in some sense equivalent if retrieve functions can be written in both directions. There is, in fact, a one-to-one correspondance[5] between elements of both models. It can be useful to build a specification around two or more equivalent models. For example, one model may require a minimal invariant, while another may offer a state with many sub-components, thus shortening the specifications of operations which affect only some of the sub-components. In such a case, two models should be used and the appropriate retrieve functions given. This is an alternative to the creation of extra functions which define alternative views of one basic model.

Exercises

1. Exercise 2 of Section 4.4 introduces a students-in-class problem. Define a representation in terms of lists; provide retrieve functions and adequacy proofs; specify operations on the lists; and prove that they model those on the abstract state.

2. Exercise 3 of Section 4.4 and Exercise 3 of Section 6.3 use two different states for the same family of operations. Show that the specification based on a pair of sets can be thought of as a reification of that based on a map (expand and check the proof obligations for the state and the operations).

3. The spell-checker application can be used to show that the proof obligation given in this section caters for non-determinism in representation operations. Respecify *ADDWORDa* to insert the new word anywhere in the list and show that the revised operation specification models *ADDWORD*. Specify operations to work on *Dictb* of the preceding Section and show that they model those of the specification in Section 4.2.

4. It is easy to specify operations which allocate elements onto two distinct lists. If there is not a reasonable upper size bound for at least one of the lists, the representation in a normal linearly addressed store presents problems. (Such a situation arises with the stack and heap in some programming languages.) One well-known technique is to reserve a large contiguous area for both lists and to allocate their space

---

[5]They are isomorphic.

from opposite ends of the space. Describe the abstract problem and its solution using two models and show that one is a reification of the other (consider the initial state).

5. Section 6.3 includes a discussion of virtual store showing abstract and implemented models. Justify the correctness of the development in terms of the proof obligations of this chapter.

6. Complete the development begun in Exercise 4 of Section 8.1 by specifying and justifying the operations on *Setrep* (consider the initial state).

7. * The equivalence relation application has been specified three times (Sections 4.4, 6.1, and 6.3). Show that the second and third are each reifications of the first and sketch the argument that the third is a reification of the second (consider the initial state).

8.3   Exercises in Reification

This section presents a larger exercise in data reification. As well as development from abstraction to representation of the sort discussed above, the way in which the same techniques can be used to handle given interfaces is explained.

The preceding section has shown that a simple form of binary tree can be used to store representations of sets. The advantage of the binary tree representation is that it facilitates efficient[6] search and update operations. A great many computer applications rely in some way on large associations between keys and data. An extended form of binary tree can be used to provide similar performance advantages for representations of such maps. In contrast to those used for set representations (cf. *Setrep*), these trees have nodes which contain a *Key/Data* pair. A top-level specification of a map from *Keys* to *Data* is made trivial by the availability of suitable base objects. Thus:

$Kdm = \text{map } Key \text{ to } Data$

The initial object in *Kdm* is:

---

[6]The number of steps is proportional to the logarithm—base 2—of the number of elements, provided the tree is balanced.

$$m_0 = \{\}$$

Operations can be defined:

> *FIND* $(k\!:Key)$ $d\!:Data$
>
> ext rd $m\!:Kdm$
>
> pre $k \in$ dom m
>
> post $d = m(k)$

> *INSERT* $(k\!:Key, d\!:Data)$
>
> ext wr $m\!:Kdm$
>
> pre $k \notin$ dom m
>
> post $m = \overleftarrow{m} \cup \{k \mapsto d\}$

> *DELETE* $(k\!:Key)$
>
> ext wr $m\!:Kdm$
>
> pre $k \in$ dom m
>
> post $m = \{k\} \triangleleft \overleftarrow{m}$

The maps (Kdm) can be represented by:

> $Mrep = [Mnode]$
>
> $Mnode\!:: Mrep\ Key\ Data\ Mrep$
> where
> $inv\text{-}Mnode(mk\text{-}Mnode(lt, mk, md, rt)) \quad \triangleq$
> $\quad (\forall lk \in collkeys(lt) \cdot lk < mk) \wedge$
> $\quad (\forall rk \in collkeys(rt) \cdot mk < rk)$

> $collkeys\!: Mrep \rightarrow$ set of Key
> $collkeys(t) \quad \triangleq$
> $\quad$ cases t of
> $\quad$ nil $\qquad\qquad\qquad\qquad\qquad \rightarrow \{\}$
> $\quad mk\text{-}Mnode(lt, mk, md, rt) \rightarrow collkeys(lt) \cup \{mk\} \cup collkeys(rt)$
> $\quad$ end

A small theory of the *Mrep* type can now be developed. Some lemmas which are stated without proof are:

*Lemma—collkeys*1

$\forall t \in Mrep \cdot collkeys(t) \in$ set of Key
(i.e. *collkeys* is total)

*Lemma—collkeys*2

$\forall mk\text{-}Mnode(lt, mk, md, rt) \in Mnode \cdot$
$\quad is\text{-}prdisj(collkeys(lt), \{mk\}, collkeys(rt))$
where:
is-prdisj: set of $X \times$ set of $X \times$ set of $X \to \mathbf{B}$

*Lemma—collkeys*3

$\forall nd \in Mnode \cdot \forall k \in collkeys(nd) \cdot$
$\quad$ let $mk\text{-}Mnode(lt, mk, md, rt) = nd$
$\quad$ in $(k < mk \;\Rightarrow\; k \in collkeys(lt)) \wedge$
$\quad\quad (mk < k \;\Rightarrow\; k \in collkeys(rt))$

The retrieve function is:

$retr\text{-}Kdm: Mrep \to Kdm$
$retr\text{-}Kdm(t) \quad \underset{\triangle}{} $
$\quad$ cases t of
$\quad$ nil $\qquad\qquad\qquad\qquad \to \{\}$
$\quad mk\text{-}Mnode(l, k, d, r) \to \bigcup\{retr\text{-}Kdm(l), \{k \mapsto d\}, retr\text{-}Kdm(r)\}$
$\quad$ end

The totality of this retrieve function relies on lemma *collkeys*2. The adequacy of *Mrep* can be argued in a way similar to *Setrep*. Another useful lemma is:

*Lemma—collkeys*4

$\forall t \in Mrep \cdot$ dom $retr\text{-}Kdm(t) = collkeys(t)$

The development of *Setrep* above employs recursive functions which are referenced in the specifications of operations. The disadvantage of this approach is that it does not lend itself to the form of recursion which is intended in the final code. In particular, the code to be presented in Chapter 10 uses by location parameters. Rather than mirror the development of *Setrep*, operation quotation is used in the development of *Mrep*. The (read only) search operation is specified:

$FINDB\ (k\colon Key)\ d\colon Data$
ext rd $t\colon Mrep$
pre $k \in collkeys(t)$
post let $mk\text{-}Mnode(lt, mk, md, rt) = t$
  in $k = mk \wedge d = md\ \vee$
  $\quad k < mk \wedge post\text{-}FINDB(k, lt, d)\ \vee$
  $\quad mk < k \wedge post\text{-}FINDB(k, rt, d)$

The proof that $FINDB$ satisfies the specification $FIND$ uses the induction rule:

$p(\mathsf{nil});$
$mk \in Key, md \in Data,\ lt, rt \in Mrep, p(lt), p(rt) \vdash$
$$\frac{\qquad\qquad\qquad\qquad p(mk\text{-}Mnode(lt, mk, md, rt))}{t \in Mrep \vdash p(t)}$$

and lemmas $collkeys3$ and $collkeys4$.

The insertion operation on $Mrep$ is specified:

$INSERTB\ (k\colon Key, d\colon Data)$
ext wr $t\colon Mrep$
pre $k \notin collkeys(t)$
post $\overleftarrow{t} = \mathsf{nil} \wedge t = mk\text{-}Mnode(\mathsf{nil}, k, d, \mathsf{nil})\ \vee$
  $\overleftarrow{t} \in Mnode\ \wedge$
  $\quad$ let $mk\text{-}Mnode(\overleftarrow{lt}, mk, md, \overleftarrow{rt}) = \overleftarrow{t}$
  $\quad$ in $k < mk\ \wedge$
  $\qquad \exists lt \in Mrep\ \cdot$
  $\qquad\qquad post\text{-}INSERTB(k, d, \overleftarrow{lt}, lt)\ \wedge$
  $\qquad\qquad t = mk\text{-}Mnode(lt, mk, md, \overleftarrow{rt})\ \vee$
  $\qquad mk < k\ \wedge$
  $\qquad\qquad \exists rt \in Mrep\ \cdot$
  $\qquad\qquad\qquad post\text{-}INSERTB(k, d, \overleftarrow{rt}, rt)\ \wedge$
  $\qquad\qquad\qquad t = mk\text{-}Mnode(\overleftarrow{lt}, mk, md, rt)$

This completes the development of operations on $Mrep$ which can now be taken as a specification of the next step of design. The tree-like objects of $Mrep$ cannot be directly constructed in a language like Pascal. Instead, each node must be created on the heap; nested trees must be represented by pointers. Pascal-like objects can be defined by:

$Root = [Ptr]$

$Heap = \mathsf{map}\ Ptr\ \mathsf{to}\ Mnoder$

$Mnoder\ ::\quad lp\!:\![Ptr]$
$\qquad\qquad\quad mk\!:\!Key$
$\qquad\qquad\quad md\!:\!Data$
$\qquad\qquad\quad rp\!:\![Ptr]$

It is clear that the *Heap* should be well-founded (cf. Section 6.3) and that all *Ptrs* contained in *Mnoders* should be contained in the domain of the *Heap*. The retrieve function can then be defined:

$retr\text{-}Mrep\!:\!Root \times Heap \rightarrow Mrep$

$retr\text{-}Mrep(r, h)\quad \triangleq$
$\qquad \mathsf{if}\ r = \mathsf{nil}$
$\qquad \mathsf{then}\quad \mathsf{nil}$
$\qquad \mathsf{else}\quad \mathsf{let}\ mk\text{-}Mnoder(lp, mk, md, rp) = h(r)$
$\qquad\qquad\qquad \mathsf{in}\ mk\text{-}Mnode(retr\text{-}Mrep(lp), mk, md, retr\text{-}Mrep(rp))$

The function:

$collkeysh\!:\!Root \times Heap \rightarrow \mathsf{set\ of}\ Key$

is an obvious derivative of *collkeys*.

The find operation on *Heap* is specified:

$FINDH\ (k\!:\!Key, p\!:\!Ptr)\ d\!:\!Data$
$\mathsf{ext\ rd}\ h\!:\!Heap$
$\mathsf{pre}\ k \in collkeysh(p, h)$
$\mathsf{post}\ \mathsf{let}\ mk\text{-}Mnoder(lp, mk, md, rp) = h(p)$
$\qquad \mathsf{in}\ k = mk \wedge d = md\ \vee$
$\qquad\quad k < mk \wedge post\text{-}FINDH(k, lp, h, d)\ \vee$
$\qquad\quad mk < k \wedge post\text{-}FINDH(k, rp, h, d)$

This is fairly simple because the pointer can be passed by value. In the insert operation, the pointer can be changed in the case that a new node is created. Thus, in addition to the obvious write access on the heap itself, the pointer is shown as an external. In the actual code, this is achieved by using a parameter passed by location. (Section 4.1 points out that the operation specification format assumes that its parameters are passed by value.) The Pascal code for this problem is given in Section 10.

$INSERTRH \; (k\!: Key, d\!: Data)$

ext wr $h\!: Heap,$ wr $p\!: Ptr$

pre $k \notin collkeysh(p, h)$

post $\overleftarrow{p} = $ nil $\wedge$

$\qquad p \notin $ dom $\overleftarrow{h} \; \wedge$

$\qquad h = \overleftarrow{h} \cup \{p \mapsto mk\text{-}Mnoder(\text{nil}, k, d, \text{nil})\} \; \vee$

$\overleftarrow{p} \neq $ nil $\wedge$

$\qquad$ let $mk\text{-}Mnoder(\overleftarrow{lp}, mk, md, \overleftarrow{rp}) = \overleftarrow{h}\,(\overleftarrow{p})$

$\qquad$ in $k < mk \; \wedge$

$\qquad\qquad (\exists hi \in Heap, lp \in Ptr \; \cdot$

$\qquad\qquad\qquad post\text{-}INSERTRH(k, d, \overleftarrow{h}, \overleftarrow{lp}, hi, lpi) \; \wedge$

$\qquad\qquad\qquad h = hi \dagger \{\overleftarrow{p} \mapsto \mu(h(\overleftarrow{p}), lp \mapsto lpi)\} \; \wedge$

$\qquad\qquad\qquad p = \overleftarrow{p}) \; \vee$

$\qquad\quad mk < k \; \wedge$

$\qquad\qquad (\exists hi \in Heap, rp \in Ptr \; \cdot$

$\qquad\qquad\qquad post\text{-}INSERTRH(k, d, \overleftarrow{h}, \overleftarrow{rp}, hi, rpi) \; \wedge$

$\qquad\qquad\qquad h = hi \dagger \{\overleftarrow{p} \mapsto \mu(h(\overleftarrow{p}), rp \mapsto rpi)\} \; \wedge$

$\qquad\qquad\qquad p = \overleftarrow{p})$

The method of developing from an abstract type to a more concrete representation should be clear. There are, however, situations in software development where a concrete interface definition is one of the reference points in a development. There is nothing essentially wrong with this situation, and the remainder of this section shows how the data reification ideas can still be applied.

The problems which can occur with interface descriptions are, however, serious. Firstly, interfaces are often recorded with far too much syntactic detail. Information on physical control blocks is sometimes described at the bit and byte level. This militates against the modern programming ideas of abstract data types. Use of the detail can lead to efficiency but almost certainly results in systems which are not maintainable. Many very large systems have made the mistake of fixing bit/byte details and an enormous penalty has resulted. In spite of the fact that this mistake is so serious, it is not the purpose of the current book to preach ideas which have long been standard practice in better organized development groups. Here, it is necessary to show only how the data reification ideas can help avoid the problem.

An even more common failing is the lack of semantics in interface descriptions. In contrast to the excessive syntactic detail, the actual meaning or effect of fields in an interface is often suggested by no more than the field names. The programming language Ada is in danger of perpetuating this problem by using the term "interface" to describe something which only has the power to define syntactic (procedure) interface questions.

Faced with a fixed concrete interface in a development, there is a series of steps which can be used to clarify an interface and to record the understanding. These steps are:

1. write an (abstract) data type with only the essential information content;

2. record the semantics with respect to this abstract interface;

3. relate the (given) concrete details to the abstraction with a retrieve function.

These steps cannot, in large applications, be performed strictly sequentially: there is a constant interplay between them.

A major application in which the author was involved concerned the development of a compiler for the PL/I language. The interest was in the back-end (object time organization and object code) issues and it was decided to take over the front-end (parser and dictionary building) of an existing compiler. The text interface had a fairly obvious linearized version of the parse tree (see Exercise 7). Variable references in the text were represented (among other things) by pointers into the dictionary. The dictionary had been designed for compactness and was a mass of special cases. The documentation was quite good on byte values but the main part of the semantics was supposed to be deduced from examples. The proposal to follow the plan set out above was met with some scepticism as to whether the time was available. Only the impossibility of getting the interface under intellectual control in any other way convinced the group. The effect was certainly worthwhile from this point of view alone. (Some of the material is available as a technical report—see Bibliography.)

Here, a simpler—but equally representative problem—is considered. A paper by Henderson and Snowdon (see Bibliography) includes the following introduction of a problem:

> A program is required to process a stream of telegrams. This stream is available as a sequence of letters, digits and blanks on some device and can be transferred in sections of predetermined

size into a buffer area where it is to be processed. The words in the telegrams are separated by sequences of blanks and each telegram is delimited by the word "zzzz". The stream is terminated by the occurrence of the empty telegram, that is a telegram with no words. Each telegram is to be processed to determine the number of chargeable words and to check for occurrences of over-length words. The words "zzzz" and "STOP" are not chargeable and words of more than twelve letters are considered over-length. The result of the processing is to be a neat listing of the telegrams, each accompanied by the word count and a message indicating the occurrence of an over-length word.

A number of unresolved questions are easy to identify and some computing scientists have used this as a criticism of the text as a specification. Although this is not an excuse, far worse documents are used as the basis of far larger systems. The debate is, however, sterile, and here the text is treated as an indication of requirements. Questions on the text fall into two broad areas. Questions about the effect (semantics) of the operations include:

- Are over-length words to be truncated in the output?

- How are over-length words to be charged?

- What output is to be printed for over-length words?

- Does the count for over-length really not count digits?

- Is a report required for the empty telegram?

- What error handling is to be provided?

Some of the questions about how the information is represented are:

- What is the meaning of "delimit"?

- What is the meaning of "sequence" (e.g. zero occurrences)?

- What determines the buffer size?

- Can words span blocks?

- What is an "empty" telegram?

- What is a "neat listing"?

• Are leading spaces allowed in records?

It is not difficult—in this case—to find a suitable abstract description of both the input and output:

$$Input = \text{seq of } Telegram$$

$$Telegram = \text{seq of } Word$$

$$Word = \text{seq of } Character$$

$$Character = Letter \cup Digit$$

$$Output = \text{seq of } Report$$

Telegram and *Word* are non-empty sequences

$$[z, z, z, z] \notin Word$$

$$
\begin{aligned}
Report \ :: \quad &tgm: Telegram \\
&count: \mathbf{N} \\
&ovlen: \mathbf{B}
\end{aligned}
$$

This abstraction ignores the details of the blanks which delimit words or the special words used to terminate telegrams. The required meaning is given by:

$ANALYZE \ (in: \text{seq of } Telegram) \ out: \text{seq of } Report$

$\text{post len } out = \text{len } in \ \wedge$

$\qquad \forall i \in \text{dom } in \ \cdot \ out(i) = analyze\text{-}telegram(in(i))$

$analyze\text{-}telegram(wordl) \quad \triangleq$

$\qquad mk\text{-}Report(wordl, charge\text{-}words(wordl), check\text{-}words(wordl))$

$charge\text{-}words(wordl) \quad \triangleq$

$\qquad \text{card } \{j \in \text{dom } wordl \mid wordl(j) \neq [\mathsf{S},\mathsf{T},\mathsf{O},\mathsf{P}]\}$

$check\text{-}words(wordl) \quad \triangleq \quad \exists w \in \text{rng } wordl \ \cdot \ \text{len } w > 12$

This has shown how the process of recording such a description can be used to document the interpretation of open semantic questions. For this author, it was also the way of generating the list of questions about the requirements. The next step is obviously to face the other part of the problem, which is the representation details. The representation can be viewed as:

Inputr = seq of *Block*

Block = seq of *Symbol*

Symbol = *Character* ∪ BLANK

The specification is completed by documenting the relationship of *Inputr* to *Input* via a retrieve function. Here, this is left as an exercise. The important messages of this approach to interfaces is both the value for uncovering imprecision and the ability to record precisely the chosen understanding. The documentation can also be an aid in implementation: separate data types can be readily identified.

One of the reasons that the Henderson and Snowdon paper has evoked so much interest is their description of how one error got into their design. Not only was this error avoided by the development based on the abstract specification, but also other errors were uncovered in the program given in the original paper.

Exercises

1. * Another representation for the equivalence relation application would be to have two different data structures. One of these would support the *TEST* operation and would store the map discussed in Section 6.1; the other would link all elements in the same equivalence class into a ring—*EQUATE* can then locate all keys in the first data structure which need updating. Specify this development and justify its correctness.

2. * A graph consists of set of nodes and arcs. An abstract representation considers an arc as an ordered pair (of node identifiers) and the whole graph as a set of arcs. Document this abstract description and define simple operations to test if an arc is present and to add an arc.

   Two possible representations are:

   (a) a two-dimensional array (where each dimension is indexed by the node identifiers) which records whether or not the relevant pairs are linked by an arc;

   (b) a one-dimensional array of pointers (indexed by the node identifiers) to linked lists of records; the non-link information in each record is the identifier of nodes to which arcs are present.

Document and justify these two representations at sensible levels of abstraction.

3. * B-trees are generalizations of binary trees. The order (say N) of a B-tree limits the branching at each node and can be chosen to achieve efficient transfers from backing store. Any (non-root) node of a B-tree has between N and $2N$ elements; in leaf nodes, these elements are pairs of key and data; for intermediate nodes, the elements are pointers to other nodes—as with binary trees, keys which guide the search are also stored at intermediate nodes. (A full description can be found in *The Ubiquitous B-tree* by D. Comer in ACM Computing Surveys, Vol. 11, No.2, pp121-137.) Document descriptions of B-trees on several levels of abstraction.

4. * Hashing provides an alternative way of storing information for rapid searching. A hash function maps *Keys* to a subset of natural numbers. If the hash function were one-to-one, this would simply be a computed address where the information (*Key/Data*) is stored. Hash functions are, in fact, many-to-one and the interesting problems concern the handling of collisions where two or more *Keys* are mapped to the same hash address. (Much of the subtlety in developing hashing techniques for particular applications concerns the minimization of collision—these aspects are not of concern here.) Describe on two levels of abstraction the general idea of hashing where records with colliding keys are placed in the "next gap".

5. * A syntax-directed editor permits a user to enter, at a terminal, a program by placing information into an abstract syntax tree. The current content of a program (and the identification of holes) is displayed by an "unparsing scheme" which relates concrete to abstract syntax. Such syntax-directed editors are table driven in that the abstract syntax and projection schemes are stored as data. Describe the general idea of syntax directed editors.

6. * Write a retrieve function for the input to the telegram analysis problem. Fix a representation for output and document its relationship to the abstraction.

7. * Choose a simple linear form (e.g. reverse Polish) for an expression language and document the relationship to a tree form for expressions.

Chapter 9

More on Data Types

> Setting up equations is like translating from one language into another.
> *G.Polya*

A number of more subtle points about data types are considered in this chapter. The approach described above is to define the data types in terms of models. This model-oriented approach presents the danger of over-specification. In particular, models can be biased towards certain implementations. A test for bias is given in Section 9.1 together with some alternative proof rules for data reification.

Section 9.2 presents an alternative way of specifying data types. The property-oriented approach is shown to be well-suited to the basic types used above. Property-oriented specifications of the sort of data types required in applications are also explored; a comparison with the model-oriented approach is included along with an attempt to define the respective roles of the two approaches.

9.1 Implementation Bias in Models

The concept of *implementation bias* is most simply introduced by example. Section 7.1 begins by introducing a specification of a queue based on objects *Queue*. A specification which defines the identical behaviour is:

$Queueb$ :: s: seq of Qel
$\qquad\qquad\quad i$: **N**
where
$inv\text{-}Queueb(mk\text{-}Queueb(s,i))$ $\triangleq$ $i \leq$ len s

$q_0 = mk\text{-}Queueb([\ ],0)$

$ENQUEUE$ $(e: Qel)$

ext wr s: seq of Qel

post $s = \overleftarrow{s} \frown [e]$

$DEQUEUE$ () $e: Qel$

ext rd s: seq of Qel, wr i: **N**

pre $i <$ len s

post $i = \overleftarrow{i} + 1 \wedge e = \overleftarrow{s}(i)$

$ISEMPTY$ () r: **B**

ext rd s: seq of Qel, rd i: **N**

post $r \Leftrightarrow (i =$ len $s)$

The model in this specification keeps unnecessary history of the queue and this is intuitively wrong. This intuitive concern can be made more formal by considering retrieve functions. A retrieve function can easily be constructed in one direction:

$retr\text{-}Queue$: $Queueb \rightarrow Queue$

$retr\text{-}Queue(mk\text{-}Queueb(s,i))$ $\triangleq$ $s(i+1,\ldots,$ len $s)$

Thus:

$retr\text{-}Queue(mk\text{-}Queueb([a,b,c,d],1) = [b,c,d]$

A retrieve function cannot be constructed in the other direction because the unnecessary history information cannot be found in $Queue$. This discloses why the problem is referred to as "implementation bias". Using the reification proof obligations given in Sections 8.1 and 8.2, the $Queueb$ model is biased towards (proving correct) implementations which retain at least as much information. An implementation which keeps even more history (e.g. the exact order of $ENQUEUE/DEQUEUE$ operations) can be proved correct: a retrieve function can be constructed to $Queueb$.

It is important to realize that the behaviour of the operations on *Queueb* is the same as that on *Queue*. Thus it is possible to show that the operations on the former model those on the latter. It is only the acceptability of the *Queueb* model as a specification which is being challenged. As an implementation, its behaviour is as required.

The bias of the *Queueb* specification is a criticism of a specific model. Is it also an indication of a weakness of the model- oriented approach to specification? There are certainly some computer scientists who have argued in this direction. The proof rules shown below permit even a biased model to be used as a starting point for development. More importantly, it is normally possible to avoid bias. Moreover, it is possible to prove that bias is absent.

The problem which is to be avoided is that an implementation is invented such that a retrieve function from its states to those of the specification cannot be constructed. This itself cannot serve as a test of a specification since it requires consideration of possible implementations. The problem with the storage of unnecessary history information in *Queueb* can, however, be described in another way: the information is unnecessary precisely because it cannot be detected by any of the available operations. The following definition is therefore given:

A model-oriented specification is based on an underlying set of states. The model is biased (with respect to a given set of operations) if there exist different elements of the set of states which cannot be distinguished by any sequence of the operations.

In terms of the example above, there is no way of distinguishing between:

$$mk\text{-}Queueb([a, b, c], 1) \quad \text{and} \quad mk\text{-}Queueb([b, c], 0)$$

The precision of this test makes it possible to use it as a proof obligation. A model is *sufficiently abstract* (to be used as a specification) providing it can be shown to be free of bias.

It is important to realize that the bias test is relative to a particular set of operations. The *Queue* model of Section 7.1 is unbiased for the collection of operations given there. However, for a different set of operations, *Queue* is a biased model. For example, if the *DEQUEUE* operation were replaced by one which only removed, but did not show, the removed value:

$REMOVE$ ()

ext wr q: $Queue$

pre $q \neq [\,]$

post $q = tl\ \overleftarrow{q}$

there is no operation which can distinguish between the queues:

$$[a, b] \qquad [b, a] \qquad [c, d]$$

An unbiased model for this collection of operations is a natural number which records the number of elements in the queue. Furthermore, if the $REMOVE$ operation is entirely discarded, the only distinction which can be detected is between empty and non-empty queues. A sufficiently abstract model for this restricted set of operations is a single Boolean value.

The test for bias is a relatively recent discovery. It has been applied to a number of specifications which were written without its guidance. The experience is that very few specifications were found to have been biased. (Even those which were revolve around rather subtle problems.) It is therefore not envisaged that this proof obligation need normally be discharged in a formal way. The concept of sufficient abstractness is more likely to be useful in general discussions about alternative models.

One cause of failure is where an invariant on the specification state has been overlooked.

It must be understood that there is not a unique sufficiently abstract model for any particular application. Different models can pass the bias test. With such a class of models, it will be possible to construct retrieve functions in either direction between any pair[1].

Among the class of unbiased models, some are more complex than others. Consider, for example, a problem in which a set can be used to define the needed operations. A model based on a list is likely to be biased—state values might, for instance, store a history of the order of operations which cannot be detected. It is, however, possible to reduce the equivalent states to single values by adding an invariant. If the elements of a list are required to be in a particular order (e.g. numeric order), there is then a one-to-one correspondance between the lists (with invariants) and sets. The restricted lists are not biased—but the model is certainly more complicated.

---

[1]Technically, the unbiased models form an isomorphism class—they partition the possible behaviour histories into equal sets.

This appears to suggest another criterion for the choice of models: in general, it is better to choose a state which minimizes the need for invariants. There are, however, exceptions to this guideline, and the reader is reminded of the discussion in Section 8.3 about the use of more than one isomorphic model. One such model may have a minimum invariant while another might be more complicated; if the more complicated model makes some operations easier to define, it can pay its way.

All of the above comments about bias relate to the choice of models for specifications. Reification certainly brings in bias. In fact, the commitments which are made by the designer are intended to introduce implementation bias. At each successive step of data reification, the range of models (which can be justified using retrieve functions) is intentionally reduced. The designer's goal is to arrive at a final, single implementation.

The remainder of this section is concerned with proof rules for handling development from biased specifications. There are two reasons for what may appear to be a *volte-face*. Firstly, bias may occur by accident. Although the point is made above that specifications do have to be rewritten, not all industrial environments are prepared to accept this austere advice. It is shown below that there are ways of handling development from biased specifications. Some users of formal methods may choose to employ the more general reification rules.

The other reason for presenting ways of handling the more general situation is that there are places where a specification which is technically biased should be used! The most common situation where (technical) bias is justified is when the full extent of the set of operations is unknown. Michael Jackson presents examples in his books (see Bibliography) in which attempts to tailor the state too closely to a particular collection of operations makes subsequent extension all but impossible. It is argued in Section 8.3 that the state represents the essence of the operations. When the operations are not a fixed collection, the state must be chosen to be the essence of the application itself. The extent to which this rather vague goal is achieved, will govern the difficulty of subsequent modifications.

There are some cases where a biased state can lead to a clearer specification than an unbiased one. Such cases are rare. An example is forming the average and standard deviation of a collection of values. An obvious specification first stores all of the numbers; to avoid bias, a specification has to rely on subtle properties of the definitions.

There is one more case where the state of a specification has more information that that of correct implementations. This is the most technical of the cases. It is sometimes necessary for the state of the specification to contain information which defines the range of non-determinacy. An implementation which resolves the non-determinacy in a particular way may need less information in the state. A representative example of this situation can be built around a symbol table. A specification can use the state:

$$Symtab = \mathsf{map}\ Sym\ \mathsf{to}\ Addr$$

$$Addr = \mathbf{N}$$

A non-deterministic operation to allocate addresses is:

$ALLOC\ (s: Sym)\ a: Addr$

ext wr $t: Symtab$

pre $s \notin \mathsf{dom}\ t$

post $a \notin \mathsf{rng}\ \overleftarrow{t} \wedge t = \overleftarrow{t} \cup \{s \mapsto a\}$

An implementation of this specification can use:

$Symtabrep = \mathsf{seq\ of}\ Sym$
where
$inv\text{-}Symtabrep(t) \quad \triangleq \quad is\text{-}uniques(t)$

with:

$ALLOCR\ (s: Sym)\ a: Addr$

ext wr $t: Symtabrep$

pre $s \notin \mathsf{rng}\ t$

post $t = \overleftarrow{t} \frown [s] \wedge a = \mathsf{len}\ t$

An attempt to use the reification rules of Chapter 8 may lead to the retrieve function:

$retr\text{-}Symtab: Symtabrep \rightarrow Symtab$

$retr\text{-}Symtab(t) \quad \triangleq \quad \{t(i) \mapsto i \mid i \in \mathsf{dom}\ t\}$

But this clearly shows that *Symtabrep* is not adequate: any value of *Symtab* with gaps in the allocated addresses cannot be represented. The need to provide a general model in the specification was to express the potential non-determinacy; the decision to yield particular addresses in the implementation renders this information redundant.

One way of handling this situation is to generate a special proof obligation for steps of development which reduce non-determinacy in this way. Although straightforward, this avenue is not pursued here since the more general proof rule covers this somewhat rare case.

It has been made clear that the behaviour of a data type is what is to be specified and verified. But there are steps of reification which cannot be proved correct by the rules of Chapter 8 even though the putative implementation manifests the same behaviour as the specification. Thus, it is clear that the given rules are too weak in some sense[2]. Although they cover a very large percentage of the development steps which one is likely to meet, it is useful to know the more general rule.

The key to the more general rule is to realize that the retrieve function must revert to a relation. The proof rules of Chapter 8 capitalized on the one-to-many situation brought about by the lack of bias. If this restriction no longer applies, the many-to-many situation can be represented by:

$$rel: Abs \times Rep \to \mathbf{B}$$

Suppose the biased $Queueb$ from the beginning of this section were to have been used in a specification; the relation to $Queue$ (now taken as an implementation!) could be recorded by:

$$rel\text{-}Queue: Queueb \times Queue \to \mathbf{B}$$
$$rel\text{-}Queue(mk\text{-}Queueb(l, i), s) \quad \triangleq \quad l(i+1, \ldots, \text{len } l) = s$$

There is no adequacy proof obligation. The domain rule is similar to that of Chapter 8:

$$rel\text{-}Queue(qb, q) \wedge pre\text{-}OPA(qb) \Rightarrow pre\text{-}OPR(q)$$

Notice that OPA works on $Queueb$ and OPR on $Queue$. The result rule is:

$$rel\text{-}Queue(\overleftarrow{qb}, \overleftarrow{q}) \wedge pre\text{-}OPA(\overleftarrow{qb}) \wedge post\text{-}OPR(\overleftarrow{q}, q) \Rightarrow$$
$$\exists qb \in Queueb \cdot post\text{-}OPA(\overleftarrow{qb}, qb) \wedge rel\text{-}Queue(qb, q)$$

The proofs of these results are left as exercises. In general, they become more difficult than proofs using the rules of Chapter 8, if for no other reason than

---

[2]They are sufficient but not necessary.

the appearance of the existential quantifier[3]. It is also necessary to handle initial states—the rule should be obvious from the corresponding rule in Chapter 8.

There are other ways of handling situations where bias occurs in the specification. In early work on formal development of compilers, Peter Lucas (see Bibliography) showed how "ghost variables" can be erected in the implementation state. These variables initially retain any redundant information but can be disposed of once there are no essential references to them.

Exercises

1. Justify *Queueb* as an implementation with respect to the *Queue* specification given in Section 7.1.

2. Design an implementation of the queue operations which retains the full history of the queue. Since this is even more information than is contained in *Queueb*, it is possible to use the (biased) *Queueb* operations as a specification. Sketch a justification which illustrates this fact.

3. Justify *Queue* as an implementation of the specification *Queueb*—since this latter is biased, the more general proof rule of this section must be used.

4. Produce a biased specification of a stack (cf. Exercise 2 of Section 7.3).

5. The first conjunct in *invp* (Section 4.3) bars an empty set from a partition. One reason for needing this is the equivalence relation specification mentioned in Section 4.4. Discuss the problem in terms of bias.

6. Outline the proof of the operation *ALLOC* for the *Symtabrep* representation of *Symtab*. The proof obligation will have to use the more general rule.

---

[3]It is, however, the existential quantifier in the result rule which ensures that this more general rule covers the sort of non-deterministic situation which arose in the symbol table example.

7. * It is standard practice to define the rational numbers as a pair of integers. Set up such a model and define some functions (e.g. addition of rationals). Discuss the problem of bias in this, functional, context.

9.2 Property-Oriented Specifications of Data Types

The preceding section should have allayed some fears about being forced into over-specification in the model-oriented approach. But the concern has been fruitful in that it is one of the stimuli which have led computer scientists to develop a way of specifying data types without using a model at all. The idea goes back to the concept of a data type being a pattern of behaviour. The *property-oriented* approach to specifying data types defines properties of these behaviours by a series of equations[4].

This chapter does not aim to provide a complete course on the property-oriented approach. This section explores the presentations, given in Chapters 4 to 7 above, for the basic data types, and discusses the role of property-oriented specifications in data types required in applications.

It has already been seen that the equations for sequences etc. present a convenient basis for proofs. In Chapter 7 the generating operators are given as:

$[\,]$: seq of X

$cons$: $X \times$ seq of $X \to$ seq of X

There, these generators are closed off by an induction rule; in a property-oriented specification, the induction rule is subsumed by the *interpretation* which is ascribed to the equations.

The properties of concatenation are given by the equations:

$_\frown{}_{}$: seq of $X \times$ seq of $X \to$ seq of X

$[\,]^\frown t = t$

$cons(e, t_1)^\frown t_2 = cons(e, t_1 {}^\frown t_2)$

Viewed innocently, the equalities in these equations indicate that terms of one form can be rewritten into another form. In the *initial interpretation*, the objects denoted by terms are equal exactly when the terms can be proven

---

[4]What is referred to here as the property-oriented approach is known in the literature under a number of different names: "(equational) presentations of algebras"; "the axiomatic approach" (viewing the equations as axioms); or even "*the* algebraic approach"

to be equal from the equations. This appears to be a very plausible position but it is not the only one possible. In fact, the consequence that inequalities can be established only by showing that a term cannot be deduced is extremely aggravating.

The reader should remember that Chapter 4 introduced the set constructors ($\{\}, \oplus$) by equations which, apart from the symbols, are identical to those given above for sequences. But clearly the sets denoted by the terms:

$$e_1 \oplus (e_2 \oplus \{\}) \quad \text{and} \quad e_2 \oplus (e_1 \oplus (e_1 \oplus \{\}))$$

should be equal. In the initial interpretation, it is necessary to add extra equations in order to ensure that term equality defines object equality. The need for these equations can be avoided in the alternative final interpretation of such equations. In the *final interpretation*, objects are assumed to be equal unless the terms which they denote can be proved unequal. The normal way to show that terms are unequal is by using some external (already understood) type. In the final interpretation for sets, there would be no need to add the absorptive and commutative equations for $\oplus$. It would, however, be necessary to add some operators in order to prevent the complete collapse of the value space. In this case the membership operator could be used (see below).

To make these points clear, the specification of three data types (sequences, bags and sets) are considered under the two interpretations. A useful concept in this discussion is a word algebra. Given some set of operators, the *word algebra* is the set of all terms which can be generated such that each application respects the types. (This set of terms could be formalized using an abstract syntax.)

With the equations:

null: *Colln*

$\oplus: X \times Colln \rightarrow Colln$

the initial model of *Colln* is exactly the sequence values. In fact, the word algebra of these generators can be thought of as providing a model on which other operators (e.g. concatenation) can be defined. The initial interpretation of these equations is a natural match for sequences. The operator:

$\_ + \_: Colln \times Colln \rightarrow Colln$

null $+ c = c$

$(e \oplus c_1) + c_2 = e \oplus (c_1 + c_2)$

automatically becomes sequence concatenation.

The same generators can be used for the bags, but here the word algebra for the operators above needs breaking into equivalence classes. Since bags do not have the concept of the order of their elements, any terms which differ only by position denote the same objects. This fact can be captured by the single equation:

$$e_1 \oplus (e_2 \oplus b) = e_2 \oplus (e_1 \oplus b)$$

This equation can be used (cf. Section 4.3) to show the commutative properties of bag operators defined over these generators (e.g. + on bags becomes union). In some sense, the initial interpretation is not such a good match for bags. The values now correspond to sets of words. One possibility is to think of choosing a representative member of each equivalence class (e.g. relying on some ordering over the elements).

For sets, the equivalence classes have to be made yet coarser. The necessary effect can again be achieved by adding one more equation:

$$e \oplus (e \oplus s) = e \oplus s$$

One can picture what has been done by considering the set of all possible words formed from null/$\oplus$ and partitioning this set into equivalence classes as indicated by the equations defining the commutativity and absorption of $\oplus$. To each such (infinite) set of terms, there corresponds one set value which is the value denoted by each of the terms in the set.

In the final interpretation, the equivalence classes of terms are as coarse as possible. Thus, the final interpretation comes closest to matching sets. However, there is nothing about the generating operators which prevents even the terms:

$$e_1 \oplus \text{null} \qquad \text{null}$$

from being treated as equal. The danger is that all terms are in one equivalence class. This is avoided by adding an operator which yields values in another type. For sets, an appropriate operator is membership. Equations for:

$$\_ \in \_ : X \times Colln \rightarrow \mathbf{B}$$

which show:

$$\neg(e \in \text{null}) \qquad and \qquad e \in (e \oplus s)$$

result in the appropriate algebra.

For bags (cf. Section 6.3), the equivalence relation on words must be made finer. This can be done by replacing the membership operator with:

$$count\colon X \times Colln \to \mathbf{N}$$

$$count(e, \mathsf{null}) = 0$$
$$count(e_1, (e_2 \oplus b)) = count(e_1, b) \qquad e_1 \neq e_2$$
$$count(e_1, (e_1 \oplus b)) = count(e_1, b) + 1$$

The equivalence class so defined still has:

$$e_1 \oplus (e_2 \oplus t) \qquad\qquad e_2 \oplus (e_1 \oplus t)$$

in the same partition since they cannot be proved unequal. To make *Colln* behave, in the final interpretation, like sequences, one could add:

$$\mathsf{hd}\_\colon Colln \to X$$

$$\mathsf{hd}(e \oplus c) = e$$

There are then at least two interpretations of a set of equations. Clearly, if specifications of data types are to be given by properties, the interpretation must be defined.

The choice is closely related to the question of how one shows that an implementation is correct with respect to a property-oriented specification. The obvious approach to such proofs might be to check that all terms which are in the same equivalence classes denote the same value in the implementation. Chapter 8 shows that, in an implementation, there may be several representations for the same abstract object. The equality of terms cannot, therefore, be used as the criterion for the correctness of implementations.

The (equivalence classes of) terms are, however, the basis for such implementation proofs. Where, as for sequences, the equivalence classes contain exactly one term, it is possible to use a style of implementation proof similar to that of Chapter 8 (i.e. based on retrieve functions). In the case that the equivalence classes contain more than one element, another technique is required. The basis of this technique is to define a homomorphism from the set of terms to the implementation. This is like a retrieve function in reverse. It can always be constructed (at least in the deterministic case) since the word algebra is the finest possible partition. The proof obligation is, then, to show that the equivalence classes represented by the equations are respected.

The remainder of this section considers the extent to which the property-oriented approach can be applied to specifications of applications. Property-oriented specifications are given by a signature part and a set of equations. The *signature* defines the syntactic information about the functions. The *equations* fix the semantics of the functions.

Just as the factorial program is a standard example for program proof methods, the stack is the standard example for data type specifications. The signature part of a property-oriented specification is:

init: $\to$ *Stack*
push: $\mathbf{N} \times$ *Stack* $\to$ *Stack*
top: *Stack* $\to (\mathbf{N} \cup$ ERROR$)$
remove: *Stack* $\to$ *Stack*
isempty: *Stack* $\to \mathbf{B}$

Several comments are in order. The standard texts on algebra consider functions rather than (what are called in this book) operations. It is possible to generalize functions to return more than one result and then operations can be viewed as functions which receive and deliver an extra (state) value. Here, the operation *POP* (cf. Section 7.3) has been split into two functions (i.e. top, remove). Another restriction is that functions are deterministic. Thus, the post-condition idea does not have an immediate counterpart here. Nor, at first sight, do the pre-conditions and their role in defining partial functions. There is a considerable literature on the algebraic treatment of errors in algebraic presentations of data types. In this section, special error values are used.

The semantics of the stack functions are fixed by the equations:

$top(init()) =$ ERROR
$top(push(i, s)) = i$
$remove(init()) = init()$
$remove(push(i, s)) = s$
$isempty(init()) =$ true
$isempty(push(i, s)) =$ false

Only the first and third of these equations should require comment. The third is somewhat artificial in that it extends the domain of *remove* to avoid introducing an error value for stacks. The first shows when it is not possible to generate a natural-number result from *top*.

When the restrictions implied by the comments above are acceptable, one might prefer a property-oriented to a model-oriented specification because a

definition without a model would appear to avoid problems like implementation bias. As is shown below, however, it is not always straightforward to
find a property-oriented specification.

The reader would have no difficulty in providing a model-oriented specification of the above stacks. Nor would there be any difficulty in showing the
changes required to define a queue. The signature of the property-oriented
specification is also easy to change:

$$init: \rightarrow Queue$$
$$enq: \mathbf{N} \times Queue \rightarrow Queue$$
$$first: Queue \rightarrow \mathbf{N}$$
$$deq: Queue \rightarrow Queue$$
$$isempty: Queue \rightarrow \mathbf{B}$$

The changes to the equations are, however, less obvious. Clearly:

$$first(enq(e, init())) = e$$

but this covers only half of the corresponding stack equation (the second
above). The remaining case must be specified:

$$first(enq(e_1, enq(e_2, q))) = first(enq(e_2, q))$$

A similar split is required for:

$$deq(enq(e, init())) = init()$$
$$deq(enq(e_1, enq(e_2, q))) = enq(e_1, deq(enq(e_2, q)))$$

This second equation is particularly disappointing since it has the feeling of
recreating the queue in a very operational way, whereas a state automatically
defines an equivalence over the histories.

In fact property-oriented specifications can be thought of as being built
on models. The model is the word algebra of the generating functions. This,
in some sense, has more mathematical economy than introducing a separate
model. But predetermining the model in this way has the disadvantage
that it is sometimes less convenient than others. For stacks the model is
convenient; for queues it is less so.

It is also possible that the generating functions do not provide an unbiased model. An example can be constructed for the integers with 0 and
succ (as for the natural numbers) and a general *minus* operator: there are
then many terms corresponding to each negative number.

The generators can be taken as guidance to the equations which are needed. The specific choice of equations is, however, a task requiring some mathematical sophistication. For example, sets could be introduced via the union operator and its properties. Another example is apparent if one considers the wide range of axiomatizations of propositional calculus.

There are also some technical points which must be considered. A set of equations (axioms) must be shown to be consistent and complete. There are also data types which cannot be characterized by a finite set of equations (Veloso's stack—cf. Exercise 2(d) in Section 7.3—is an example).

Rather than criticize the property-oriented approach, the intention here is to determine the correct roles for property-oriented and model-oriented specifications. It would be useful if all of the data types which were to be used in other specifications were given property-oriented specifications. This, basically, has been done in Chapters 4 to 7. The advantages of this approach include its firm mathematical framework, which is particularly needed to define type parameterization. Such specifications should, however, be constructed with great care and—at least—checked by a mathematician. The model-oriented approach can, in contrast, be used relatively safely for specifications of applications which are to be implemented (e.g. a database system). The state model itself can provide considerable insight into a system and makes it possible to consider operations separately. Given an understanding of the concept of implementation bias, it should be possible to provide model-oriented specifications which are sufficiently abstract.

A number of examples above have shown how properties can be deduced from a model-oriented specification. Such properties can be used as a check against the intuitive requirements for a system. This section shows that sets of properties can be completed in a way which elevates them to a property-oriented specification. This book adopts the position that the effort required to do this is rarely justified for applications[5].

Exercises

1. Present a property-oriented specification of maps.

2. The first paper to introduce the idea of abstract syntax was by John Mc Carthy. In that paper (what are called here) make-functions and

---

[5]The respective roles suggested here correspond closely to those for denotational and axiomatic semantics of programming languages.

selectors were presented by their properties. Experiment with this idea on some abstract syntax.

3. It is possible to characterize the equivalence-relation specification by a property-oriented specification. Write an appropriate signature and set of equations.

Chapter 10

Operation Decomposition

> Make haste slowly, for the man who manages a matter safely and with no mistakes is better than one who is rash and overconfident.
> *Octavius Augustus*

It is proposed above that specifications be built around abstract states with each operation being specified by pre- and post-conditions. Chapter 8 describes techniques by which abstract objects (particularly states) are reified onto data types which are available in the implementation language. The operations are, however, still specified: their pre- and post-conditions say what should be done and not how to do it. Post-conditions are not—in general—executable.

The process of *operation decomposition* develops implementations (for operations) in terms of the primitives available in the language and support software. Thus, a specified operation might be decomposed into a Pascal while loop. The body of the loop might, in a simple case, contain a few assignment statements; in larger problems the body might be an operation whose specification is recorded for subsequent development. Thus operation decomposition is normally an iterative design process.

A design can be presented as a combination of (specified) sub-problems. A *compositional* development method permits the verification of a design in terms of the specification of its (syntactic) sub-programs. Thus, one step of development is independent of subsequent steps in the sense that any implementation of a sub-program can be used to form the implementation of the specification which gave rise to the sub-specification. In a non-compositional

247

development method, the correctness of one step of development might depend on the subsequent development of the sub-programs.

The control constructs (e.g. while) can be thought of as combinators for specifications. The specific combinators available vary from one language to another. Here fairly general forms of the main combinators for structured coding are discussed. It is interesting to note that this is the first place in this book that there is a clear commitment to procedural programming languages. Although operations are introduced in Chapter 4, all of the ideas of using abstract objects could be employed in the specification of functional programs—the data refinement technique could be applied to the arguments and results of functions.

As the reader would by now expect, the process of operation decomposition gives rise to proof obligations. Section 10.1 explains the proof obligations and exhibits a style in which programs can be annotated with their correctness arguments. There are similarities between such texts and the natural deduction style of proof used in the preceding chapters. Ways in which the proof ideas can be used in the development of programs are discussed in Section 10.2.

The placing of the material on operation decomposition reflects the fact that it applies to the later stages of the design process. Other textbooks treat this material at far greater length—normally at the expense of adequate discussion of data abstraction and reification. The reader who wishes to pursue the material on operation decomposition is recommended to follow through one of the books listed in the Bibliography using the proof methods described in this chapter. The majority of the examples in this chapter are arithmetic; some of the non-numeric applications from above are considered at the end of the chapter.

10.1   Program Proofs

This section presents proof rules[1] for some simple programming language constructs. The general form of these rules is similar to those of logic. Here, the conditions under which a rule can be applied require that certain properties hold for sub-operations and the conclusions are that (other) properties

---

[1]The proof rules which are required in this book differ from the standard Hoare-logic (see Bibliography) because of the use here of post-conditions of two states. It is, in part, the form of these rules which prompted the decision to mark initial values with a hook (rather than priming the final values).

hold for the appropriate combinations of the sub-operations.

The proof rules facilitate proofs that pieces of program satisfy specifications. Thus it can be shown that:

> if $i < 0$ then $i, j := -i, -j$ else skip

satisfies:

> $MAKEPOS$
>
> ext wr $i: \mathbf{Z}$, wr $j: \mathbf{Z}$
>
> pre true
>
> post $0 \leq i \wedge i * j = \overleftarrow{i} * \overleftarrow{j}$

The meaning of the multiple assignment is simply that the list of expressions in the right-hand side is evaluated and then these values are assigned to the variables on the left-hand side. There is an obvious restriction that the same variable must not occur in more than one left-hand side.

For small examples, it is convenient to record the specification and its implementation together:

> $MAKEPOS$
>
> ext wr $i: \mathbf{Z}$, wr $j: \mathbf{Z}$
>
> pre true
>
> > if $i < 0$ then $i, j := -i, -j$ else skip
>
> post $0 \leq i \wedge i * j = \overleftarrow{i} * \overleftarrow{j}$

Such an annotated program is written when the code has been shown to satisfy the specification. The name of the operation and the externals line are sometimes omitted when they are obvious from context.

A natural extension of this style is to record specifications for sub-operations—rather than (just) their code; see Figure 10.1. This can be read as saying that the composition of the two sub-operations $MAKEPOS$ and $POSMULT$ would satisfy the specification of $MULT$. The sub-operations are not (yet) coded—rather, their specifications are given. The proof rule for sequential execution is discussed below.

When whole programs are presented in this way, the effect is intentionally similar to natural deduction proofs. The program code can be thought of as an argument from the assumptions (pre/from) to the conclusion (post/infer). Nesting plays a similar role in the two styles of presentation. There are, however, some important differences which are discussed at the end of this section.

$MULT$
ext wr $i, j, m: \mathbf{Z}$
pre true

$\quad MAKEPOS$
$\quad$ ext wr $i, j: \mathbf{Z}$
$\quad$ pre true
$\quad$ post $i \geq 0 \wedge i * j = \overleftarrow{i} * \overleftarrow{j}$

$\quad ;$

$\quad POSMULT$
$\quad$ pre $i \geq 0$
$\quad$ post $m = \overleftarrow{i} * \overleftarrow{j}$
post $m = \overleftarrow{i} * \overleftarrow{j}$

Figure 10.1: Example of Specifications in Place of Code

There are proof rules governing valid proofs which are somewhat similar to the deduction rules for logic. Broadly, there is one proof rule for each programming construct. In order to present the proof rules[2] in a compact way, the pre- and post-conditions are written in braces before and after the piece of code to which they relate—thus:

$$\{pre\} S \{post\}$$

Notice that this is using the braces as in Pascal comments and has nothing to do with sets. It is sometimes necessary to use information from a pre-condition in the post-condition. Decorating P with a hook to denote a logical expression which is the same as P except that all free variables are decorated with a hook, the relevant proof rule is:

$$\frac{\{P\} S \{R\}}{\{P\} S \{\overleftarrow{P} \wedge R\}}$$

Thus, for example, from:

pre $fn = 1$

post $fn = \overleftarrow{fn} * \overleftarrow{n}!$

---

[2]Readers who are familiar with the original form of Hoare-logic should be reassured that the assertions written here are for total correctness: termination is required for all states satisfying *pre*.

it follows that:

pre $fn = 1$

post $fn = \overline{fn} * \overleftarrow{n}! \wedge \overleftarrow{fn} = 1$

or:

pre $fn = 1$

post $fn = \overleftarrow{n}!$

Notice that the hooking of P (and thus its free variables) is crucial—it is not true that, in the final state:

$$fn = 1$$

The most basic way of combining two operations is to execute them in sequence. It would be reasonable to expect that the first operation must leave the state in a situation where the pre-condition of the second operation is satisfied. In order to write this, a distinction must be made between the relational and single-state properties guaranteed by the first statement. The names of the truth-valued functions have been chosen as a reminder of the distinction between:

$$P: \Sigma \to \mathbf{B}$$
$$R: \Sigma \times \Sigma \to \mathbf{B}$$

Writing:

$$R_1 \mid R_2$$

for:

$$\exists \sigma_i \cdot R_1(\overleftarrow{\sigma}, \sigma_i) \wedge R_2(\sigma_i, \sigma)$$

the sequence rule is:

$$\frac{\{P_1\} S_1 \{P_2 \wedge R_1\}, \ \{P_2\} S_2 \{R_2\}}{\{P_1\} S_1; S_2 \{R_1 \mid R_2\}}$$

An example of an application of this rule is given above in the implementation of *MULT* by composing *MAKEPOS* and *POSMULT*. The post-condition of *MAKEPOS* includes, as its first conjunct, the pre-condition of *POSMULT* (cf. P_2 in the rule); P_1 of the rule is true in this case; the (remainder of) *post-MAKEPOS* can be written as:

$$\textit{post-MAKEPOS}(\overleftarrow{\imath}\,,\overleftarrow{\jmath}\,,\overleftarrow{m},i,j,m) \;\;\triangleq\;\; i*j = \overleftarrow{\imath}\,*\,\overleftarrow{\jmath} \wedge m = \overleftarrow{m}$$

The non-appearance of m in the external clause justifies the second conjunct. Also:

$$\textit{post-POSMULT}(\overleftarrow{\imath}\,,\overleftarrow{\jmath}\,,\overleftarrow{m},i,j,m) \;\;\triangleq\;\; m = \overleftarrow{\imath}\,*\,\overleftarrow{\jmath}$$

Thus:

$$\textit{post-MAKEPOS} \mid \textit{post-POSMULT}$$

becomes:

$$\exists i_i, j_i, m_i \cdot i_i * j_i = \overleftarrow{\imath}\,*\,\overleftarrow{\jmath} \wedge m_i = \overleftarrow{m} \wedge m = i_i * j_i$$

from which:

$$m = \overleftarrow{\imath}\,*\,\overleftarrow{\jmath}$$

follows.

In practice, it is not normally necessary to proceed formally with such proofs. It becomes rather easy, with practice, to check an annotated text like that for *MULT*. The only care required is the association of the hooked variables with the values at the beginning of the appropriate operation. A good visual check is given by the nesting. The generalization to a sequence of more than two statements is straightforward.

The proof rule for conditional statements is:

$$\frac{\{P \wedge B\}\,TH\,\{R\},\ \{P \wedge \neg B\}EL\{R\}}{\{P\}\ \textsf{if}\ B\ \textsf{then}\ TH\ \textsf{else}\ EL\{R\}}$$

A simple example can again be taken from the multiplication example:

MAKEPOS
ext wr $i,j\colon \mathbf{Z}$
pre true
    If $i < 0$
    then   pre $i < 0$
            post $i = -\overleftarrow{\imath} \wedge j = -\overleftarrow{\jmath} \wedge i \geq 0$
    else   pre $i \geq 0$
            post $i = \overleftarrow{\imath} \wedge j = \overleftarrow{\jmath} \wedge i \geq 0$
post $i \geq 0 \wedge i * j = \overleftarrow{\imath}\,*\,\overleftarrow{\jmath}$

Formally, this argument uses—in addition to the rule for conditional—a rule which permits stronger pre-conditions or weaker post-conditions:

$$\frac{\{P\}S\{RR\},\ PP\ \Rightarrow\ P,\ RR\ \Rightarrow\ R}{\{PP\}S\{R\}}$$

The proof obligation[3] for iteration—as would be expected—is the most interesting. The rule is:

$$\frac{\{P \wedge B\}S\{P \wedge R\}}{\{P\}\ \text{while}\ B\ \text{do}\ S\{P \wedge \neg B \wedge R^*\}}$$

R is required to be well-founded. The logical expression R might anyway be irreflexive, for example:

$$x < \overleftarrow{x}$$

Since the body of the loop might not be executed at all, the state might not be changed by the while loop. Thus the overall post-condition can only assume R^* which is the reflexive closure of R—for example:

$$x \leq \overleftarrow{x}$$

There is a significant advantage in requiring that R be well-founded (and thus irreflexive) since the above proof obligation then establishes termination. The rest of this rule should be easy to understand. The expression P is an invariant which is true after any number (including zero!) iterations of the loop body. This is, in fact, just a special use of data type invariants. Notice that such an invariant could fail to be satisfied within the body of the loop. The falseness of B after the loop follows immediately from the meaning of the loop construct.

Returning again to the multiplication example, *POSMULT* might be implemented as in Figure 10.2. The reader should check carefully how the terms in these logical expressions relate to the proof rule. Notice that the rel is well-founded, since i is always positive and cannot be decreased indefinitely (cf. inv).

The above implementation is slow in that it is linear in the value of i. Using the ability of a binary computer to detect even/odd numbers (by checking the least significant bit) and to multiply/divide by two (by shifting),

---

[3]These proof obligations have all been justified with respect to the satisfaction notion.

POSMULT
ext wr $i, j, m: \mathbf{Z}$
pre $i \geq 0$

    $m := 0$

    ;

    pre $i \geq 0$

        while $i \neq 0$ do
        inv $i \geq 0$

            $i, m := i - 1, m + j$

        rel $m + i * j = \overleftarrow{m} + \overleftarrow{i} * \overleftarrow{j} \wedge i < \overleftarrow{i}$

      post $m = \overleftarrow{m} + \overleftarrow{i} * \overleftarrow{j}$

post $m = \overleftarrow{i} * \overleftarrow{j}$

Figure 10.2: Development for Multiplication Example

POSMULT
ext wr $i, j, m: \mathbf{Z}$
pre $i \geq 0$

    $m := 0$

    ;

    pre $i \geq 0$

        while $i \neq 0$ do
        inv $i \geq 0$

            ext wr $i, j: \mathbf{Z}$
            pre $i \neq 0$

                while *is-even*(i) do
                inv $i \geq 1$

                    $i, j := i/2, j * 2$

                rel $i * j = \overleftarrow{i} * \overleftarrow{j} \wedge i < \overleftarrow{i}$

              post $i * j = \overleftarrow{i} * \overleftarrow{j} \wedge i \leq \overleftarrow{i}$
            ;

            $m, i := m + j, i - 1$

        rel $m + i * j = \overleftarrow{m} + \overleftarrow{i} * \overleftarrow{j} \wedge i < \overleftarrow{i}$

      post $m = \overleftarrow{m} + \overleftarrow{i} * \overleftarrow{j}$

post $m = \overleftarrow{i} * \overleftarrow{j}$

Figure 10.3: Alternative Development for Multiplication Example

an algorithm which takes time proportional to the logarithm (base 2) of i is shown in Figure 10.3. The outer loop of these two algorithms is the same. It should now be clear why the rel clause is written so as not to determine the precise amount by which i is decreased.

The comparison is made above between annotated program texts and natural deduction proofs. Although this similarity can be useful, it is important to notice the differences. In the program texts, the same expression denotes different things in different places. The effect of assignment statements is to destroy so-called "referential transparency". It is therefore *not* possible to simply refer to any earlier line in a text in the same way as is done in natural deduction proofs.

It would be reasonable, at this point, to discuss how the inv/rel expressions are discovered. A path different from the discovery of proofs from code is planned for the next section, and this discussion is thus avoided. It is, however, already possible to observe that the proof step is, in some sense, the inverse of the program design activity. As such it serves as a check in the same way that differentiation of an expression derived by integration is a standard check in the infinitesimal calculus.

Another interesting comparison is between the type checking in high-level languages and proofs. The proofs here are using logical expressions as assertions. The type information associated with variables in, for example, Pascal also provides assertions about the values of variables. The type checking performed by a compiler is simply a check that the type assertions are justified. Here the assertions needed go beyond what can be checked by a compiler. In fact, the sub-range information in Pascal is also not—in general—checkable.

Exercises

1. Complete the annotations in the following program:

pre $j \geq 0$

    $t := 0; r := i$

    ;

    pre $t \leq j$

        while $t \neq j$ do

        inv ?

            $t := t + 1;$

            $r := r + 1$

      rel ?

    post $r = \overleftarrow{i} + \overleftarrow{j}$

post $r = \overleftarrow{i} + \overleftarrow{j}$

2. Create annotations for the following program:

pre $j \geq 0$

    $r := i$

    ;

    pre ?

        while $j \neq 0$ do

        inv ?

            $j := j - 1;$

            $r := r + 1$

      rel ?

    post ?

post $r = \overleftarrow{i} + \overleftarrow{j}$

10.2 Design by Decomposition

The preceding section introduces the decomposition proof rules by showing their use on given programs. This section shows how the proof obligations can be used to stimulate program design steps. It is, however, important that the reader is not led to expect too much from this idea. Design requires intuition and cannot, in general, be automated. What is offered is a framework into which the designer's commitments can be placed. If done with care, the verification then represents almost no extra burden. Even so, false steps of design cannot be avoided in the sense that even a verified decision can lead to a blind alley (e.g. a decomposition which has unacceptable performance implications). If this happens, there is no choice but to reconsider the design decision which led to the problem. Once again, what is being offered is a framework into which a final design explanation can be fitted. This section aims only to show that the need for verification can also help the design process.

An obvious example of the way in which a proof rule can help a designer's thinking about decomposition is given by the rule for sequence—the assertion P_2 fixes an interface between the two sub-operations. The discussion of the factorial example in Section 4.1 indicates that there are advantages in not making such interfaces unnecessarily restrictive. The choice of a general pre-condition for the second operation can result in the specification—and eventual implementation—of a piece of software which has applicability outside the context of the first operation. Such meaningful decompositions are to be sought in all cases of design.

The design problems presented by iterative constructs are more interesting. Here, judicious use of the rel/inv clauses can lead to the specification of the loop body. The reader's experience with the exercises of the preceding section may have already suggested that loops with and without temporary variables differ. In the first exercise the overall post-condition is:

$$r = \overleftarrow{i} + \overleftarrow{j}$$

The design decision to introduce a temporary variable suggests setting up the relation:

$$r = i + t$$

This is easy to establish by initialization and can be used as a loop invariant. The relation need, in this case, only ensure that i and j are unchanged (this could also be done by an externals list). In the second program, the decision to avoid a temporary variable gives rise to a different pattern. The initialization does not obviously establish an invariant which relates three variables. The plan to reduce j suggests something like:

$$r = i + (\overleftarrow{j} - j)$$

but this is not an expression in a single state. However, rel does not have to be, and noting the initialization, gives:

$$r + j = \overleftarrow{r} + \overleftarrow{j}$$

for rel. This time the invariant is simpler because it only plays a part in checking that rel is well-founded.

pre $0 \leq n$

    $fn, t := 1, 0$

    ;

    pre $t \leq n \wedge fn = t!$

      while $t \neq n$ do

      inv $t \leq n \wedge fn = t!$

        $t := t + 1; \ fn := fn * t$

      rel $n = \overleftarrow{n} \wedge \overleftarrow{t} < t$

    post $fn = t! \wedge t = n = \overleftarrow{n}$

post $fn = \overleftarrow{n}!$

Figure 10.4: Development of Factorial

Applying the two approaches to the task of computing factorial yields a similar analysis. The overall post-condition is:

    $fn = \overleftarrow{n}!$

Taking this as an invariant leaves only the preservation of n and well-foundedness for rel—see Figure 10.4. The body of the loop can be completed with the assignments shown.

With the version of the program which does not have a temporary variable, the factorial is computed backwards $(n * (n - 1) * \ldots)$. This is done by overwriting the value in n, and rel captures this with:

    $fn * n! = \overleftarrow{fn} * \overleftarrow{n}!$

This gives rise to the development shown in Figure 10.5.

The specification of integer division is discussed in Exercise 3 of Section 4.1. A straightforward development of this specification is shown in Figure 10.6. Here, the crux of the matter is to spot that the expression which is to remain constant is:

    $j * q + i$

As an illustration of a more interesting problem, consider describing how a mechanical calculator performs the same task. In a first stage (SL), j is

pre $0 \leq n$

  $fn := 1$

  ;

  pre $0 \leq n$

    while $n \neq 0$ do

    inv $0 \leq n$

      $fn, n := fn * n, n - 1$

    rel $fn * n! = \overleftarrow{fn} * \overleftarrow{n}! \wedge n < \overleftarrow{n}$

  post $fn = \overleftarrow{fn} * \overleftarrow{n}!$

post $fn = \overleftarrow{n}!$

Figure 10.5: Alternative Development of Factorial

pre $j \neq 0$

  $q := 0$

  ;

  pre

    while $i \geq j$ do

    inv true

      $i, q := i - j, q + 1$

    rel $j * q + i = \overleftarrow{j} * \overleftarrow{q} + \overleftarrow{i} \wedge j = \overleftarrow{j} \wedge i < \overleftarrow{i}$

  post $\overleftarrow{j} * q + i = \overleftarrow{j} * \overleftarrow{q} + \overleftarrow{i} \wedge i < \overleftarrow{j}$

post $\overleftarrow{j} * q + i = \overleftarrow{i} \wedge i < \overleftarrow{j}$

Figure 10.6: Development of Integer Division Algorithm

pre $j \neq 0$

   pre $j \neq 0$ $\{SL\}$

      ext rd i, wr j, q, n

      $n := 0;$

      while $j \leq i$ do

      inv true

         $j, n := j * 10, n + 1$

      rel $j * 10^{\overleftarrow{n}} = \overleftarrow{j} * 10^n \wedge j > \overleftarrow{j}$

   post $j = \overleftarrow{j} * 10^n \wedge i < j$

   $; q := 0;$

   pre 10^n divides $j \wedge i < j$ $\{SR\}$

      while $n \neq 0$ do

      inv 10^n divides $j \wedge i < j$

         $n, j, q := n - 1, j/10, q * 10;$ $\{SRS\}$

         while $j \leq i$ $\{SRC\}$ext wr i, q, rd j

         inv $(0 \leq i)$

            $i, q := i - j, q + 1$

        rel $\overleftarrow{j} * \overleftarrow{q} + \overleftarrow{i} = j * q + i \wedge i < \overleftarrow{i}$

      rel $j/10^n = \overleftarrow{j}/10^{\overleftarrow{n}} \wedge j * q + i = \overleftarrow{j} * \overleftarrow{q} + \overleftarrow{i} \wedge n < \overleftarrow{n}$

   post $j = \overleftarrow{j}/10^{\overleftarrow{n}} \wedge j * q + i = \overleftarrow{j} * \overleftarrow{q} + \overleftarrow{i} \wedge i < j$

post $\overleftarrow{j} * q + i = \overleftarrow{i} \wedge i < \overleftarrow{j}$

Figure 10.7: Development of Alternative Integer Division Algorithm

shifted left until it is larger than i—the number of shifts is counted in n. The second stage (SR) shifts j back and at each step keeps the expression $j * q + i$ constant. There are two places this must be done: shifting at SRS and re-establishing $i < j$ by stepping down i at SRC. The presentation in Figure 10.7 is made simpler by assuming that all variables are natural numbers.

As a further example of a decomposition proof, the binary tree problem is picked up from Chapters 5 and 8. The Pascal equivalent of the data objects in Chapter 8 are:

```
type Ptr = ↑ Binoderep
Binnoderep =
        record
              lp: Ptr
              mk: Key
              md: Data
              rp: Ptr
        end
```

The $FINDBH$ function can be coded (with auxiliary functions $findbhn$ and $depth$ for the assertions) as shown in Figure 10.8.

It must now be obvious why arithmetic examples have been used in the bulk of this chapter: the examples with interesting data structures often result in fairly trivial code once the representation problem has been solved. The same is true of the equivalence relation problem shown in Figure 10.9. This leads immediately to code for $TESTF$ and $EQUATEF$.

Exercises

1. Develop two different algorithms for multiplication, showing how the inv/rel might be found.

2. * Develop algorithms for sorting using the method explained in this chapter (use a standard reference as a source for the algorithms).

```
function
FINDBH (k: Key) d: Data
ext rd rt: Ptr, rd h: Heap
pre k ∈ collkeysh(rt, h)
    var p: Ptr;
    begin
    p : = rt
    ;
    pre k ∈ collkeysh(p, h)
        while k ≠ p ↑ mk do
        inv k ∈ collkeysh(p, h)
            with p ↑ do
            if k < mk
            then    p : = lp
            else    p : = rp;
        rel findbhn(k, p) = findbhn(k, ⃖p ) ∧ depth(p) < depth(⃖p )
    post p = findbhn(k, p)
    ;
    FINDBH : = p ↑ md
post d = md(findbhn(k, ⃖rt ))
end
```

Figure 10.8: Development of *FIND*

$ROOTF\ (e\!:X)\ X$
ext rd $m\!:Forest(X)$
pre true
    var$v\!:X$;
    begin
    pre
        $v\,:\,=\,e$
        ;
        while $v \in$ dom m do
        inv true
            $v\,:\,=\,m(v)$
        rel $root(v,m) = root(\overleftarrow{v},m) \wedge depth(v,m) < depth(\overleftarrow{v},m)$
    post $v = root(e,m)$
    ;
    $ROOTF\,:\,=\,v$

post $v = root(e,m)$

end

Figure 10.9: Development of $ROOT$

Postscript

> If we try to solve society's problems without over-
> coming the confusion and aggression in our own
> state of mind, then our efforts will only contribute
> to the basic problems, instead of solving them.
> *Chögyam Trungpa*

The decision to write a personal postscript to this book was partly prompted
by my involvement in a panel discussion on Social Responsibility at the
1985 TAPSOFT conference in Berlin. Computer systems are now so widely
used that computer scientists must consider where they stand on issues
relating to the systems they build. We should not expect others to accept
our judgements, but we should provoke discussion and be prepared to accept
criticism. A crucial issue is the reliance being put on computer systems. The
probability of (physical) hardware errors has been decreased significantly
over the last twenty years, but software errors persist.

One clear personal responsibility is not to oversell our ideas. This
postscript attempts to put the proposals made in this book into a slightly
wider context. One must first recognise that there are many problems associated with the development of computer systems. Some of these problems
have nothing at all to do with specifications (formal or otherwise).

The material relating to specifications in this book attempts to show
how mathematical notation can be used to increase the precision of a specification. The basic objects such as maps can, when used with care, achieve
conciseness of expression as well as precision. I believe that these ideas are
important.

But a major issue relating to specifications is whether they match the
user's requirements. The idea of proving properties of formal specifications
is proposed above. But it is also conceded that this can never ensure a

match with the, inherently informal, requirements. One can argue that this match can only be tested in the same way in which a scientific theory is tested. It is also possible to claim that Popper's arguments for refutability are a support for formality on the specification side of the comparison—and experience supports this claim. But the fact that there is no way of proving that a system matches the user's requirements should force us to consider, in every system with which we are involved, the danger of a mismatch.

The material in this book relating to design aims to provide developers with ways to increase their confidence that the systems they create satisfy the specifications. This must be a part of a software engineer's training. With machine-checked proofs, an enormous increase in confidence would be justified, but it must be understood that nothing can ever provide absolute certainty of correctness. The same is, of course, true of physical systems. It is simply a question of comparing probabilities.

There is a great danger associated with people's perception of new concepts. If improved methods are used to tackle the same sort of problems previously handled by *ad hoc* methods, the systems created could be far safer. If, on the other hand, the improved methods are used to justify tackling systems of even greater complexity, no progress will have been made.

Appendix A

Rules of Logic

Conventions

1. $E, E_1, \ldots$ denote logical expressions.

2. $x, y, \ldots$ denote variables over proper elements in a universe.

3. $c, c_1, \ldots$ denote constants over proper elements in a universe.

4. $s, s_1, \ldots$ denote terms which may contain partial functions.

5. $E(x)$ denotes a formula in which x occurs free.

6. $E(s/x)$ denotes a formula obtained by substituting all free occurrences of x by s in E. If a clash between free and bound variables would occur, suitable renaming is performed before the substitution.

7. $E[s_2/s_1]$ denotes a formula obtained by substituting some occurrences of s_1 by s_2. If a clash between free and bound variables would occur, then suitable renaming is performed before the substitution.

8. X is a non-empty set.

9. An "arbitrary" variable is one about which no results have been established.

266

General Properties

inf
$$\frac{E_1 \vdash E_2;\ E_1}{E_2}$$

var-I
$$\overline{x^1 \in X}$$

commutativity ($\vee / \wedge / \Leftrightarrow$-comm)

$$\frac{E_1 \vee E_2}{E_2 \vee E_1} \qquad \frac{E_1 \wedge E_2}{E_2 \wedge E_1} \qquad \frac{E_1 \Leftrightarrow E_2}{E_2 \Leftrightarrow E_1}$$

associativity ($\vee / \wedge / \Leftrightarrow$-ass)

$$\frac{(E_1 \vee E_2) \vee E_3}{E_1 \vee (E_2 \vee E_3)} \qquad \frac{(E_1 \wedge E_2) \wedge E_3}{E_1 \wedge (E_2 \wedge E_3)} \qquad \frac{(E_1 \Leftrightarrow E_2) \Leftrightarrow E_3}{E_1 \Leftrightarrow (E_2 \Leftrightarrow E_3)}$$

transitivity ($\Rightarrow / \Leftrightarrow$-trans)

$$\frac{E_1 \Rightarrow E_2;\ E_2 \Rightarrow E_3}{E_1 \Rightarrow E_3} \qquad \frac{E_1 \Leftrightarrow E_2;\ E_2 \Leftrightarrow E_3}{E_1 \Leftrightarrow E_3}$$

substitution

=t-subs
$$\frac{s_1 = s_2;\ E}{E[s_2/s_1]}$$

=v-subs
$$\frac{s \in X;\ x \in X \vdash E(x)}{E(s/x)}$$

=-comm
$$\frac{s_1 = s_2}{s_2 = s_1}$$

=-trans
$$\frac{s_1 = s_2;\ s_2 = s_3}{s_1 = s_3}$$

$f : D \rightarrow R$

$f(d) \overset{\Delta}{=} e$

$e_0 = e(d_0/d)$

---

[1] x is arbitrary

$\triangleq$-subs
$$\frac{d_0 \in D;\ E(e_0)}{E[f(d_0)/e_0]}$$

$\triangleq$-inst
$$\frac{d_0 \in D;\ E(f(d_0))}{E[e_0/f(d_0)]}$$

$f(d) \quad \triangleq \quad$ if e then et else ef

if-subs
$$\frac{d_0 \in D;\ e_0;\ E(et_0)}{E[f(d_0)/et_0]} \qquad\qquad \frac{d_0 \in D;\ \neg e_0;\ E(ef_0)}{E[f(d_0)/ef_0]}$$

Definitions of Connectives

f-defn
$$\frac{\neg\text{true}}{\text{false}}$$

$\wedge$-defn
$$\frac{\neg(\neg E_1 \vee \neg E_2)}{E_1 \wedge E_2}$$

$\Rightarrow$-defn
$$\frac{\neg E_1 \vee E_2}{E_1 \Rightarrow E_2}$$

$\Leftrightarrow$-defn
$$\frac{(E_1 \Rightarrow E_2) \wedge (E_2 \Rightarrow E_1)}{E_1 \Leftrightarrow E_2}$$

$\forall$-defn
$$\frac{\neg \exists x \in X \cdot \neg E(x)}{\forall x \in X \cdot E(x)}$$

Relationships between Operators

deM
$$\frac{\neg(E_1 \vee E_2)}{\neg E_1 \wedge \neg E_2} \qquad\qquad \frac{\neg(E_1 \wedge E_2)}{\neg E_1 \vee \neg E_2}$$

$$\frac{\neg \exists x \in X \cdot E(x)}{\forall x \in X \cdot \neg E(x)} \qquad\qquad \frac{\neg \forall x \in X \cdot E(x)}{\exists x \in X \cdot \neg E(x)}$$

dist
$$\frac{E_1 \lor E_2 \land E_3}{(E_1 \lor E_2) \land (E_1 \lor E_3)} \qquad \frac{E_1 \land (E_2 \lor E_3)}{E_1 \land E_2 \lor E_1 \land E3}$$

$\exists\lor$-dist
$$\frac{\exists x \in X \cdot E_1(x) \lor E_2(x)}{(\exists x \in X \cdot E_1(x)) \lor (\exists x \in X \cdot E_2(x))}$$

$\exists\land$-dist
$$\frac{\exists x \in X \cdot E_1(x) \land E_2(x)}{(\exists x \in X \cdot E_1(x)) \land (\exists x \in X \cdot E_2(x))}$$

$\forall\lor$-dist
$$\frac{(\forall x \in X \cdot E_1(x)) \lor (\forall x \in X \cdot E_2(x))}{\forall x \in X \cdot E_1(x) \lor E_2(x)}$$

$\forall\land$-dist
$$\frac{(\forall x \in X \cdot E_1(x)) \land (\forall x \in X \cdot E_2(x))}{\forall x \in X \cdot E_1(x) \land E_2(x)}$$

Substitution

$\land$-subs
$$\frac{E_1 \land \ldots \land E_i \land \ldots \land E_n; \ E_i \vdash E}{E_1 \land \ldots \land E \land \ldots \land E_n}$$

$\lor$-subs
$$\frac{E_1 \lor \ldots \lor E_i \lor \ldots \lor E_n; \ E_i \vdash E}{E_1 \lor \ldots \lor E \lor \ldots \lor E_n}$$

$\exists$-subs
$$\frac{\exists x \in X \cdot E_1(x); \ E_1(x) \vdash E(x)}{\exists x \in X \cdot E(x)}$$

contr
$$\frac{E_1; \ \neg E_1}{E_2}$$

$\Rightarrow$-contrp
$$\frac{E_1 \Rightarrow E_2}{\neg E_2 \Rightarrow \neg E_1}$$

$$\textit{INTRODUCTION}(op\text{-}I) \quad \textit{ELIMINATION}(op\text{-}E)$$

$\neg\neg$

$$\frac{E}{\neg\neg E} \qquad\qquad \frac{\neg\neg E}{E}$$

$\vee$

$$\frac{E_i}{E_1 \vee E_2 \vee \ldots \vee E_n} \qquad \frac{\begin{array}{c}E_1 \vee \ldots \vee E_n; \\ E_1 \vdash E; \ldots; E_n \vdash E\end{array}}{E}$$

$\wedge$

$$\frac{E_1; E_2; \ldots; E_n}{E_1 \wedge E_2 \wedge \ldots \wedge E_n} \qquad \frac{E_1 \wedge E_2 \wedge \ldots \wedge E_n}{E_i}$$

$\neg\vee$

$$\frac{\neg E_1; \neg E_2; \ldots; \neg E_n}{\neg(E_1 \vee E_2 \vee \ldots \vee E_n)} \qquad \frac{\neg(E_1 \vee E_2 \vee \ldots \vee E_n)}{\neg E_i}$$

$\neg\wedge$

$$\frac{\neg E_i}{\neg(E_1 \wedge \ldots \wedge E_n)} \qquad \frac{\begin{array}{c}\neg(E_1 \wedge \ldots \wedge E_n); \\ \neg E_1 \vdash E; \ldots; \neg E_n \vdash E\end{array}}{E}$$

$\Rightarrow$

$$\frac{E_1 \vdash E_2; E_1 \in \mathbf{B}}{E_1 \Rightarrow E_2}$$

$\text{vac} \Rightarrow$

$$\frac{E_2}{E_1 \Rightarrow E_2} \qquad \frac{E_1 \Rightarrow E_2; \neg E_2}{\neg E_1}$$

$$\frac{\neg E1}{E_1 \Rightarrow E_2} \qquad \frac{E_1 \Rightarrow E_2; E_1}{E_2}$$

$\Leftrightarrow$

$$\frac{E_1 \wedge E_2}{E_1 \Leftrightarrow E_2} \qquad \frac{E_1 \Leftrightarrow E_2}{E_1 \wedge E_2 \vee \neg E_1 \wedge \neg E_2}$$

$$\frac{\neg E_1 \wedge \neg E_2}{E_1 \Leftrightarrow E_2}$$

$\neg \Leftrightarrow$

$$\frac{E_1 \wedge \neg E_2}{\neg(E_1 \Leftrightarrow E_2)} \qquad \frac{\neg(E_1 \Leftrightarrow E_2)}{E_1 \wedge \neg E_2 \vee \neg E_1 \wedge E_2}$$

$$\frac{\neg E_1 \land E_2}{\neg(E_1 \Leftrightarrow E_2)}$$

∃
$$\frac{s \in X;\ E(s/x)}{\exists x \in X \cdot E(x)}$$

$$\frac{\exists x \in X \cdot E(x);\ y^2 \in X, E(y/x) \vdash E_1}{E_1}$$

∀
$$\frac{x^3 \in X \vdash E(x)}{\forall x \in X \cdot E(x)}$$

$$\frac{\forall x \in X \cdot E(x);\ s \in X}{E(s/x)}$$

¬∃
$$\frac{x \in X \vdash \neg E(x)}{\neg \exists x \in X \cdot E(x)}$$

$$\frac{\neg \exists x \in X \cdot E(x);\ s \in X}{\neg E(s/x)}$$

¬∀
$$\frac{s \in X;\ \neg E(s/x)}{\neg \forall x \in X \cdot E(x)}$$

$$\frac{\neg \forall x \in X \cdot E(x);\ y^4 \in X, \neg E(y/x) \vdash E}{E}$$

Miscellaneous

∃split
$$\frac{\exists x \in X \cdot E(x, x)}{\exists x, y \in X \cdot E(x, y)}$$

∀fix
$$\frac{\forall x, y \in X \cdot E(x, y)}{\forall x \in X \cdot E(x, x)}$$

∀ → ∃
$$\frac{\forall x \in X^5 \cdot E(x)}{\exists x \in X \cdot E(x)}$$

$$\frac{\exists x \in X \cdot \forall y \in Y \cdot E(x, y)}{\forall y \in Y \cdot \exists x \in X \cdot E(x, y)}$$

---

[2] y is arbitrary and not free in E_1

[3] x is arbitrary

[4] y is arbitrary and not free in E

[5] X is non-empty

$$\frac{\forall x \in X \cdot E_1(x) \Leftrightarrow E_2(x)}{(\forall x \in X \cdot E_1(x)) \Leftrightarrow (\forall x \in X \cdot E_2(x))}$$

=-contr $\qquad \dfrac{\neg(s = s)}{E}$

=-term $\qquad \dfrac{s \in X}{s = s}$

=-comp $\qquad \dfrac{s_1, s_2 \in X}{(s_1 = s_2) \vee \neg(s_1 = s_2)}$

Δ-I $\qquad \dfrac{E}{\Delta E} \qquad\qquad\qquad \dfrac{\neg E}{\Delta E}$

Δ-E $\qquad \dfrac{\Delta E; \ E \vdash E_1; \ \neg E \vdash E_1}{E_1}$

$\neg\Delta$-I $\qquad \dfrac{\Delta E \vdash E_1; \ \Delta E \vdash \neg E_1}{\neg\Delta E}$

$\neg\Delta$-E $\qquad \dfrac{\neg\Delta E \vdash E_1; \ \neg\Delta E \vdash \neg E_1}{\Delta E}$

==-refl $\qquad \dfrac{}{s == s}$

==-subs $\qquad \dfrac{s_1 == s_2; \ E}{E[s_2/s_1]}$

==-comm $\qquad \dfrac{s_1 == s_2}{s_2 == s_1}$

==-trans $\qquad \dfrac{s_1 == s_2; \ s_2 == s_3}{s_1 == s_3}$

==$\rightarrow$= $\qquad \dfrac{s_1 == s_2; \ s_i \in X}{s_1 = s_2}$

=$\rightarrow$== $\qquad \dfrac{s_1 = s_2}{s_1 == s_2}$

Appendix B

Properties of Data

Relations

Ordering: Transitive, Reflexive, Antisymmetric.
Equivalence: Transitive, Reflexive, Symmetric.

Natural Numbers (cf. Section 3.2)

$0 \colon \mathbf{N}$
$succ \colon \mathbf{N} \to \mathbf{N}$

N-ind
$$\frac{p(0); \quad n \in \mathbf{N}, p(n) \vdash p(n+1)}{n \in \mathbf{N} \vdash p(n)}$$

N-indp
$$\frac{p(0); \quad n \in \mathbf{N_1}, p(n-1) \vdash p(n)}{n \in \mathbf{N} \vdash p(n)}$$

N-cind
$$\frac{n, m \in \mathbf{N}, m < n \;\Rightarrow\; p(m) \vdash p(n)}{n \in \mathbf{N} \vdash p(n)}$$

Sets (cf. Section 4.3)

s, s_i are sets

$\{\} \colon$ set of X

$\_ \oplus \_ \colon X \times$ set of $X \to$ set of X

$\oplus$-comm
$$\frac{e_1, e_2 \in X; \; s \in \text{set of } X}{e_1 \oplus (e_2 \oplus s) = e_2 \oplus (e_1 \oplus s)}$$

$\oplus$-abs
$$\frac{e \in X; \; s \in \text{set of } X}{e \oplus (e \oplus s) = e \oplus s}$$

set-ind
$$\frac{p(\{\}); \; e \in X, s \in \text{set of } X, p(s) \vdash p(e \oplus s)}{s \in \text{set of } X \vdash p(s)}$$

set-ind2
$$\frac{p(\{\}); \; s \in \text{set of } X, e \in s, p(s - \{e\}) \vdash p(s)}{s \in \text{set of } X \vdash p(s)}$$

$\_ \cup \_ :$ set of $X \times$ set of $X \to$ set of X

$\_ \cap \_ :$ set of $X \times$ set of $X \to$ set of X

$\cup, \cap$ are commutative, associative, and distribute in both directions

$\{\} \cup s = s$

$s \cup s = s$

$s \cap \{\} = \{\}$

$s \cap s = s$

$\bigcup \_ :$ set of $(\text{set of } X) \to$ set of X

$\bigcup (es_1 \cup es_2) = \bigcup es_1 \cup \bigcup es_2$

$\_ - \_ :$ set of $X \times$ set of $X \to$ set of X

$s - \{\} = s$

$s - s = \{\}$

$(s_1 - s_2) \cap s_3 = (s_1 \cap s_3) - s_2$

$s_1 \cup (s_1 - s_2) = s_1$

$s_1 \cup (s_2 - s_1) = s_1 \cup s_2$

$s_1 \cap (s_1 - s_2) = s_1 - s_2$

$s_1 \cap (s_2 - s_1) = \{\}$

$\_ \subseteq \_ :$ set of $X \times$ set of $X \rightarrow \mathbf{B}$

$\{\} \subseteq s$

$\subseteq$ is a (partial) order

$(s_1 \cap s_2) \subseteq s_1$

$s_1 \subseteq (s_1 \cup s_2)$

$\_ \diamond \_ :$ set of $X \times$ set of $X \rightarrow$ set of X

$s_1 \diamond s_2 = (s_1 \cup s_2) - (s_1 \cap s_2)$

$s_1 \diamond s_2 = (s_1 - s_2) \cup (s_2 - s_1)$

Partitions (cf. Section 4.3)

$Partition(X) =$ set of (set of X)
where
$inv\text{-}Partition(p) \quad \triangleq \quad \{\} \notin p \wedge \bigcup p = X \wedge is\text{-}prdisj(p)$

$\{\{x\} \mid x \in X\} \in Partition(X)$

$p \in Partition(X) \vdash$
$\qquad (\{s \in p \mid \neg tvf(s)\} \cup \{\bigcup s \in p \mid tvf(s)\}) \in Partition(X)$

Maps (cf. Section 6.2)

m, m_i are maps; s is a set

$\_ \dagger \_ :$ map D to $R \times$ map D to $R \rightarrow$ map D to R
$\dagger$ is associative

$m \dagger \{\} = m = \{\} \dagger m$

dom $\_ :$ map D to $R \rightarrow$ set of D

rng $\_ :$ map D to $R \rightarrow$ set of R

$\_ \cup \_ :$ map D to $R \times$ map D to $R \rightarrow$ map D to R

$m_1, m_2 \in$ map D to $R, is\text{-}disj(\text{dom } m_1, \text{dom } m_2) \vdash$
$\qquad m_1 \cup m_2 \in$ map D to R

$\cup$ (when defined) is commutative

$\lhd$: set of D $\times$ map D to R $\rightarrow$ map D to R

$s \lhd \{\} = \{\}$

$\{\} \lhd m = \{\}$

$\_\blacktriangleleft\_$: set of D $\times$ map D to R $\rightarrow$ map D to R

$\{\}\blacktriangleleft m = m$

$m_1 \dagger m_2 = (\text{dom } m_2 \blacktriangleleft m_1) \cup m_2$

Sequences (cf. Section 7.2)

t is a sequence

$[\,]$: seq of X

$cons: X \times$ seq of X $\rightarrow$ seq of X

seq-ind
$$\frac{p([\,]); \; e \in X, t \in \text{ seq of } X, p(t) \vdash p(cons(e, t))}{t \in \text{ seq of } X \vdash p(t)}$$

seq-ind2
$$\frac{p([\,]); \; t \in \text{ seq of } X, t \neq [\,], p(\text{tl } t) \vdash p(t)}{t \in \text{ seq of } X \vdash p(t)}$$

$\_\frown\_$: seq of X $\times$ seq of X $\rightarrow$ seq of X

$\frown$ is associative

$[\,] \frown t = t = t \frown [\,]$

Appendix C

Proof Obligations

Implementability

functions:

$$\forall d \in D \cdot \textit{pre-f}(d) \;\Rightarrow\; \exists r \in R \cdot \textit{post-f}(d, r)$$

operations:

$$\forall \overleftarrow{\sigma} \in \Sigma \cdot \textit{pre-OP}(\overleftarrow{\sigma}) \;\Rightarrow\; \exists \sigma \in \Sigma \cdot \textit{post-OP}(\overleftarrow{\sigma}, \sigma)$$

Remember the role of invariants in such proofs.

Satisfaction of Specification

functions:

$$\forall d \in D \cdot \textit{pre-f}(d) \;\Rightarrow\; f(d) \in R \wedge \textit{post-f}(d, f(d))$$

operations:

$$
\begin{aligned}
&\forall \overleftarrow{\sigma} \in \Sigma \cdot \\
&\quad \textit{pre-OP}(\overleftarrow{\sigma}) \Rightarrow \\
&\qquad \exists \sigma \in \Sigma \cdot (\overleftarrow{\sigma}, \sigma) \in OP \wedge \\
&\qquad \forall \sigma \in \Sigma \cdot (\overleftarrow{\sigma}, \sigma) \in OP \Rightarrow \textit{post-OP}(\overleftarrow{\sigma}, \sigma)
\end{aligned}
$$

Data Reification

adequacy:

$$\forall a \in A \cdot \exists r \in R \cdot retr(r) = a$$

initial state:

$$retr(r_0) = a_0$$

domain:

$$\forall r \in R \cdot pre\text{-}A(retr(r)) \Rightarrow pre\text{-}R(r)$$

result:

$$\forall \overleftarrow{r}, r \in R \cdot pre\text{-}A(retr(\overleftarrow{r})) \wedge post\text{-}R(\overleftarrow{r}, r) \Rightarrow$$
$$post\text{-}A(retr(\overleftarrow{r}), retr(r))$$

Operation Decomposition

inherit pre-condition:

$$\frac{\{P\}S\{R\}}{\{P\}S\{\overleftarrow{P} \wedge R\}}$$

sequence

$$\frac{\{P_1\}S_1\{P_2 \wedge R_2\}, \ \{P_2\}S_2\{R_2\}}{\{P_1\}S_1; S_2\{R_1 \mid R_2\}}$$

conditional

$$\frac{\{P \wedge B\}\, TH\{R\}, \ \{P \wedge \neg B\}EL\{R\}}{\{P\}\text{if } B \text{ then } TH \text{ else } EL\{R\}}$$

while

$$\frac{\{P \wedge B\}S\{P \wedge R\}}{\{P\} \text{ while } B \text{ do } S \ \{P \wedge \neg B \wedge R^*\}}$$

Appendix D

Glossary of Terms

Abstract syntax : the abstract syntax of a language defines the set of objects which are in the language; in contrast to the strings of the concrete syntax, the syntactic clues for parsing are omitted and only the necessary information content remains (cf. semantics).

Adequacy : the adequacy proof obligation establishes that there is at least one representation for each abstract value.

ADJ diagram : a graphical representation of the signatures of the operators of a data type.

Antecedent : the left hand side of an implication.

Application : a function is applied to an element in its domain; the result is an element of the range of the function.

Associativity : an operator is associative if, for all valid operands:

$$x \text{ op } (y \text{ op } z) = (x \text{ op } y) \text{ op } z$$

Backus-Naur Form : the notation used to define the concrete syntax of ALGOL 60; BNF or some variant thereof is now used in most language descriptions.

Bag : a Bag is an unordered collection of values where values can be contained more than once (thus it is possible to count the occurrences).

Basis : in an inductive proof, the basis is the sub-proof that the required expression is true for the minimum element of the set of values.

Behaviour : the behaviour of a data type determines (for a functional data type) the result of its operators and functions or (for a state-based data type) of its operations.

Bias : *see* implementation bias.

BNF : *see* Backus-Naur Form.

Body : the body of a quantified expression is that part following the raised dot.

Bound identifiers : in a quantified expression the bound identifiers are those appearing after the quantifier; all free occurrences of the identifier in the body of such an expression are bound in the overall quantified expression. There are other ways of binding identifiers—for example, the names corresponding to the values of parameters and external variables are bound within an operation specification.

Cardinality : the cardinality of a finite set is the number of elements contained in the set.

Commutativity : an operator is commutative if, for all valid operands:

$$x \text{ op } y = y \text{ op } x$$

Complete : an axiomatization is complete with respect to a model if all statements which are true in that model can be proved from the axioms using the rules of inference.

Composite object : composite objects are tagged and can contain a number of fields; they are created by make-functions.

Composite type : a composite type defines a set of composite objects.

Concatenation : the operator which creates a sequence from the elements of its two operands.

Conclusion : in a sequent, the conclusion is the logical expression on the right of a turnstile.

Concrete syntax : the concrete syntax of a language defines exactly the set of strings which form sentences of the language; the rules define a certain structure on the sentences but convey no meaning.

Conjunction : a logical expression whose principal operator is "and" ($\wedge$).

Consequent : the right-hand side of an implication.

Constraint : the constraint of a quantified expression fixes the type of the identifier bound by the quantifier; it governs the values over which the variable ranges.

Contingent : a logical expression is contingent if there are contexts in which it evaluates to true while in others it evaluates to false.

Contradiction : a logical expression is a contradiction if there is no context in which it evaluates to true.

Data reification : abstract objects are reified to chosen representations in the early stages of system design.

Data type : a data type is a set of values together with ways of manipulating those values; functional data types (e.g. natural numbers or sequences) have operators or functions whose results depend only on their arguments; state-based data types are manipulated by operations whose result is affected by and whose execution affects a state.

Data type invariant : a data type invariant is a truth-valued function which defines a subset of a class of objects defined by a syntax.

Decidable : a logical calculus is decidable if an algorithm exists which can determine, for any expression of the calculus, whether the formula is true or not.

Decomposition : *see* operation decomposition.

Definition (direct) : a direct definition of a function provides a rule for computing the result of application.

Derived rules : results proved with general propositional variables can be used as inference rules in proofs; such inference rules are derived from the basic axiomatization.

Difference : the difference of two sets is the set containing exactly those elements of the first set which are absent from the second.

Disjoint sets : disjoint sets are those with no common elements.

Disjunction : a logical expression whose principal operator is "or" (∨).

Distributed union : the distributed union of a set of sets is the set containing exactly those elements of the sets which are elements of the operand.

Distributivity : an operator (opa) is said to left distribute over another operator (opb) if, for all valid operands:

$$x \text{ opa } (y \text{ opb } z) = (x \text{ opa } y) \text{ opb } (x \text{ opa } z)$$

and similarly for right-distributivity.

Domain : the domain of a function is the set of values to which the function can be applied.

Equations : the equations of a property-oriented specification provide the semantics (without giving a model).

Equivalence : a logical expression whose principal operator is an equivalence symbol (⇔).

Equivalence relation : an equivalence relation is reflexive, symmetric and transitive.

Equivalent : two logical expressions are equivalent if they yield the same value for all possible values of their free variables.

Exception : the specification of exceptions can be separated from the normal pre-/post-conditions by minor extensions to the specification format.

Existential quantifier : (∃) "there exists (one or more)"

Final interpretation : the final interpretation of a (property-oriented) specification is one in which values are considered to be equivalent if and only if their denoting expressions can not be proved to be different from the equations.

Formal language : a language having precise syntax and semantics.

Formal proof : a formal proof is one in which all steps are mechanical; thus a formal proof can be checked by a computer program.

Frame problem : the statement of those entities which are not changed by an operation.

Free variables : the free variables of an expression are (the identifiers) which are not bound (e.g. by a quantifier).

Function : a function is a mapping between two sets of values (i.e. from elements in the domain to elements in the range).

Functional specification : defines the intended input/output behaviour of a computer system: *what* the system should do.

Generators : the generators of a type are the functions which can, in suitable combinations, generate all values of the type (e.g. 0 and *succ* for the natural numbers).

Hypothesis : a logical expression on left of a sequent.

Implementability : the use of implicit specification gives rise to a proof obligation known as implementability: for all acceptable inputs there must be some possible result.

Implementation bias : a model-oriented specification is biased (towards certain implementations) if equality on the states cannot be defined in terms of the available operations; in other words, there are two, or more, state values which cannot be distinguished by the operations.

Implication : a logical expression whose principal operator is an implication sign ($\Rightarrow$).

Implicit specification : an implicit specification characterizes *what* is to be done without (if possible) saying anything about *how* the result is to be achieved.

Indexing : the application of a sequence to a valid index is called indexing; it yields an element of the sequence.

Induction step : in an inductive proof, the inductive step shows that the required expression inherits over the successor function for the type.

Inductive hypothesis : in the induction step of an inductive proof, the induction hypothesis is the assumption of the required property from which its inheritance has to be proved.

Inductive proof : an inductive proof is one which uses the induction principle for a type.

Inference rule : an inference rule consists of a number of hypotheses and a conclusion separated by a horizontal line; an appropriate instance of the conclusion is justified if corresponding matches can be made with the hypotheses.

Initial interpretation : the initial interpretation of a property-oriented specification is one in which values are considered to be equivalent if and only if their denoting expressions can be proven to be equal from the equations.

Intersection : the intersection of two sets is the set containing exactly those elements contained in both sets.

Invariants : *see* data type invariant.

Logic of partial function : a logic which copes with undefined terms. An axiomatization of this logic is given in Appendix A.

LPF : *see* logic of partial functions.

Make-function : each composite type has an associated make-function which forms elements of the type from elements of the sets of values for the fields of the composite object.

Map : map values define a finite (many-to-one) relationship between two sets; the map can be applied to elements in its domain to find the corresponding element in the range.

Maplet : the ordered pairs of an explicitly given map are written as maplets with the two values separated by a small arrow ($\mapsto$).

Model oriented : a model-oriented specification of a data type defines the behaviour in terms of a class of objects; these objects are built from ones which already exist; operations transform the objects.

Model theory : a model theory for a calculus associates its formulae with a collection of mathematical objects.

Modus ponens : an inference rule which from $E_1 \Rightarrow E_2$ and E_1 justifies E_2.

Monotone : a function is monotone if its application preserves some stated ordering.

Multiset : *see* Bag.

Natural deduction : a particular style for presenting formal proofs in propositional and predicate calculus.

Negation : a logical expression whose principal operator is "not" ($\neg$).

Non-deterministic : an operation whose specification permits more than one result is said to be non-deterministic.

Operation : a program or piece thereof (often a procedure); an operation depends on and changes external variables (its state).

Operation decomposition : operations are decomposed into constructs which combine operations (e.g. while loops); proof obligations to check operation decomposition are given.

Operator : common functions are written as infix or prefix operators in order to shorten expressions and make the statement of algebraic properties clearer.

Partial function : a partial function is one which is not defined for all of the values indicated in the domain part of its signature; the values to which it can be safely applied are defined by a pre-condition.

Partition : a partition of a set S is a set of disjoint subsets of S whose union is S.

Post-condition : a truth-valued function which defines the required relation between input and output values for a function (operation).

Power Set : the power set of a set S is the set of all subsets of S.

Pre-condition : a truth-valued function which defines the elements of the domain of a partial function (operation) for which the existence of a result is guaranteed.

Predicate : a predicate is a truth-valued expression which contains free variables.

Predicate calculus : expressions of the predicate calculus are built up from truth-valued functions, propositional operators and quantifiers.

Proof obligations : claims such as "this piece of code satisfies that specification" give rise to proof obligations; if formal notation is used, these proof obligations are sequents to be proved.

Proof theory : A proof theory for a calculus provides a way of deducing formulae; deductions begin with (instances of) axioms and use the given rules of inference.

Proper subset : one set is a proper subset of another set if it is a subset and if the second set contains some elements absent from the first set.

Property oriented : a property-oriented specification of a data type consists of a signature and a collection of equations.

Proposition : an expression which, in classical logic, has the value true or false; in LPF, propositions can be undefined by virtue of undefined terms.

Propositional calculus : the expressions of the propositional calculus are built up from propositions and the operators $\neg, \wedge, \vee, \Rightarrow, \Leftrightarrow$; laws relate expressions and form a calculus.

Quantifiers : symbols of the predicate calculus ($\forall$ "for all", $\exists$ "there exists (one or more)", $\exists!$ "there exists exactly one").

Quoting : the specification of one data type can be made to depend on the specification of another by quoting the pre- and post-conditions of its operators.

Range : the range of a function is a specified set which contains the results of function application.

Recursive definition (abstract syntax)): a recursively defined abstract syntax defines a class of finite, but arbitrarily deeply nested, objects.

Recursive definition (function): a recursive definition of a function is one in which the name of the function being defined is used within the definition.

Reflexive : a relation R is reflexive if for all x:

$$(x, x) \in R$$

Reification : development of an abstract data type to a (more) concrete representation.

Relation : a relation can be viewed as a subset of the Cartesian product of two sets. Many of the relations of interest in this book (e.g. equivalence relations) are such that the same set (X) constitutes the domain and range; such relations are said to be "on X".

Retrieve function : a retrieve function relates a representation to an abstraction by mapping the former to the latter. Retrieve functions provide the basic link for data reification proofs.

Rigorous arguments : a rigorous argument outlines how a proof could be constructed; the reason for accepting such an argument is the knowledge of how it could be made formal.

Satisfy (specification) : an implementation is said to satisfy a specification if, over the range of values required by the (pre-condition of the) specification, the implementation produces results which agree with the (post-condition of the) specification.

Satisfy (truth-valued function) : values satisfy a truth-valued function if its application to those values yields the value true.

Selectors : the selectors for a composite type can be applied to values of that type to yield values of the components.

Semantics : the meaning of, for example, a language.

Sequence : a sequence is an ordered collection of values in which values can occur more than once; elements are of a specified type and the sequence itself is of finite size.

Sequent : a sequent consists of a list of logical expressions (the assumptions), followed by a turnstile, followed by another logical expression (its conclusion); it is to be read as a claim that, in all contexts where all of the assumptions are true, the conclusion is true.

Set : a set is an unordered collection of distinct objects.

Set comprehension : a set can be defined by set comprehension to contain all elements satisfying some property.

Signature : the signature of a function gives its domain and range.

Specification : strictly, a precise statement of all external characteristics of a system used here as a shorthand for "functional specification".

State : a collection of variables; the state of a state-based data type is such that the externals of all of its operations have compatible names and types with the state.

Structural induction : a way of generating induction rules for composite types.

Subset : one set is a subset of another set if all of the elements of the first set are contained in the second. A set is thus a subset of itself—*see* proper subset.

Sufficiently abstract : a model-oriented specification is said to be sufficiently abstract if it is not biased towards some particular implementations.

Symmetric : a relation R is symmetric if for all x, y:

$$(x, y) \in R \;\Rightarrow\; (y, x) \in R$$

Syntax : *see* abstract syntax/concrete syntax.

Tautology : a logical expression which evaluates to true for any values of its constituent propositions.

Term : an expression involving constants, identifiers and operators; such a term denotes a value.

Transitive : a relation R is transitive if for all x, y, z:

$$(x, y) \in R \wedge (y, z) \in R \;\Rightarrow\; (x, z) \in R$$

Truth table : tabular presentations of truth values which can be used either to define propositional operators or to verify facts about propositional expressions.

Truth-valued function : a function whose range is the truth values (**B**).

Turnstile : the turnstile symbol ($\models$) is used in model theory to show that the conclusion is true in all cases where all hypotheses are true; (in proof theory $\vdash$ shows that the conclusion can be deduced from the hypotheses).

Union : the union of two sets is the set containing exactly the elements contained in either (or both) sets.

Universal quantifier : ($\forall$) "for all"

VDM : *see* Vienna Development Method.

Vienna Development Method : a collection of notation and ideas which grew out of the work of the IBM Laboratory, Vienna. The original application was the denotational description of programming languages. The same specification technique has been applied to many other systems. Design rules which show how to prove that a design satisfies its specification have been developed. (See Bibliography).

Well-founded : a well-founded relation is one in which there are no infinite descending chains.

Appendix E

Glossary of Symbols

Numbers

$\mathbf{N_1} = \{1, 2, \ldots\}$
$\mathbf{N} = \{0, 1, 2, \ldots\}$
$0, \text{succ}$ as generators
$\mathbf{Z} = \{\ldots, -1, 0, 1, \ldots\}$
$\mathbf{R}$ = real numbers
normal arithmetic operators (e.g. $+, -, <$)
   mod   modulus

Functions

$f : D_1 \times D_2 \rightarrow R$ signature
$f(d)$ application
$\lambda x \in T \cdot t$ abstraction
if ... then ... else ...   conditional
let $x = \ldots$ in ...   local definition

Logic

$\mathbf{B} = \{\text{true}, \text{false}\}$
E_i are logical expressions, Γ is a list of logical expressions

$\neg E$	negation [1]
$E_1 \wedge E_2$	conjunction
$E_1 \vee E_2$	disjunction
$E_1 \Rightarrow E_2$	implication
$E_1 \Leftrightarrow E_2$	equivalence
$\forall x \in T \cdot E$	universal quantifier [2]
$\exists x \in T \cdot E$	existential quantifier
$\exists! x \in T \cdot E$	unique existence
$\Gamma \vdash E$	sequent E can be proved from Γ (hypothesis $\vdash$ conclusion)
$\Gamma \models E$	sequent (E is true in all worlds where Γ all true)
$\dfrac{\Gamma}{E}$	inference rule
$\dfrac{E_1}{E_2}$	bidirectional inference rule

Sets

S, T are sets, t_i are terms

set of T	all finite subsets of T
$\{t_1, t_2, \ldots, t_n\}$	set enumeration
$\{\}$	empty set
$\oplus$	generator
$\{x \in T \mid E\}$	set comprehension
$\{i, \ldots, j\}$	subset of integers
$t \in S$	set membership
$t \notin S$	$\neg(t \in S)$
$S \subseteq T$	set containments (subset of)
$S \subset T$	strict set containment

---

[1] The five propositional operators are given in decreasing order of priority

[2] With all of the quantifiers, the scope extends as far as possible to the right; no parentheses are required but they can be used for extra grouping.

$S \cap T$	set intersection [3]
$S \cup T$	set union
$S - T$	set difference
$S \diamond T$	symmetric set difference
$\bigcup S$	distributed union
card S	cardinality of a set

Maps

M is a map

map D to R	finite maps
dom M	domain
rng M	range
$\{d_1 \mapsto r_1, d_2 \mapsto r_2, \ldots, d_n \mapsto r_n\}$	map enumeration
$\{\}$	empty map
$\oplus$	generator
$\{d \mapsto f(d) \mid E\}$	map comprehension
$m(d)$	application
$S \lhd M$	domain restriction
$S \ntriangleleft M$	domain deletion
$M_1 \dagger M_2$	overwriting

Sequences

s, t are sequences

seq of T	finite sequences
len s	length
$[t_1, t_2, \ldots, t_n]$	sequence enumeration
$[\,]$	empty sequence
cons	generator
$s \frown t$	concatenation
hd s	head
tl s	tail
$s(i, \ldots, j)$	sub-sequence

[3]Intersection is higher priority than union.

Composite Objects

o is a composite object

compose N of $\ldots$ end	
where $inv\text{-}N()$ $\triangleq$ $\ldots$	invariant
$::$	compose
nil	omitted object
$mk\text{-}N()$	generator
$s_1(o)$	selector
$\mu(o, s_1 \mapsto t)$	modify a component

Function Specification

$f(d\!:\!D)\ r\!:\!R$

pre $\ldots d \ldots$

post $\ldots d \ldots r \ldots$

Operation Specification

$OP\ (p\!:\!Tp)\ r\!:\!Tr$

ext rd $e_1\!:\!T_1,$ wr $e_2\!:\!T_2$

pre $\ldots p \ldots e_1 \ldots e_2 \ldots$

post $\ldots p \ldots e_1 \ldots \overleftarrow{e_2} \ldots r \ldots e_2 \ldots$

Appendix F

Annotated Bibliography

This book uses VDM. The research of the Vienna group was first described in research reports and papers. The first book—which contains references to the papers—was *The Vienna Development Method: The Meta-Language* edited by D. Bjørner and C. B. Jones (Springer-Verlag, Lecture Notes in Computer Science, no. 61, 1978). The program development aspects of VDM were described in *Software Development: a Rigorous Approach* by C. B. Jones (Prentice/Hall International, 1980). This book was used in many industrial courses. The current book includes a number of developments which have occurred recently. Notably the emphasis on proof using the natural deduction presentations and the specific use of LPF have a large influence on the material presented here. Although parallelism is not covered here, the author's work in this area has also prompted some changes of notation—cf. *Specification and Design of (Parallel) Programs* by C. B. Jones (Elsevier Science Publishers B. V. (North-Holland), Information Processing 83, pp. 321–332, 1983). The application of VDM to programming language semantics is covered in *Formal Specification and Software Development* by D. Bjørner and C. B. Jones (Prentice/Hall International, 1982). This book largely supercedes the earlier LNCS volume. The outstanding work of one of the Vienna group is recorded in *Programming Languages and Their Definitions* by H. Bekič (Springer-Verlag, Lecture Notes in Computer Science, no. 177, 1984).

There are many applications of VDM to significant system specification and development tasks. The scale of some of these (e.g. PL/I description) does not suit them for normal publication. One interesting book is *Towards a Formal Description of Ada* Edited by D. Bjørner and O. N. Oest (Springer-Verlag, Lecture Notes in Computer Science, no. 98, 1980). The Teacher's

Notes, mentioned in the Preface, will include a more extensive Bibliography of VDM material.

There are other formal specification methods, some of which are in the process of acquiring the related development methods. The method known as "Z" is described in *Non-Deterministic System Specification* by J. R. Abrial and S. A. Schuman in *Semantics of Concurrent Computation* edited by G. Kahn (Springer-Verlag, Lecture Notes in Computer Science, no. 70, pp. 34–50, 1979). More recent references are *Specification of the UNIX Filing System* by C. Morgan and B. Sufrin in *IEEE Transactions on Software Engineering*, vol. 10 no. 2, March, 1984 and *Applying Formal Specification to Software Development in Industry* by I. J. Hayes in *IEEE Transactions on Software Engineering*, vol. 11, no. 2, 1985.

A very interesting specification language is described in *An Informal Introduction to specification using Clear* by R. M. Burstall in *The Correctness Problem in Computer Science* edited by R. S. Boyer and J. S. Moore (Academic Press, International Lecture Series in Computer Science, pp.185–212, 1981).

One of the most recent and interesting specification languages is described in *Larch in Five Easy Pieces* by J. V. Guttag, J. J. Horning, and J. M. Wing (Digital Research Report, no. 5, 1985).

There are other books ranging, from monographs to textbooks, on formal methods. The reader who wishes to try VDM on some standard examples could extract them from these references. This would be particularly useful for the operation decomposition method described in Chapter 10. The method here differs from the referenced books because of the use of postconditions of pairs of states. The references are *A Discipline of Programming* by E. W. Dijkstra (Prentice/Hall, 1976), *The Craft of Programming* by J. C. Reynolds (Prentice/Hall International, 1981), *The Science of Programming* by D. Gries (Springer-Verlag, 1981), *The Logic of Programming* by E. C. R. Hehner (Prentice/Hall International, 1984).

There are many good textbooks on classical logic—a recent one is *Numbers, Sets and Axioms: the apparatus of Mathematics* by A. G. Hamilton (Cambridge University Press, 1982). A textbook which describes natural deduction proofs very clearly is *Logic: An Introductory Course* by W. H. Newton-Smith (Routledge and Kegan Paul, 1985). The work on LPF is described in *A Logic Covering Undefinedness in Program Proofs* by H. Barringer, J. H. Cheng and C. B. Jones (Acta Informatica, vol. 21, pp 251–269, 1984). This paper also refers to other approaches to the same problem. The related work on PL/CV2 is described in *An Introduction to the PL/CV2 Programming Logic* by R. L. Constable, S. D. Johnson, and C. D. Eichenlaub (Springer-Verlag, Lecture Notes in Computer Science, no. 135, 1982).

There are many approaches to machine support for formal methods. One of the systems most relevant to VDM is described in *The IOTA Programming System: A Modular Programming Environment* edited by R. Nakajima and T. Yuasa (Springer-Verlag, Lecture Notes in Computer Science, no. 160, 1983). Other theorem provers are described in *A Computational Logic* by R. S. Boyer and J. S. Moore (Academic Press, ACM Monograph Series, 1979) and *Edinburgh LCF* by M. J. Gordon, A. J. Milner and C. P. Wadsworth (Springer-Verlag, Lecture Notes in Computer Science, no. 78, 1979).

An application of a theorem prover to the task of compiler development is described in *Compiler Specification and Verification* by W. Polak, (Springer-Verlag, Lecture Notes in Computer Science, no. 124, 1981). The work of the Manchester group in providing a support system (known as "Mule") for VDM is outlined in *Project Support Environments for Formal Methods* by I. D. Cottam, C. B. Jones, T. Nipkow, A. C. Wills, M. I. Wolczko and A. Yaghi in *Integrated Project Support Environments* edited by J. A. McDermid (Peter Peregrinus, 1985). In addition to the material already referenced, work on constructing theories of data types is discussed in *Constructing a Theory of a Data Structure as an Aid to Program Development* by C. B. Jones (Acta Informatica, vol. 11, pp. 119–137, 1979).

Work on specifying exceptions is described in *The Rigorous Development of a System Version Control Program* by I. D. Cottam in *IEEE Transactions on Software Engineering*, vol. 10, no. 2, pp. 143–154, March, 1984. This contains references to other approaches to the problem.

The source reference for the telegram-analysis problem is *An Experiment in Structured Programming* by P. Henderson, and R. A. Snowdon (BIT, vol. 12, pp. 38–53, 1972). The PL/I compiler interface description is given in *A Formal Interface Specification* by F. Weissenböck (IBM Laboratory, Vienna, TR 25.141, 1975).

An approach to developing programs (by reflecting, in their design, the reality in which the system is to be embedded) is described in *System Development* by M. Jackson (Prentice/Hall International, 1983). Recent research on data reification is described in *Nondeterministic Data Types: Models and Implementations* by T. Nipkow (accepted for publication by Acta Informatica, 1985) and *Data Refinement Refined* by J. He, C. A. R. Hoare and J. W. Sanders, (Oxford University, 1985).

Index